Canto is a paperback imprint
which offers a broad range of titles,
both classic and more recent,
representing some of the best
and most enjoyable of Cambridge
publishing.

Nations and nationalism since 1780

Programme, myth, reality

SECOND EDITION

E. J. HOBSBAWM

CAMBRIDGE
UNIVERSITY PRESS

PUBLISHED BY THE PRESS SYNDICATE OF THE UNIVERSITY OF CAMBRIDGE
The Pitt Building, Trumpington Street, Cambridge, United Kingdom

CAMBRIDGE UNIVERSITY PRESS
The Edinburgh Building, Cambridge CB2 2RU, UK
40 West 20th Street, New York, NY 10011–4211, USA
477 Williamstown Road, Port Melbourne, VIC 3207, Australia
Ruiz de Alarcón 13, 28014 Madrid, Spain
Dock House, The Waterfront, Cape Town 8001, South Africa

http://www.cambridge.org

First published 1990
Reprinted 1990, 1991
Canto edition 1991
Second edition 1992
Reprinted 1993, 1994, 1995, 1997, 1999, 2000, 2002 (twice)

Printed in the United Kingdom at the University Press, Cambridge

A catalogue record for this book is available from the British Library

Library of Congress Cataloguing in Publication data
Hobsbawm. E. J. (Eric J.), 1917–
Nations and nationalism since 1780: programme, myth, reality /
E. J. Hobsbawm. – 2nd ed.
p.   cm.
Includes index.
ISBN 0 521 43961 2 (paperback)
1. Nationalism – History. I. Title.
JC311.H577   1992
320.5′4–dc20   92–14949   CIP

ISBN 0 521 43961 2 paperback

Cover illustration: *The Tower of Babel*. Peter Bruegel the Elder.
Kunsthistorisches Museum, Vienna/Bridgeman Art Library

CE

Contents

Preface

This book is based on the Wiles Lectures which I had the honour to give at the Queen's University of Belfast in May 1985. The location suggested the topic. For the sake of convenience the somewhat concentrated contents of the four lectures to which the Lectureship commits the visitor have been spread out. There are now five chapters of unequal length, an introduction and some concluding reflections. The manuscript has also been revised, partly to take account of some later material, but mainly in the light of the discussions with the invited group of experts, which is one of the chief attractions of the Wiles Lectures for those fortunate enough to give them. I am grateful to all those who organized the lectures and those who took part in the discussions, and in particular to Perry Anderson, John Breuilly, Judith Brown, Ronan Fanning, Miroslav Hroch, Victor Kiernan, Joe Lee, Shula Marks, Terence Ranger and Göran Therborn, for criticism and stimulation and especially for making me think further about non-European nationalism. However, I have concentrated mainly on the nineteenth and earlier twentieth centuries, when the subject is rather Eurocentric or at any rate centred in the 'developed' regions. Since I have been some time talking and asking questions about nations and nationalism, there are many others who have given me ideas, information or references to books I would not otherwise have known about. At the risk of unfairness I single out Kumari Jayawardene and the other South Asian scholars at the World Institute for Development Economics Research in Helsinki, and my colleagues and students at the New School for Social Research in New York, who have heard and discussed some of this material. Much of the research for this book was made possible by a Leverhulme Emeritus Fellowship, and I should like to express my appreciation for the generous assistance thus provided by the Leverhulme Trust.

'The national question' is a notoriously controversial subject. I have not sought to make it any less controversial. However, I hope that these lectures in their printed form will advance the study of the historical phenomena with which they attempt to come to grips.

London 1989

The last chapter has been extended and largely rewritten to take account of events since the text of the first edition was completed.

London, March 1992

Introduction

Suppose that one day, after a nuclear war, an intergalactic historian lands on a now dead planet in order to enquire into the cause of the remote little catastrophe which the sensors of his galaxy have recorded. He or she – I refrain from speculating on the problem of extraterrestrial physiological reproduction – consults the terrestrial libraries and archives which have been preserved, because the technology of mature nuclear weaponry has been designed to destroy people rather than property. Our observer, after some study, will conclude that the last two centuries of the human history of planet Earth are incomprehensible without some understanding of the term 'nation' and the vocabulary derived from it. This term appears to express something important in human affairs. But what exactly? Here lies the mystery. He will have read Walter Bagehot, who presented the history of the nineteenth century as that of 'nation-building', but who also observed, with his usual common sense: 'We know what it is when you do not ask us, but we cannot very quickly explain or define it.'[1] This may be true for Bagehot and for us, but not for extragalactic historians who have not the human experience which appears to make the idea of the 'nation' so convincing.

I think it would today be possible, thanks to the literature of the past fifteen to twenty years, to provide such a historian with a short reading list to help him, her, or it with the desired analysis, and to supplement A. D. Smith's 'Nationalism: A Trend Report and Bibliography', which contains most references in the field up to that

---

[1] Walter Bagehot, *Physics and Politics* (London 1887), pp. 20–21.

date.[2] Not that one would wish to recommend all that much that was written in earlier periods. Our reading list would contain very little that was written in the classic period of nineteenth-century liberalism, for reasons which should become clear later, but also because very little other than nationalist and racist rhetoric was being written then. And the best work produced at that time was actually very brief, like John Stuart Mill's passages on the subject in his *Considerations on Representative Government* and Ernest Renan's famous lecture 'What is a nation?'[3]

The reading list would contain some historically necessary, as well as some optional reading from the first major effort to apply dispassionate analysis to the subject, the important and under-estimated debates among the Marxists of the Second International on what they called 'the national question'. We shall see later why the best minds in the international socialist movement – and it contained some extremely powerful intellects – applied themselves to this problem: Kautsky and Luxemburg, Otto Bauer and Lenin, to name but a few.[4] Probably it would contain some of Kautsky, certainly Otto Bauer's *Die Nationalitätenfrage*, but it would also need to contain Stalin's *Marxism and the National and Colonial Question*, not so much for its modest, but not negligible – if somewhat derivative – intellectual merits, but rather for its subsequent political influence.[5]

[2] A. D. Smith, 'Nationalism, A Trend Report and Bibliography' in *Current Sociology* XXI/3, The Hague and Paris 1973. See also the bibliographies in the same author's *Theories of Nationalism* (London, 2nd edn 1983) and *The Ethnic Origins of Nations* (Oxford 1986). Professor Anthony Smith is at present the main guide in this field for readers of the English language.

[3] Ernest Renan, *Qu'est ce que c'est une nation?* (Conférence faite en Sorbonne le 11 mars 1882) (Paris 1882); John Stuart Mill, *Considerations on Representative Government* (London 1861), chapter XVI.

[4] For a convenient introduction, including a selection of writings by the chief Marxist authors of the time, Georges Haupt, Michel Lowy and Claudie Weill, *Les Marxistes et la question nationale 1848–1914* (Paris 1974). Otto Bauer, *Die Nationalitätenfrage und die Sozialdemokratie* (Vienna 1907, the second edition of 1924 contains an important new introduction), appears, unaccountably, not to have been translated into English. For a recent attempt, Horace B. Davis, *Toward a Marxist Theory of Nationalism* (New York 1978).

[5] The 1913 text was published together with later writings in Joseph Stalin, *Marxism and the National and Colonial Question* (London 1936) in a volume which had considerable international influence, not only among communists, especially in the dependent world.

It would not, in my judgment, deserve to contain much from the age of those who have been called 'the twin founding fathers' of the academic study of nationalism, after World War I: Carleton B. Hayes and Hans Kohn.[6] Nothing was more natural than that the subject should attract attention in a period when the map of Europe was, for the first – and as it turned out for the only – time redrawn according to the principle of nationality, and when the vocabulary of European nationalism came to be adopted by new movements of colonial liberation or Third World assertion, to which Hans Kohn at least paid considerable attention.[7] Nor is there any doubt that the writings of this period contain a mass of material drawn from the earlier literature, which can save the student a good deal of primary reading. The chief reason for the obsolescence of so much of it is that the main innovation of the period, which had incidentally been anticipated by the Marxists, has become commonplace, except among nationalists. Nations, we now know – not least through the efforts of the Hayes–Kohn era – are not, as Bagehot thought, 'as old as history'.[8] The modern sense of the word is no older than the eighteenth century, give or take the odd predecessor. The academic literature on nationalism multiplied, but did not advance greatly in the following decades. Some would regard the work of Karl Deutsch, who stressed the role of communication in the formation of nations, as a major addition to it, but I would not regard this author as indispensable.[9]

It is not altogether clear why the literature on nations and nationalism entered so fruitful a phase about twenty years ago, and indeed the question only arises for those who believe that it did so. This is not yet a universally established view. The problem will be considered in the final chapter, though not in great detail. At all

---

6 Carleton B. Hayes, *The Historical Evolution of Modern Nationalism* (New York 1931) and Hans Kohn, *The Idea of Nationalism. A Study in its Origin and Background* (New York 1944) contain valuable historical material. The phrase 'founding fathers' comes from the valuable study in philological and conceptual history, A. Kemiläinen, *Nationalism. Problems Concerning the Word, the Concept and Classification* (Jyväskylä 1964).
7 See his *History of Nationalism in the East* (London 1929); *Nationalism and Imperialism in the Hither East* (New York 1932).
8 Bagehot, *Physics and Politics*, p. 83.
9 Karl W. Deutsch, *Nationalism and Social Communication. An Enquiry into the Foundations of Nationality* (Cambridge MA 1953).

events, in the opinion of the present author, the number of works genuinely illuminating the question of what nations and national movements are and what role in historical development they play is larger in the period 1968–88 than for any earlier period of twice that length. The text which follows should make it clear which of them I have found particularly interesting, but it may be convenient to mention a few important titles, among which the author refrains from including all but one of his own writings on the subject.[10] The following brief list may serve as an introduction to the field. It is an alphabetical order of authors, except for the work of Hroch, which opened the new era in the analysis of the composition of national liberation movements.

Hroch, Miroslav. *Social Preconditions of National Revival in Europe* (Cambridge 1985). This combines the findings of two works published by the author in Prague in 1968 and 1971.

Anderson, Benedict. *Imagined Communities* (London 1983)

Armstrong, J. *Nations before Nationalism* (Chapel Hill 1982)

Breuilly, J. *Nationalism and the State* (Manchester 1982)

John W. Cole and Eric R. Wolf. *The Hidden Frontier: Ecology and Ethnicity in an Alpine Valley* (New York and London 1974)

J. Fishman (ed.) *Language Problems of Developing Countries* (New York 1968)

Ernest Gellner. *Nations and Nationalism* (Oxford 1983)

Hobsbawm, E. J. and Ranger, Terence (eds.) *The Invention of Tradition* (Cambridge 1983)

Smith, A. D. *Theories of Nationalism* (2nd edn, London 1983)

Szücs, Jenö. *Nation und Geschichte: Studien* (Budapest 1981)

---

[10] These are, in addition to chapters on the subject in *The Age of Revolution 1789–1848* (1962), *The Age of Capital 1848–1875* (1975) and *The Age of Empire 1875–1914* (1987): 'The attitude of popular classes towards national movements for independence' (Celtic parts of Great Britain) in Commission Internationale d'Histoire des Mouvements Sociaux et Structures Sociales, *Mouvements nationaux d'indépendence et classes populaires aux XIXe et XXe siècles en Occident et en Orient*, 2 vols. (Paris 1971), vol. I, pp. 34–44; 'Some reflections on nationalism' in T. J. Nossiter, A. H. Hanson, Stein Rokkan (eds.), *Imagination and Precision in the Social Sciences: Essays in Memory of Peter Nettl* (London 1972 pp. 385–406); 'Reflections on "The Break-Up of Britain"' (*New Left Review*, 105, 1977); 'What is the worker's country?' (ch. 4 of my *Worlds of Labour*, London 1984); 'Working-class internationalism' in F. van Holthoon and Marcel

Tilly, C. (ed.) *The Formation of National States in Western Europe* (Princeton 1975)

To these I cannot resist adding a brilliant essay written from within the subjective identification with a 'nation', but with a rare sense of its historical context and malleability, Gwyn A. Williams, 'When was Wales?' in this author's *The Welsh in their History* (London and Canberra 1982).

Most of this literature has turned on the question: What is a (or the) nation? For the chief characteristic of this way of classifying groups of human beings is that, in spite of the claims of those who belong to it that it is in some ways primary and fundamental for the social existence, or even the individual identification, of its members, no satisfactory criterion can be discovered for deciding which of the many human collectivities should be labelled in this way. That is not in itself surprising, for if we regard 'the nation' as a very recent newcomer in human history, and the product of particular, and inevitably localized or regional, historical conjunctures, we would expect it to occur, initially as it were, in a few colonies of settlement rather than in a population generally distributed over the world's territory. But the problem is that there is no way of telling the observer how to distinguish a nation from other entities *a priori*, as we can tell him or her how to recognize a bird or to distinguish a mouse from a lizard. Nation-watching would be simple if it could be like bird-watching.

Attempts to establish objective criteria for nationhood, or to explain why certain groups have become 'nations' and others not, have often been made, based on single criteria such as language or ethnicity or a combination of criteria such as language, common territory, common history, cultural traits or whatever else. Stalin's definition is probably the best known among these, but by no means the only one.[11] All such objective definitions have failed, for the obvious reason that, since only some members of the large class

van der Linden (eds.), *Internationalism in the Labour Movement* (Leiden–New York–Copenhagen–Cologne 1988, pp. 2–16).

[11] 'A nation is a historically evolved, stable community of language, territory, economic life and psychological make-up manifested in a community of culture.' Joseph Stalin, *Marxism and the National and Colonial Question*, p. 8. The original was written in 1912.

of entities which fit such definitions can at any time be described as 'nations', exceptions can always be found. Either cases corresponding to the definition are patently not (or not yet) 'nations' or possessed of national aspirations, or undoubted 'nations' do not correspond to the criterion or combination of criteria. How indeed could it be otherwise, given that we are trying to fit historically novel, emerging, changing and, even today, far from universal entities into a framework of permanence and universality?

Moreover, as we shall see, the criteria used for this purpose – language, ethnicity or whatever – are themselves fuzzy, shifting and ambiguous, and as useless for purposes of the traveller's orientation as cloud-shapes are compared to landmarks. This, of course, makes them unusually convenient for propagandist and programmatic, as distinct from descriptive purposes. An illustration of the nationalist use of such an 'objective' definition in recent Asian politics may make this clear:

> The Tamil-speaking people in Ceylon constitute a nation distinct from that of the Singalese by every fundamental test of nationhood, firstly that of a separate historical past in the island at least as ancient and as glorious as that of the Singalese [sic], secondly by the fact of their being a linguistic entity entirely different from that of the Sinhalese, with an unsurpassed classical heritage and a modern development of language which makes Tamil fully adequate for all present-day needs, and finally by reason of their territorial habitation of definite areas.[12]

The purpose of this passage is clear: it is to demand autonomy or independence for an area described as 'over one third of the island' of Sri Lanka, on grounds of Tamil nationalism. Nothing else about it is as it seems. It obscures the fact that the territorial habitation consists of two geographically separate areas inhabited by Tamil speakers of different origins (indigenous and recent Indian immigrant labour respectively); that the area of continuous Tamil settlement is also, in certain zones, inhabited by anything up to a third of Sinhalese and anything up to 41% of Tamil speakers who refused to consider themselves national Tamils and prefer identifi-

---

[12] Ilankai Tamil Arasu Kadchi, 'The case for a federal constitution for Ceylon', Colombo 1951, cited in Robert N. Kearney, 'Ethnic conflict and the Tamil separatist movement in Sri Lanka' (*Asian Survey*, 25, 9 September 1985, p. 904).

cation as Muslims (the 'Moors'). In fact, even leaving aside the central region of immigrants, it is not at all clear that the territory of major continuous Tamil settlement, comprising as it does areas of solid Tamil settlement (from 71 to 95% – Batticaloa, Mullaitivu, Jaffna) and areas where self-identified Tamils form 20 or 33% (Amparal, Trincomalee) should be described, except in purely cartographic terms, as a single space. In fact, in the negotiations which led to the end of the Sri Lankan civil war in 1987, the decision to do so was a straightforward political concession to the demands of the Tamil nationalists. As we have already seen the 'linguistic entity' conceals the unquestionable fact that indigenous Tamils, immigrant Indians and Moors are – so far – a homogeneous population in no other than the philological sense, and, as we shall see, probably not even in this sense. As for the 'separate historical past', the phrase is almost certainly anachronistic, question-begging or so vague as to be meaningless. It may, of course, be objected that patently propagandist manifestos should not be scrutinized as though they were contributions to the social sciences, but the point is that almost any classification of some community as a 'nation' on the grounds of such purportedly objective criteria would be open to similar objections, unless the fact that it was a 'nation' could be established on other grounds.

But what other grounds? The alternative to an objective definition is a subjective one, whether collective (along the lines of Renan's 'a nation is a daily plebiscite') or individual, in the manner of the Austro-Marxists, for whom 'nationality' could attach to persons, wherever they lived and whoever they lived with, at any rate if they chose to claim it.[13] Both are evident attempts to escape from the constraints of *a priori* objectivism, in both cases, though in a different manner, by adapting the definition of 'nation' to territories in which persons of different languages or other 'objective' criteria coexist, as they did in France and the Habsburg empire. Both are open to the objection that defining a nation by its

[13] Karl Renner specifically compared the individual's national membership with his (her) membership of a religious confession, i.e. a status 'freely chosen, *de jure*, by the individual who has reached the age of majority, and on behalf of minors, by their legal representatives'. Synopticus, *Staat und Nation* (Vienna 1899) pp. 7ff.

members' consciousness of belonging to it is tautological and provides only an *a posteriori* guide to what a nation is. Moreover, it can lead the incautious into extremes of voluntarism which suggests that all that is needed to be or to create or recreate a nation is the will to be one: if enough inhabitants of the Isle of Wight wanted to be a Wightian nation, there would be one.

[margin note: not just the individual groups can class themselves as a nation esp if they lock the power to.]

While this has, especially since the 1960s, led to some attempts at nation-building by consciousness-raising, it is not a legitimate criticism of observers as sophisticated as Otto Bauer and Renan, who knew perfectly well that nations also had objective elements in common. Nevertheless, to insist on consciousness or choice as the criterion of nationhood is insensibly to subordinate the complex and multiple ways in which human beings define and redefine themselves as members of groups, to a single option: the choice of belonging to a 'nation' or 'nationality'. Politically or administratively such a choice must today be made by virtue of living in states which supply passports or ask questions about language in censuses. Yet even today it is perfectly possible for a person living in Slough to think of himself, depending on circumstances, as – say – a British citizen, or (faced with other citizens of a different colour) as an Indian, or (faced with other Indians) as a Gujarati, or (faced with Hindus or Muslims) as a Jain, or as a member of a particular caste, or kinship connection, or as one who, at home, speaks Hindi rather than Gujarati, or doubtless in other ways. Nor indeed is it possible to reduce even 'nationality' to a single dimension, whether political, cultural or otherwise (unless, of course, obliged to do so by *force majeure* of states). People can identify themselves as Jews even though they share neither religion, language, culture, tradition, historical background, blood-group patterns nor an attitude to the Jewish state. Nor does this imply a purely subjective definition of 'the nation'.

[margin note: identity is changeable depending on what group you are identifying against.]

Neither objective nor subjective definitions are thus satisfactory, and both are misleading. In any case, agnosticism is the best initial posture of a student in this field, and so this book assumes no *a priori* definition of what constitutes a nation. As an initial working assumption any sufficiently large body of people whose members regard themselves as members of a 'nation', will be treated as such.

However, whether such a body of people does so regard itself cannot be established simply by consulting writers or political spokesmen of organizations claiming the status of 'nation' for it. The appearance of a group of spokesmen for some 'national idea' is not insignificant, but the word 'nation' is today used so widely and imprecisely that the use of the vocabulary of nationalism today may mean very little indeed.

Nevertheless, in approaching 'the national question' 'it is more profitable to begin with the concept of "the nation" (i.e. with "nationalism") than with the reality it represents'. For 'The "nation" as conceived by nationalism, can be recognized prospectively; the real "nation" can only be recognized *a posteriori*.'[14] This is the approach of the present book. It pays particular attention to the changes and transformations of the concept, particularly towards the end of the nineteenth century. Concepts, of course, are not part of free-floating philosophical discourse, but socially, historically and locally rooted, and must be explained in terms of these realities.

For the rest, the position of the writer may be summarized as follows.

(1) I use the term 'nationalism' in the sense defined by Gellner, namely to mean 'primarily a principle which holds that the political and national unit should be congruent.'[15] I would add that this principle also implies that the political duty of Ruritanians to the polity which encompasses and represents the Ruritanian nation, overrides all other public obligations, and in extreme cases (such as wars) all other obligations of whatever kind. This implication distinguishes modern nationalism from other and less demanding forms of national or group identification which we shall also encounter.

(2) Like most serious students, I do not regard the 'nation' as a primary nor as an unchanging social entity. It belongs exclusively to a particular, and historically recent, period. It is a social entity only insofar as it relates to a certain kind of modern territorial state,

[marginal handwritten note: unchanging social entity]

---

[14] E. J. Hobsbawm, 'Some reflections on nationalism', p. 387.
[15] Ernest Gellner, *Nations and Nationalism*, p. 1. This basically political definition is also accepted by some other writers, e.g. John Breuilly, *Nationalism and the State*, p. 3.

the 'nation-state', and it is pointless to discuss nation and nationality except insofar as both relate to it. Moreover, with Gellner I would stress the element of artefact, invention and social engineering which enters into the making of nations. 'Nations as a natural, God-given way of classifying men, as an inherent ... political destiny, are a myth; nationalism, which sometimes takes pre-existing cultures and turns them into nations, sometimes invents them, and often obliterates pre-existing cultures: *that* is a reality.'[16] In short, for the purposes of analysis nationalism comes before nations. Nations do not make states and nationalisms but the other way round.

(3) The 'national question', as the old Marxists called it, is situated at the point of intersection of politics, technology and social transformation. Nations exist not only as functions of a particular kind of territorial state or the aspiration to establish one – broadly speaking, the citizen state of the French Revolution – but also in the context of a particular stage of technological and economic development. Most students today will agree that standard national languages, spoken or written, cannot emerge as such before printing, mass literacy and hence, mass schooling. It has even been argued that popular spoken Italian as an idiom capable of expressing the full range of what a twentieth-century language needs outside the domestic and face-to-face sphere of communication, is only being constructed today as a function of the needs of national television programming.[17] Nations and their associated phenomena must therefore be analysed in terms of political, technical, administrative, economic and other conditions and requirements.

(4) For this reason they are, in my view, dual phenomena, constructed essentially from above, but which cannot be understood unless also analysed from below, that is in terms of the assumptions, hopes, needs, longings and interests of ordinary people, which are not necessarily national and still less nationalist. If I have a major criticism of Gellner's work it is that his preferred

---

16 Gellner, *Nations and Nationalism*, pp. 48–9.
17 Antonio Sorella, 'La televisione e la lingua italiana' (*Trimestre. Periodico di Cultura*, 14, 2–3–4 (1982), pp. 291–300.

perspective of modernization from above, makes it difficult to pay adequate attention to the view from below.

That view from below, i.e. the nation as seen not by governments and the spokesmen and activists of nationalist (or non-nationalist) movements, but by the ordinary persons who are the objects of their action and propaganda, is exceedingly difficult to discover. Fortunately social historians have learned how to investigate the history of ideas, opinions and feelings at the sub-literary level, so that we are today less likely to confuse, as historians once habitually did, editorials in select newspapers with public opinion. We do not know much for certain. However, three things are clear.

First, official ideologies of states and movements are not guides to what it is in the minds of even the most loyal citizens or supporters. Second, and more specifically, we cannot assume that for most people national identification – when it exists – excludes or is always or ever superior to, the remainder of the set of identifications which constitute the social being. In fact, it is always combined with identifications of another kind, even when it is felt to be superior to them. Thirdly, national identification and what it is believed to imply, can change and shift in time, even in the course of quite short periods. In my judgment this is the area of national studies in which thinking and research are most urgently needed today.

(5) The development of nations and nationalism within old-established states such as Britain and France, has not been studied very intensively, though it is now attracting attention.[18] The existence of this gap is illustrated by the neglect, in Britain, of any problems connected with English nationalism – a term which in itself sounds odd to many ears – compared to the attention paid to Scots, Welsh, not to mention Irish nationalism. On the other hand there have in recent years been major advances in the study of national movements aspiring to be states, mainly following Hroch's pathbreaking comparative studies of small European national movements. Two points in this excellent writer's analysis

---

[18] For the range of such work, see Raphael Samuel (ed.), *Patriotism. The Making and Unmaking of British National Identity* (3 vols., London 1989). I have found the work of Linda Colley particularly stimulating, e.g. 'Whose nation? Class and national consciousness in Britain 1750–1830' (*Past & Present*, 113, 1986), pp. 96–117.

are embodied in my own. First, 'national consciousness' develops unevenly among the social groupings and *regions* of a country; this regional diversity and its reasons have in the past been notably neglected. Most students would, incidentally, agree that, whatever the nature of the social groups first captured by 'national consciousness', the popular masses – workers, servants, peasants – are the last to be affected by it. Second, and in consequence, I follow his useful division of the history of national movements into three phases. In nineteenth-century Europe, for which it was developed, phase A was purely cultural, literary and folkloric, and had no particular political or even national implications, any more than the researches (by non-Romanies) of the Gypsy Lore Society have for the subjects of these enquiries. In phase B we find a body of pioneers and militants of 'the national idea' and the beginnings of political campaigning for this idea. The bulk of Hroch's work is concerned with this phase and the analysis of the origins, composition and distribution of this *minorité agissante*. My own concern in this book is more with phase C when – and not before – nationalist programmes acquire mass support, or at least some of the mass support that nationalists always claim they represent. The transition from phase B to phase C is evidently a crucial moment in the chronology of national movements. Sometimes, as in Ireland, it occurs before the creation of a national state; probably very much more often it occurs afterwards, as a consequence of that creation. Sometimes, as in the so-called Third World, it does not happen even then.

Finally, I cannot but add that no serious historian of nations and nationalism can be a committed political nationalist, except in the sense in which believers in the literal truth of the Scriptures, while unable to make contributions to evolutionary theory, are not precluded from making contributions to archaeology and Semitic philology. Nationalism requires too much belief in what is patently not so. As Renan said: 'Getting its history wrong is part of being a nation.'[19] Historians are professionally obliged not to get it wrong,

[19] Ernest Renan, *Qu'est que c'est une nation?* pp. 7–8: 'L'oubli et je dirai même l'erreur historique, sont un facteur essentiel de la formation d'une nation et c'est ainsi que le progrès des études historiques est souvent pour la nationalité un danger.'

or at least to make an effort not to. To be Irish and proudly attached to Ireland – even to be proudly Catholic-Irish or Ulster-Protestant Irish – is not in itself incompatible with the serious study of Irish history. To be a Fenian or an Orangeman, I would judge, is not so compatible, any more than being a Zionist is compatible with writing a genuinely serious history of the Jews; unless the historian leaves his or her convictions behind when entering the library or the study. Some nationalist historians have been unable to do so. Fortunately, in setting out to write the present book I have not needed to leave my non-historical convictions behind.

Author is interested in WHEN, nationalist programmes acquire mass support.

changing history = Nation building

CHAPTER 1

The nation as novelty: from revolution to liberalism

The basic characteristic of the modern nation and everything connected with it is its modernity. This is now well understood, but the opposite assumption, that national identification is somehow so natural, primary and permanent as to precede history, is so widely held that it may be useful to illustrate the modernity of the vocabulary of the subject itself. The Dictionary of the Royal Spanish Academy, whose various editions have been scrutinized for this purpose[1] does not use the terminology of state, nation and language in the modern manner before its edition of 1884. Here, for the first time, we learn that the *lengua nacional* is 'the official and literary language of a country, and the one generally spoken in that country, as distinct from dialects and the languages of other nations'. The entry under 'dialect' establishes the same relation between it and the national language. Before 1884 the word *nación* simply meant 'the aggregate of the inhabitants of a province, a country or a kingdom' and also 'a foreigner'. But now it was given as 'a State or political body which recognizes a supreme centre of common government' and also 'the territory constituted by that state and its individual inhabitants, considered as a whole', and henceforth the element of a common and supreme state is central to such definitions, at least in the Iberian world. The *nación* is the 'conjunto de los habitantes de un país *regido por un mismo gobierno*' (emphasis added).[2] The *nação* of the (recent) *Enciclopé-*

[1] Lluis Garcia i Sevilla, 'Llengua, nació i estat al diccionario de la real academia espanyola' (*L'Avenç*, 16 May 1979, pp. 50–5).
[2] *Enciclopedia Universal Ilustrada Europeo-Americana* (Barcelona 1907–34), vol. 37, pp. 854–67: 'nación'.

dia Brasileira Mérito[3] is 'the community of the citizens of a state, living under the same regime or government and having a communion of interests; the collectivity of the inhabitants of a territory with common traditions, aspirations and interests, *and subordinated to a central power which takes charge of maintaining the unity of the group* (emphasis added); the people of a state, excluding the governing power'. Moreover, in the Dictionary of the Spanish Academy the final version of 'the nation' is not found until 1925 when it is described as 'the collectivity of persons who have the same ethnic origin and, in general, speak the same language and possess a common tradition'.

def of Nation-alism

Gobierno, the government, is not therefore specifically linked with the concept of *nación* until 1884. For indeed, as philology would suggest, the first meaning of the word 'nation' indicates origin or descent: 'naissance, extraction, rang' to quote a dictionary of ancient French, which cites Froissart's 'je fus retourné au pays de ma nation en la conté de Haynnau' (I was returned to the land of my birth/origin in the county of Hainault).[4] And, insofar as origin or descent are attached to a body of men, it could hardly be those who formed a state (unless in the case of rulers or their kin). Insofar as it was attached to a territory, it was only fortuitously a political unit, and never a very large one. For the Spanish dictionary of 1726 (its first edition) the word *patria* or, in the more popular usage, *tierra*, 'the homeland' meant only 'the place, township or land where one is born', or 'any region, province or district of any lordship or state'. This narrow sense of *patria* as what modern Spanish usage has had to distinguish from the broad sense as *patria chica*, 'the little fatherland', is pretty universal before the nineteenth century, except among the classically educated, with a knowledge of ancient Rome. Not until 1884 did *tierra* come to be attached to a state; and not until 1925 do we hear the emotional note of modern patriotism, which defines *patria* as 'our own nation, with the sum total of material and immaterial things, past, present and future that enjoy the loving loyalty of patriots'.

---

[3] (São Paulo–Rio–Porto Alegre 1958–64), vol. 13, p. 581.
[4] L. Curne de Sainte Pelaye, *Dictionnaire historique de l'ancien langage françois* (Niort n.d.), 8 vols.; 'nation'.

Admittedly, nineteenth-century Spain was not exactly in the van-guard of ideological progress, but Castile – and we are talking about the Castilian language – was one of the earliest European kingdoms to which it is not totally unrealistic to attach the label 'nation-state'. At any rate it may be doubted whether eighteenth-century Britain and France were 'nation-states' in a very different sense. The development of its relevant vocabulary may therefore have a general interest.   *Inquirtio → the meaning of "nation"*

In Romance languages the word 'nation' is indigenous. Else-where, insofar as it is used, it is a foreign loan. This allows us to trace distinctions in the usage more clearly. Thus in High and Low German the word *Volk* (people) clearly has some of the same associations today as the words derived from 'natio', but the interaction is complex. It is clear that in medieval Low German the term (*natie*), insofar as it is used – and one would guess from its Latin origin it would hardly be used except among the literate or those of royal, noble or gentle birth – does not yet have the connotation *Volk*, which it only begins to acquire in the sixteenth century. It means, as in medieval French, birth and descent group (*Geschlecht*)[5]

As elsewhere, it develops in the direction of describing larger self-contained groups such as guilds or other corporations which require to be distinguished from others with whom they coexist: hence the 'nations' as a synonym for foreigner, as in Spanish, the 'nations' of foreign merchants ('foreign communities, especially of traders, living in a city and enjoying privileges there'),[6] the familiar 'nations' of students in ancient universities. Hence also the less familiar 'a regiment from the nation of Luxemburg'.[7] However, it seems clear that the evolution could tend to stress the place or territory of origin – the *pays natal* of one old French definition which readily becomes, at least in the minds of later lexicographers the equivalent of 'province',[8] while others stress rather the common descent group, and thus move into the direction of ethnicity, as in

[5] Dr E. Verwijs and Dr J. Verdam, *Middelnederlandsch Woordenboek*, vol. 4 (The Hague 1899), col. 2078.
[6] *Woordenboek der Nederlandsche Taal*, vol. 9 (The Hague 1913), cols. 1586–90.
[7] Verwijs and Verdam, *Middelenderlandsch Woordenboek*, vol. 4.
[8] L. Huguet, *Dictionnaire de la langue française du 16e siècle*, vol. 5 (Paris 1961), p. 400.

the Dutch insistence on the primary meaning of *natie* as 'the totality of men reckoned to belong to the same "stam"'.

Either way, the problem of the relation of even such an extended but indigenous 'nation' to the state remained puzzling, for it seemed evident that in ethnic, linguistic or any other terms, most states of any size were not homogeneous, and could therefore not simply be equated with nations. The Dutch dictionary specifically singles out as a peculiarity of the French and English that they use the word 'nation' to mean the people belonging to a state even when not speaking the same language.[9] A most instructive discussion of this puzzle comes from eighteenth-century Germany.[10] For the encyclopedist Johann Heinrich Zedler in 1740 the nation, in its real and original meaning meant a united number of *Bürger* (it is best, in mid-eighteenth-century Germany, to leave this word its notorious ambiguity) who share a body of customs, mores and laws. From this it follows that it can have no territorial meaning, since members of different nations (divided by 'differences in ways of life – *Lebensarten* – and customs') can live together in the same province, even quite a small one. If nations had an intrinsic connection with territory, the Wends in Germany would have to be called Germans, which they patently are not. The illustration naturally comes to the mind of a Saxon scholar, familiar with the last – and still surviving – Slav population within linguistic Germany, which it does not yet occur to him to label with the question-begging term 'national minority'. For Zedler the word to describe the totality of the people of all 'nations' living within the same province or state is *Volck*. But, alas for terminological tidiness, in practice the term 'Nation' is often used in he same sense as 'Volck'; and sometimes as a synonym for 'estate' of society (*Stand, ordo*) and sometimes for any other association or society (*Gesellschaft, societas*).

Whatever the 'proper and original' or any other meaning of 'nation', the term is clearly still quite different from its modern meaning. We may thus, without entering further into the matter,

[9] *Woordenboek* (1913), col. 1588.
[10] John. Heinrich Zedler, *Grosses vollständiges Universal-Lexicon aller Wissenschaften und Künste...*, vol. 23 (Leipzig–Halle 1740, repr. Graz 1961), cols. 901–3.

accept that in its modern and basically political sense the concept *nation* is historically very young. Indeed, this is underlined by another linguistic monument, the *New English Dictionary* which pointed out in 1908, that the old meaning of the word envisaged mainly the ethnic unit, but recent usage rather stressed 'the notion of political unity and independence'.[11]

Given the historical novelty of the modern concept of 'the nation', the best way to understand its nature, I suggest, is to follow those who began systematically to operate with this concept in their political and social discourse during the Age of Revolution, and especially, under the name of 'the principle of nationality' from about 1830 onwards. This excursus into *Begriffsgeschichte* is not easy, partly because, as we shall see, contemporaries were too unselfconscious about their use of such words, and partly because the same word simultaneously meant, or could mean, very different things.

The primary meaning of 'nation', and the one most frequently ventilated in the literature, was political. It equated 'the people' and the state in the manner of the American and French Revolutions, an equation which is familiar in such phrases as 'the nation-state', the 'United Nations', or the rhetoric of late-twentieth-century presidents. Early political discourse in the USA preferred to speak of 'the people', 'the union', 'the confederation, 'our common land', 'the public', 'public welfare' or 'the community' in order to avoid the centralizing and unitary implications of the term 'nation' against the rights of the federated states.[12] For it was, or certainly soon became, part of the concept of the nation in the era of the Revolutions that it should be, in the French phrase, 'one and indivisible'.[13] The 'nation' so considered, was the body of citizens

[11] *Oxford English Dictionary*, vol. VII (Oxford 1933), p. 30.
[12] John J. Lalor (ed.), *Cyclopedia of Political Science* (New York 1889), vol. II, p. 932: 'Nation'. The relevant entries are largely reprinted, or rather translated, from earlier French works.
[13] 'It would follow from this definition that a nation is destined to form only one state and that it constitutes one indivisible whole' (*ibid.* p. 923). The definition from which this 'would follow' is that a nation is 'an aggregate of men speaking the same language, having the same customs, and endowed with certain moral qualities which distinguish them from other groups of a like nature'. This is one of the numerous exercises in the art of begging questions to which nationalist argument has so often been prone.

whose collective sovereignty constituted them a state which was their political expression. For, whatever else a nation was, the element of citizenship and mass participation or choice was never absent from it. John Stuart Mill did not merely define the nation by its possession of national sentiment. He also added that the members of a nationality 'desire to be under the same government, and desire that it should be government by themselves or a portion of themselves exclusively'.[14] We observe without surprise that Mill discusses the idea of nationality not in a separate publication as such, but, characteristically – and briefly – in the context of his little treatise on Representative Government, or democracy.

The equation nation = state = people, and especially sovereign people, undoubtedly linked nation to territory, since structure and definition of states were now essentially territorial. It also implied a multiplicity of nation-states so constituted, and this was indeed a necessary consequence of popular self-determination. As the French Declaration of Rights of 1795 put it:

> Each people is independent and sovereign, whatever the number of individuals who compose it and the extent of the territory it occupies. This sovereignty is inalienable.[15]

But it said little about what constituted a 'people'. In particular there was no logical connection between the body of citizens of a territorial state on one hand, and the identification of a 'nation' on ethnic, linguistic or other grounds or of other characteristics which allowed collective recognition of group membership. Indeed, it has been argued that the French Revolution 'was completely foreign to the principle or feeling of nationality; it was even hostile to it' for this reason.[16] As the Dutch lexicographer noted perceptively, language had nothing to do *in principle* with being English or French, and indeed, as we shall see, French experts were to fight

---

[14] J. S. Mill, *Utilitarianism, Liberty and Representative Government* (Everyman edition, London 1910), pp. 359–66.

[15] It may be observed that there is no reference to the right of peoples to sovereignty and independence in the Declarations of Rights of 1789 or 1793. See Lucien Jaume, *Le Discours jacobin et la démocratie* (Paris 1989), Appendices 1–3, pp. 407–14. However, O. Dann and J. Dinwiddy (eds.), *Nationalism in the Age of the French Revolution* (London 1988), p. 34, for the same view in 1793.

[16] Maurice Block, 'Nationalities, principle of' in J. Lalor (ed.), *Cyclopedia of Political Science*, vol. II, p. 939.

stubbornly against any attempt to make the spoken language a criterion of nationality which, they argued, was determined purely by French citizenship. The language Alsatians or Gascons spoke remained irrelevant to their status as members of the French people.

Indeed, if 'the nation' had anything in common from the popular-revolutionary point of view, it was not, in any fundamental sense, ethnicity, language and the like, though these could be indications of collective belonging also. As Pierre Vilar has pointed out,[17] what characterized the nation–people as seen from below was precisely that it represented the common interest against particular interests, the common good against privilege, as indeed is suggested by the term Americans used before 1800 to indicate nationhood while avoiding the word itself. Ethnic group differences were from this revolutionary-democratic point of view as secondary as they later seemed to socialists. Patently what distinguished the American colonists from King George and his supporters was neither language nor ethnicity, and conversely, the French Republic saw no difficulty in electing the Anglo-American Thomas Paine to its National Convention.

We cannot therefore read into the revolutionary 'nation' anything like the later nationalist programme of establishing nation-states for bodies defined in terms of the criteria so hotly debated by the nineteenth-century theorists, such as ethnicity, common language, religion, territory and common historical memories (to cite John Stuart Mill yet again).[18] As we have seen, except for a territory whose extent was undefined (and perhaps skin colour) none of these united the new American nation. Moreover, as the 'grande nation' of the French extended its frontiers in the course of the revolutionary and Napoleonic wars to areas which were French by none of the later criteria of national belonging, it was clear that none of them were the basis of its constitution.

Nevertheless, the various elements later used to discover definitions of non-state nationality, were undoubtedly present, either

[17] P. Vilar, 'Sobre los fundamentos de las estructuras nacionales' (*Historia*, 16/Extra V (Madrid, April 1978), p. 11.

[18] John Stuart Mill, *Utilitarianism, Liberty and Representative Government*, pp. 359–66.

associated with the revolutionary nation or creating problems for it; and the more one and indivisible it claimed to be, the more heterogeneity within it created problems. There is little doubt that for most Jacobins a Frenchman who did not speak French was suspect, and that in practice the ethno-linguistic criterion of nationality was often accepted. As Barère put it in his report on languages to the Committee of Public Safety:

> Who, in the Departments of Haut-Rhin and Bas-Rhin, has joined with the traitors to call the Prussian and the Austrian on our invaded frontiers? It is the inhabitant of the [Alsatian] countryside, who speaks the same language as our enemies, and who consequently considers himself their brother and fellow-citizen rather than the brother and fellow-citizen of Frenchmen who address him in another language and have other customs.[19]

The French insistence on linguistic uniformity since the Revolution has indeed been marked, and at the time it was quite exceptional. We shall return to it below. But the point to note is, that in theory it was not the native use of the French language that made a person French – how could it when the Revolution itself spent so much of its time proving how few people in France actually used it?[20] – but the willingness to acquire this, among the other liberties, laws and common characteristics of the free people of France. In a sense acquiring French was one of the conditions of full French citizenship (and therefore nationality) as acquiring English became for American citizenship. To illustrate the difference between a basically linguistic definition of nationality and the French, even in its extreme form, let us recall the German philologist whom we shall encounter below convincing the International Statistical Congress of the need to insert a question on language into state censuses (see below pp. 98–9). Richard Böckh, whose influential publications in the 1860s argued that language was the only adequate

19 Cited in M. de Certeau, D. Julia, and J. Revel, *Une Politique de la langue. La Révolution Française et les patois: L'enquête de l'Abbé Grégoire* (Paris 1975), p. 293. For the general problem of the French Revolution and the national language, see also Renée Balibar and Dominique Laporte, *Le Français national. Politique et pratique de la langue nationale sous la Révolution* (Paris 1974). For the specific problem of Alsace, see E. Philipps, *Les Luttes linguistiques en Alsace jusqu'en 1945* (Strasbourg 1975) and P. Lévy, *Histoire linguistique d'Alsace et de Lorraine* (2 vols., Strasbourg 1929).
20 De Certeau, Julia and Revel, *Une Politique de la langue, passim.*

indicator of nationality, an argument well-suited to German nationalism, since Germans were so widely distributed over central and eastern Europe, found himself obliged to classify the Ashkenazic Jews as Germans, since Yiddish was unquestionably a German dialect derived from medieval German. This conclusion as he was well aware, was not likely to be shared by German anti-Semites. But French revolutionaries, arguing for the integration of Jews into the French nation, would neither have needed nor understood this argument. From their point of view Sephardic Jews speaking medieval Spanish and Ashkenazic ones speaking Yiddish – and France contained both – were equally French, once they accepted the conditions of French citizenship, which naturally included speaking French. Conversely, the argument that Dreyfus could not 'really' be French because he was of Jewish descent, was rightly understood as challenging the very nature of the French Revolution and its definition of the French nation.

Nevertheless, it is at the point of Barère's report that two quite different concepts of the nation meet: the revolutionary-democratic and the nationalist. The equation state = nation = people applied to both, but for nationalists the creation of the political entities which would contain it derived from the prior existence of some community distinguishing itself from foreigners, while from the revolutionary-democratic point of view the central concept was the sovereign citizen-people = state which, in relation to the remainder of the human race, constituted a 'nation'.[21] Nor should we forget that henceforth states, however constituted, would also have to take account of their subjects, for in the Age of Revolution it had become more difficult to rule them. As the Greek liberator Kolokotrones put it, it was no longer true that 'the people thought that kings were gods upon earth and that they were bound to say that what they did was well done'.[22] Divinity no longer hedged them. When Charles X of France revived the ancient ceremony of coronation at Rheims in 1825 and (reluctantly) the

[21] 'In relation to the state, the *citizens* constitute the *people*; in relation to the human race, they constitute the *nation*', J. Hélie, 'Nation, definition of,' in Lalor, *Cyclopedia of Political Science*, vol. II, p. 923.

[22] Quoted in E. J. Hobsbawm, *The Age of Revolution 1789–1848* (London 1962), pp. 91–2.

ceremony of magical healing, a mere 120 people turned up to be cured of scrofula by the royal touch. At the last coronation before him, in 1774, there had been 2,400.[23] As we shall see, after 1870 democratization would make this problem of legitimacy and the mobilization of citizens both urgent and acute. For governments the central item in the equation state = nation = people was plainly the state.

But what was the locus of the nation, or for that matter the equation state = nation = people in whatever order of terms, in the theoretical discourse of those who, after all, impressed their character most firmly on the European nineteenth century, and especially on the period when the 'principle of nationality' changed its map in the most dramatic way, namely the period from 1830 to 1880: the liberal bourgeoisies and their intellectuals? Even had they wanted to, they could not have avoided reflecting on the problem during the fifty years when the European balance of power was transformed by the emergence of two great powers based on the national principle (Germany and Italy), the effective partition of a third on the same grounds (Austria–Hungary after the Compromise of 1867), not to mention the recognition of a number of lesser political entities as independent states claiming the new status as nationally based peoples, from Belgium in the west to the Ottoman successor states in southeast Europe (Greece, Serbia, Romania, Bulgaria), and two national revolts of the Poles demanding their reconstitution as what they thought of as a nation-state. Nor did they wish to avoid it. For Walter Bagehot 'nation-making' was the essential content of nineteenth-century evolution.[24]

However, since the number of nation-states in the early nineteenth century was small, the obvious question for enquiring minds was which of the numerous European populations classifiable as a 'nationality' on some ground or another, would acquire a state (or some lesser form of separate political or administrative recognition), and which of the numerous existing states would be imbued with the character of 'nation'. The drawing up of lists of the criteria of potential or actual nationhood essentially served this purpose. It

[23] Marc Bloch, *Les Rois thaumaturges* (Paris 1924), pp. 402–4.
[24] Walter Bagehot, *Physics and Politics* (London 1887), ch.III, IV on 'Nation-making'.

seemed obvious that not all states would coincide with nations, nor the other way round. On the one hand, Renan's famous question 'why is Holland a nation, while Hanover and the Grand Duchy of Parma are not?'[25] raised one set of analytical issues. On the other hand John Stuart Mill's observation that the establishment of a national state had to be (a) feasible and (b) desired by the nationality itself, raised another. This was so even for mid-Victorian nationalists who had no doubt at all about the answer to both kinds of question as they concerned their own nationality or the state in which it found itself. For even they found themselves looking at the claims of other nationalities and states with a colder eye.

However, when we get beyond this point we encounter, in nineteenth-century liberal discourse, a surprising degree of intellectual vagueness. This is due not so much to a failure to think the problem of the nation through, as to the assumption that it did not require to be spelled out, since it was already obvious. Hence much of the liberal theory of nations emerges only, as it were, on the margins of the discourse of liberal writers. Moreover, as we shall see, one central area of liberal theoretical discourse made it difficult to consider the 'nation' intellectually at all. Our task in the remainder of this chapter is to reconstruct a coherent liberal bourgeois theory of the 'nation', rather in the manner in which archaeologists reconstruct trade routes from deposits of coins.

The best way may be to begin with the least satisfactory notion of the 'nation', namely the sense in which Adam Smith uses the word in the title of his great work. For in his context it plainly means no more than a territorial state, or, in the words of John Rae, a sharp Scottish mind wandering through early nineteenth-century North America criticizing Smith, 'every separate community, society, nation, state or people (terms which, as far as our subject is concerned, may be considered synonymous)'.[26] Yet the thought of the great liberal political economist must surely be relevant to liberal middle-class thinkers considering the 'nation' from other

[25] Ernest Renan, 'What is a nation?' in Afred Zimmern (ed.), *Modern Political Doctrines* (Oxford 1939), p. 192.

[26] John Rae, *The Sociological Theory of Capital, being a complete reprint of The New Principles of Political Economy by John Rae* (1834) (ed.) C. W. Mixter (New York 1905), p. 26.

points of view, even if they were not, like John Stuart Mill, economists themselves, or like Walter Bagehot, editors of *The Economist*. Was it, we may ask, historically fortuitous that the classic era of free trade liberalism coincided with that 'nation-making' which Bagehot saw as so central to his century? In other words, did the nation-state have a specific function as such in the process of capitalist development? Or rather: how did contemporary liberal analysts see this function?

For it is evident to the historian that the role of economies defined by state frontiers was large. The nineteenth-century world economy was *international* rather than cosmopolitan. World system theorists have tried to show that capitalism was bred as a global system in one continent and not elsewhere, precisely because of the political pluralism of Europe, which neither constituted nor formed part of a single 'world empire'. Economic development in the sixteenth–eighteenth centuries proceeded on the basis of territorial states, each of which tended to pursue mercantilist policies as a unified whole. Even more obviously, when we speak of world capitalism in the nineteenth and early twentieth centuries we do so in terms of its component national units in the developed world – of British industry, the American economy, German as distinct from French capitalism and so on. During the lengthy period from the eighteenth century to the years following World War II, there seemed to be little space and scope in the global economy for those genuinely extra-territorial, transnational or interstitial units which had played so large a part in the genesis of a capitalist world economy and which are today once again so prominent: for instance, independent mini-states whose economic significance is out of proportion to their size and resources – Lübeck and Ghent in the fourteenth century, Singapore and Hongkong once again today. In fact, looking back over the development of the modern world economy we are inclined to see the phase during which economic development was integrally linked to the 'national economies' of a number of developed territorial states as situated between two essentially transnational eras.

The difficulty for nineteenth-century liberal economists, or liberals who, as might have been expected, accepted the arguments of classical political economy, was that they could only recognize the economic significance of nations in practice, but not in theory. Classical political economy, and notably Adam Smith's, had been formulated as a critique of the 'mercantile system', i.e. of precisely the system in which governments treated national economies as ensembles to be developed by state effort and policy. Free trade and the free market were directed precisely against this concept of national economic development, which Smith thought he had demonstrated to be counter-productive. Economic theory was thus elaborated uniquely on the basis of individual units of enterprise – persons or firms – rationally maximizing their gains and minimizing their losses in a market which had no specific spatial extension. At the limit it was, and could not but be, the world market. While Smith was far from opposed to certain functions of government which were relevant to the economy, so far as the general theory of economic growth was concerned, it had no place for the nation, or any collectivity larger than the firm, which, incidentally, it did not bother to investigate much.

Thus J. E. Cairnes, at the peak of the liberal era, even spent ten pages seriously considering the proposition that a theory of international trade was unnecessary, as distinct from any other trade between individuals.[27] He concluded that, while international transactions were undoubtedly becoming steadily easier, there were still enough frictions left to justify separate consideration of the problem of trade between states. The German liberal economist Schönberg doubted whether the concept of 'national income' had any meaning. Those not content with superficial ideas might be tempted to believe this, but they were probably going too far even though estimates of 'national wealth' in monetary terms were mistaken.[28] Edwin Cannan[29] thought Adam Smith's 'nation' consisted only of the collection of individuals living on the territory of a state and considered whether the fact that in a hundred years' time

---

[27] J. E. Cairnes, *Some Leading Principles of Political Economy Newly Expounded* (London 1874), pp. 355–65.

[28] Dr Gustav Schönberg (ed.), *Handbuch der politischen Oekonomie*, vol. I (Tübingen 1882), pp. 158ff.

[29] Edwin Cannan, *History of the Theories of Production and Distribution in English Political Economy from 1776 to 1848* (London 1894), pp. 10ff.

all these people would be dead, made it impossible to speak of the 'nation' as a continuously existing entity. In policy terms this meant the belief that only the allocation of resources through the market was optimal, and that by means of its operation the interests of individuals would automatically produce the interests of the whole – insofar as there was room in theory for such a concept as the interests of the whole community. Conversely, John Rae wrote his 1834 book specifically to demonstrate against Smith that individual and national interests were not identical, i.e. that the principles that guided the individual's pursuit of self-interest did not necessarily maximize the wealth of the nation.[30] As we shall see, those who refused to take to Smith unconditionally were not to be neglected, but their economic theories could not compete with the classical school. The term 'national economy' only appears in Palgrave's *Dictionary of Political Economy* in connection with German economic theory. The term 'nation' itself had disappeared from the equivalent French work of the 1890s.[31]

John Rae vs. Adam Smith.

And yet, even the purest of classical economists were obliged to operate with the concept of a national economy. As the Saint-Simonian Michel Chevalier announced apologetically or tongue-in-cheek in his inaugural lesson as Professor of Political Economy at the Collège de France:

> We are commanded to concern ourselves with the general interests of human societies, and we are not prohibited from considering the particular situation in the society within which we are living.[32]

Or, as Lord Robbins was to put it, once again in relation to classical political economists, 'there is little evidence that they often went beyond the test of national advantage as a criterion of policy, still less that they were prepared to contemplate the dissolution of national bonds'.[33] In short, they neither could nor wanted to get

---

[30] Rae, *The Sociological Theory of Capital.*
[31] *Nouveau Dictionnaire d'Economie Politique* (ed.), Léon Say and Joseph Chailley (Paris 1892).
[32] Michel Chevalier, *Cours d'economie politique fait au Collège de France*, vol. 1 (Paris 1855), p. 43. The lecture was originally given in 1841.
[33] L. Robbins, *The Theory of Economic Policy in English Classical Political Economy* (2nd edn, London 1977), pp. 9–10. An exception should, however, be made for the genuinely global Bentham.

away from 'the nation', whose progress Porter monitored with self-satisfaction from 1835 onwards because, he thought, one wished 'to ascertain the means by which any community has attained the eminence among nations'. By 'any community' he meant, one need hardly add, 'one's own community'.[34]

How indeed could the economic functions and even benefits of the nation-state be denied? The existence of states with a monopoly of currency and with public finances and therefore fiscal policies and activities was a fact. These economic activities could not be abolished, even by those who wished to eliminate their harmful interventions into the economy. Moreover, even extreme libertarians could accept, with Molinari, that 'the division of humanity into autonomous nations is essentially economic'.[35] For the state – in the post-revolutionary era the nation-state – after all guaranteed the security of property and contracts, and as J. B. Say put it – notoriously no friend to public enterprise – 'no nation has ever attained a level of wealth without being under a regular government'.[36] Government functions could even be rationalized by liberal economics in terms of free competition. Thus Molinari argued that 'the fragmentation of humanity into nations is useful, inasmuch as it develops an extremely powerful principle of economic emulation'.[37] He cited the Great Exhibition of 1851 in support. But even without such justifications, the function of government in economic development was assumed. J. B. Say, who could see no more difference between a nation and its neighbours than between two neighbouring provinces, nevertheless accused France – i.e. the French state and government – of neglecting to develop the country's domestic resources and indulging in foreign conquest instead. In short, no economist of even the most extreme liberal persuasion could overlook or fail to take account of the national economy. Only liberal economists did not like to, or quite know how to, talk about it.

34 George Richardson Porter, *The progress of the Nation, in its various social and economic relations, from the beginning of the nineteenth century to the present time*, 2 pts (London 1836), Preface.
35 Molinari in *Dictionnaire d'economie politique* (Paris 1854) repr. in Lalor, *Cyclopedia of Political Science*, vol. II, p. 957: 'Nations in political economy'.
36 *Ibid.* pp. 958–9.   37 *Ibid.* p. 957.

But in countries pursuing national economic development against the superior economy of Britain, Smithian free trade seemed less attractive. There we find no shortage of men who were anxious to talk about the national economy as a whole. The neglected Scottish-Canadian Rae has already been mentioned. He propounded theories which appear to anticipate the import-substituting and technology-importing doctrines of the UN Economic Commission for Latin America in the 1950s. More obviously the great Federalist Alexander Hamilton in the USA linked nation, state and economy, using this link to justify the strong national government he favoured against less centralizing politicians. The list of his 'great national measures' drawn up by the author of the article 'nation' in a later American work of reference is exclusively economic: the foundation of a national bank, national responsibility for state debts, the creation of a national debt, the protection of national manufactures by high tariffs, and compulsory excise.[38] It may be that, as the admiring author suggests, all these measures 'were intended to develop the germ of nationality', or it may be that, as in the case of other Federalists who talked little of the nation and much in economic argument, he felt that the nation would take care of itself if the Federal government took care of economic development: in any case nation implied national economy and its systematic fostering by the state, which in the nineteenth century meant protectionism.

Nineteenth-century American development economists were, in general, too mediocre to make much of a theoretical case for Hamiltonianism, as the miserable Carey and others attempted to do.[39] However, that case was made both lucidly and eloquently by German economists, headed by Friedrich List, who had acquired his ideas, which were frankly inspired by Hamilton, during his stay in the USA in the 1820s, when he had actually taken part in the national economic debates of that period.[40] For List the task of

[handwritten: economic reason for Nationalism.]

[38] *Ibid.* p. 933.
[39] Cf. J. Schumpeter, *History of Economic Analysis* (Oxford 1954), pp. 515–16.
[40] He wrote an *Outline of American Political Economy* (Philadelphia 1827), which anticipates his later views. For List in America see W. Notz 'Friedrich List in Amerika' (*Weltwirtschaftliches Archiv*, 29, 1925, pp. 199–265 and vol. 22, 1925, pp. 154–82 and 'Frederick List in America' (American Economic Review, 16, 1926, pp. 249–65).

economics, which Germans henceforth tended to call 'national economy' (Nationaloekonomie) or 'people's economy' (Volkswirthschaft) rather than 'political economy', was to 'accomplish the economic development of the nation and to prepare its entry into the universal society of the future'.[41] One need hardly add that this development would take the form of capitalist industrialization pressed forward by a vigorous bourgeoisie.

However, what is interesting from our point of view about List, and the later 'historical school' of German economists who took him as their inspiration – as did economic nationalists of other countries like Arthur Griffith of Ireland[42] – is that he clearly formulated a characteristic of the 'liberal' concept of the nation which was usually taken for granted. It had to be of sufficient size to form a viable unit of development. If it fell below this threshold, it had no historic justification. This seemed too obvious to require argument, and was rarely argued out. The *Dictionnaire politique* of Garnier-Pagès in 1843 thought it 'ridiculous' that Belgium and Portugal should be independent nations, because they were patently too small.[43] John Stuart Mill justified the quite undeniable nationalism of the Irish on the ground that they were after all, all things considered, 'sufficiently numerous to be capable of constituting a respectable nationality'.[44] Others, among them Mazzini and Cavour, apostles though they were of the principle of nationality, disagreed. Indeed, the *New English Dictionary* itself defined the word 'nation' not just in the usual manner familiarized in Britain by J. S. Mill, but as 'an *extensive* aggregate of persons' with the required characteristics (emphasis added).[45]

Now List stated clearly that

> a large population and an extensive territory endowed with manifold national resources, are essential requirements of the normal nationality ... A nation restricted in the number of its population and in

41 Friedrich List, *The National System of Political Economy* (London 1885), p. 174.
42 For a good summary of his views, E. Strauss, *Irish Nationalism and British Democracy* (London 1951), pp. 218–20.
43 'Nation' by Elias Regnault, *Dictionnaire politique*, with an introduction by Garnier-Pagès (Paris 1842), pp. 623–5. 'N'y-a-t-il pas quelque chose de dérisoire d'appeler la Belgique une nation?'
44 *Considerations on Representative Government* in *Utilitarianism*, p. 365.
45 *Oxford English Dictionary*, VII, p. 30.

territory, especially if it has a separate language, can only possess a crippled literature, crippled institutions for promoting art and science. A small state can never bring to complete perfection within its territory the various branches of production.[46]

The economic benefits of large-scale states (*Grossstaaten*), thought Professor Gustav Cohn, were demonstrated by the history of Britain and France. They were no doubt less than those of a single global economy, but world unity, unfortunately, was not attainable as yet. In the mean time 'everything to which humanity aspires for the entire human race ... is at this point already (*zunächst einmal*) achieved for a significant fraction of humanity, i.e. for 30–60 millions'. And so 'it follows that the future of the civilized world will, for a long time to come, take the form of the creation of large states (*Grossstaatenbildung*)'.[47] We note, incidentally, the constant assumption, to which we shall return below, of 'nations' as a second-best to world unity.

Two consequences followed from this thesis, which was almost universally accepted by serious thinkers on the subject, even when they did not formulate it as explicitly as did the Germans who had some historical reasons for doing so.

First, it followed that the 'principle of nationality' applied in practice only to nationalities of a certain size. Hence the otherwise startling fact that Mazzini, the apostle of this principle, did not envisage independence for Ireland. As for even smaller nationalities or potential nationalities – Sicilians, Bretons, Welsh – their claims need be taken even less seriously. In fact, the word *Kleinstaaterei* (the system of mini-states) was deliberately derogatory. It was what German nationalists were against. The word 'Balkanization', derived from the division of the territories formerly in the Turkish empire into various small independent states, still retains its negative connotation. Both terms belonged to the vocabulary of political insults. This 'threshold principle' is excellently illustrated by the map of the future Europe of nations which Mazzini himself drew up in 1857: it comprised a bare dozen states and federations, only one of which (needless to say Italy) would not be obviously

[46] *Ibid.*, pp. 175–6.
[47] Gustav Cohn, *Grundlegung der Nationaloekonomie*, vol. 1 (Stuttgart 1885), pp. 447–9.

classified as multi-national by later criteria.[48] The 'principle of nationality' in the Wilsonian formulation which dominated the peace treaties after World War I, produced a Europe of twenty-six states – twenty-seven if we add the Irish Free State which was shortly to be established. I merely add that a recent study of regionalist movements in western Europe alone counts forty-two of them,[49] thus demonstrating what can happen once the 'threshold principle' is abandoned.

The point to note, however, is that in the classical period of liberal nationalism nobody would have dreamed of abandoning it. Self-determination for nations applied only to what were considered to be viable nations: culturally, and certainly economically (whatever exactly viability meant). To this extent Mazzini's and Mill's idea of national self-determination was fundamentally different from President Wilson's. We shall consider the reasons for the change from one to the other below. However, it may be worth noting en passant even here that the 'threshold principle' was not entirely abandoned even in the Wilsonian era. Between the wars the existence of Luxemburg and Liechtenstein remained a slight embarrassment, however welcome these polities were to philatelists. Nobody felt happy about the existence of the Free City of Danzig, not only in the two neighbouring states each of which wanted it within its territory, but more generally among those who felt that no city-state could be viable in the twentieth century as it had been in Hanseatic days. The inhabitants of rump Austria almost unanimously desired integration into Germany, because they simply could not believe that a small state such as theirs was independently viable as an economy ('lebensfähig'). It is only since 1945, and even more since decolonization, that we have made way in the community of nations for entities like Dominica or the Maldives or Andorra.

The second consequence is that the building of nations was seen inevitably as a process of expansion. This was another reason for the anomaly of the Irish case or of any other purely separatist

[48] See Denis Mack Smith (ed.), Il Risorgimento (Bari 1968), p. 422.
[49] Jochen Blaschke (ed.), Handbuch der westeuropäischen Regionalbewegungen (Frankfurt 1980).

nationalism. As we have seen, it was accepted in theory that social evolution expanded the scale of human social units from family and tribe to county and canton, from the local to the regional, the national and eventually the global. Nations were therefore, as it were, in tune with historical evolution only insofar as they extended the scale of human society, other things being equal.

> If our doctrine were to be summed up in the form of a proposition, we should perhaps say that, generally, the principle of nationalities is legitimate when it tends to unite, in a compact whole, scattered groups of population, and illegitimate when it tends to divide a state.[50]

In practice this meant that national movements were expected to be movements for national *unification* or expansion. All Germans and Italians thus hoped to come together in one state, as did all Greeks. Serbs would merge with Croats into a single Yugoslavia (for which there was no historical precedent whatever), and beyond this the dream of a Balkan Federation haunted the seekers after a yet larger unity. It remained a commitment of the communist movements until after World War II. Czechs would merge with Slovaks, Poles would combine with Lithuanians and Ruthenes – in fact, they had already formed a single large state in pre-partition Poland – Romanians of Moldavia would fuse with those of Wallachia and Transylvania, and so on. This was evidently incompatible with definitions of nations as based on ethnicity, language or common history, but, as we have seen, these were not the decisive criteria of liberal nation-making. In any case, nobody ever denied the actual multinationality or multilinguality or multiethnicity of the oldest and most unquestioned nation-states, e.g. Britain, France and Spain.

That 'nation-states' would be nationally heterogeneous in this way was accepted all the more readily, as there were many parts of Europe and much of the rest of the world where nationalities were so obviously mixed up on the same territory, that a purely spatial unscrambling of them seemed to be quite unrealistic. This was to be the basis of interpretations of nationality such as the later Austro-Marxist one, which attached it not to territory but to people. Nor

[50] Maurice Block in Lalor, *Cyclopedia of Political Science*, vol. II, p. 941.

was it an accident that the initiative in this matter within the Austrian social democratic party came largely from the Slovenes, who lived in an area where Slovene and German settlements, often existing as enclaves within enclaves or border zones of uncertain and shifting identification, were particularly hard to disentangle.[51] However, the national heterogeneity of nation-states was accepted, above all, because it seemed clear that small, and especially small and backward, nationalities had everything to gain by merging into greater nations, and making their contributions to humanity through these. 'Experience', said Mill, articulating the consensus of sensible observers, 'proves that it is possible for one nationality to merge and be absorbed into another.' For the backward and inferior this would be so much gain:

> Nobody can suppose that it is not more beneficial for a Breton or a Basque of French Navarre to be ... a member of the French nationality, admitted on equal terms to all the privileges of French citizenship ... than to sulk on his own rocks, the half-savage relic of past times, revolving in his own little mental orbit, without participation or interest in the general movement of the world. The same remark applies to the Welshman or the Scottish highlander as members of the British nation.[52]

Once it was accepted that an independent or 'real' nation also had to be a viable nation by the criteria then accepted, it also followed that some of the smaller nationalities and languages were doomed to disappear as such. Frederick Engels has been bitterly assailed as a great-German chauvinist for predicting the disappearance of the Czechs as a people and making uncomplimentary remarks about the future of a good few other peoples.[53] He was indeed proudly German, and inclined to compare his people favourably with others except in respect of its revolutionary tradition. He was also, without the slightest doubt, totally wrong about the Czechs, and about some other peoples. However, it is

---

[51] For the contribution of Etbin Kristan to the Brünn (Brno) Congress of the party, which elaborated its national programme, see Georges Haupt, Michel Lowy and Claudie Weill, *Les Marxistes et la question nationale 1848–1914* (Paris 1937), pp. 204–7.

[52] Mill, *Utilitarianism, Liberty and Representative Government*, pp. 363–4.

[53] Cf. Roman Rosdolsky, 'Friedrich Engels und das Problem der "geschichtslosen Völker"' (*Archiv für Sozialgeschichte*, 4/1964, pp. 87–282).

sheer anachronism to criticize him for his essential stance, which was shared by every impartial mid-nineteenth-century observer. *Some* small nationalities and languages had no independent future. So much was generally accepted, even by people far from hostile to national liberation in principle, or practice.

There was nothing chauvinist in such a general attitude. It did not imply any hostility to the languages and culture of such collective victims to the laws of progress (as they would certainly have been called then). On the contrary, where the supremacy of the state-nationality and the state-language were not an issue, the major nation could cherish and foster the dialects and lesser languages within it, the historic and folkloric traditions of the lesser communities it contained, if only as proof of the range of colours on its macro-national palette. Moreover, small nationalities or even nation-states which accepted their integration into the larger nation as something positive – or, if one prefers, which accepted the laws of progress – did not recognize any irreconcilable differences between micro-culture and macro-culture either, or were even reconciled to the loss of what could not be adapted to the modern age. It was the Scots and not the English who invented the concept of the 'North Briton' after the Union of 1707.[54] It was the speakers and champions of Welsh in nineteenth-century Wales who doubted whether their own language, so powerful a medium for religion and poetry, could serve as an all-purpose language of culture in the nineteenth-century world – i.e. who assumed the necessity and advantages of bilingualism.[55] Doubtless they were not unaware of the possibilities of all-British careers for the English-speaking Welshman, but this did not diminish their emotional bond with ancient tradition. This is evident even among those who reconciled themselves to the eventual disappearance of the idiom, like the Rev. Griffiths of the Dissenting College, Brecknock, who merely asked for natural evolution to be left to take its course:

[54] See Linda Colley, 'Whose nation? Class and national consciousness in Britain 1750–1830' (*Past and Present*, 113, 1986), pp. 96–117.
[55] Ieuan Gwynedd Jones, 'Language and community in nineteenth-century Wales' in David Smith (ed.), *A People and a Proletariat: Essays in the History of Wales 1780–1980* (London 1980), pp. 41–71, esp. pp. 59–63.

Let it [the Welsh language] die fairly, peacefully and reputably. Attached to it as we are, few would wish to postpone its euthanasy. But no sacrifice would be deemed too great to prevent its being murdered.[56]

Forty years later, another member of a small nationality, the socialist theoretician Karl Kautsky – by origin a Czech – talked in similarly resigned, but not dispassionate, terms:

National languages will be increasingly confined to domestic use, and even there they will tend to be treated like an old piece of inherited family furniture, something that we treat with veneration even though it has not much practical use.[57]

But these were problems of the smaller nationalities whose independent future seemed problematic. The English hardly gave a thought to the preoccupations of the Scots and the Welsh, as they gloried in the home-grown exoticisms of the British Isles. Indeed, as the stage-Irish soon discovered, who welcomed lesser nationalities which did not challenge the greater, all the more, the more unlike the English they behaved: the thicker the Irishness or Scottishness were laid on with the trowel. Similarly Pangerman nationalists actually encouraged the production of literature in Low German or Frisian, since these were safely reduced to appendages rather than competitors with High German, nationalist Italians prided themselves on Belli, Goldoni and songs in Neapolitan. For that matter Francophone Belgium did not object to Belgians who talked and wrote Flemish. It was the *Flamingants* who resisted French. There were indeed cases where the leading nation or *Staatsvolk* tried actively to suppress minor languages and cultures, but until the late nineteenth century this was rare outside France.

Some people or nationalities were thus destined never to become full nations. Others had attained, or would attain, full nationhood. But which had a future and which did not? The debates on what constituted the characteristics of a nationality – territorial, linguistic, ethnical, etc. – did not help much. The 'threshold principle' was naturally more useful, since it eliminated a number of small

[56] Inquiry on Education in Wales, *Parliamentary Paper*, 1847, XXVII, part II (Report on the Counties of Brecknock, Cardigan and Radnor), p. 67.
[57] Haupt, Lowy and Weill, *Les Marxistes*, p. 122.

peoples, but, as we have seen, it was not decisive either, since there existed unquestioned 'nations' of quite modest size, not to mention national movements like the Irish, about whose capacity to form viable nation-states there were divided opinions. The immediate point of Renan's question about Hanover and the Grand Duchy of Parma was, after all, to contrast them not with *any* nations but with other nation-states of the same modest order of magnitude, with the Netherlands or Switzerland. As we shall see, the emergence of national movements with mass support, demanding attention, would call for substantial revisions of judgment, but in the classic era of liberalism few of them, outside the Ottoman empire, actually as yet seemed to demand recognition as independent sovereign states, as distinct from demanding various kinds of autonomy. The Irish case was, as usual, anomalous in this respect also – at any rate it became so with the appearance of the Fenians who demanded an Irish Republic which could not but be independent from Britain.

In practice there were only three criteria which allowed a people to be firmly classed as a nation, always provided it was sufficiently large to pass the threshold. The first was its historic association with a current state or one with a fairly lengthy and recent past. Hence there was little dispute about the existence of an English or French nation-people, a (Great) Russian people or the Poles, and little dispute outside Spain about a Spanish nation with well-understood national characteristics.[58] For given the identification of nation with state, it was natural for foreigners to assume that the only people in a country were those belonging to the state-people, a habit which still irritates the Scots.

The second criterion was the existence of a long-established cultural elite, possessing a written national literary and administrative vernacular. This was the basis of the Italian and German claims to nationhood, although the respective 'peoples' had no single state with which they could identify. In both cases national identification was in consequence strongly linguistic, even though in neither case was the national language spoken for everyday purposes by more

[58] Within Spain the cultural, linguistic and institutional differences between the peoples of the kingdoms of Aragon and Castile were evident. In the Spanish empire, from which Aragon was excluded, even more so.

than a small minority – for Italy it has been estimated at 2½% at the moment of unification[59] – while the rest spoke various and often mutually incomprehensible idioms.[60]

The third criterion, it must unfortunately be said, was a proven capacity for conquest. There is nothing like being an imperial people to make a population conscious of its collective existence as such, as Friedrich List well knew. Besides, for the nineteenth century conquest provided the Darwinian proof of evolutionary success as a social species.

Other candidates for nationhood were plainly not excluded *a priori*, but neither was there any *a priori* presumption in their favour. Their safest course was probably to belong to some political entity which was, by the standards of nineteenth-century liberalism, anomalous, obsolete, and doomed by history and progress. The Ottoman empire was the most obvious evolutionary fossil of this kind, but so, it was increasingly evident, was the Habsburg empire.

Such, then, were the conceptions of nation and nation-state as seen by the ideologists of the era of triumphant bourgeois liberalism: say from 1830 to 1880. They were part of liberal ideology in two ways. First, because the development of nations was unquestionably a phase in human evolution or progress from the small group to the larger, from family to tribe to region, to nation and, in the last instance, to the unified world of the future in which, to quote the superficial and therefore typical G. Lowes Dickinson, 'the barriers of nationality which belong to the infancy of the race will melt and dissolve in the sunshine of science and art'.[61]

That world would be unified even linguistically. A single world language, no doubt coexisting with national languages reduced to the domestic and sentimental role of dialects, was in the minds of

---

[59] Tullio de Mauro, *Storia linguistica dell'Italia unita* (Bari 1963), p. 41.

[60] 'Obwohl sie alle in einem Reich "Deutscher Nation" nebeneinander lebten, darf nichts darüber hinwegtäuschen, dasz ihnen sogar die gemeinsame Umgangssprache fehlte.' Hans-Ulrich Wehler, *Deutsche Gesellschaftsgeschichte*, vol. I (Munich 1987), p. 50.

[61] B. Porter, *Critics of Empire. British Radical Attitudes to Colonialism in Africa, 1895–1914* (London 1968), p. 331, citing G. Lowes Dickinson's *A Modern Symposium* (1908).

both President Ulysses S. Grant and Karl Kautsky.[62] Such predictions, as we now know, were not entirely beside the mark. The attempts to construct artificial world languages which were made from the 1880s, following the international telegraphic and signalling codes of the 1870s, were indeed unsuccessful, even though one of them, Esperanto, still survives among small groups of enthusiasts, and under the protection of some regimes deriving from the socialist internationalism of the period. On the other hand Kautsky's sensible scepticism of such efforts and his prediction that one of the major state languages would be transformed into a *de facto* world language, has indeed been proved correct. English has become that global language, even though it supplements rather than replaces national languages.

Thus in the perspective of liberal ideology, the nation (i.e. the viable large nation) was the stage of evolution reached in the mid-nineteenth century. As we have seen, the other face of the coin 'nation as progress' was therefore, logically, the assimilation of smaller communities and peoples to larger ones. This did not necessarily imply the abandonment of old loyalties and sentiments, though of course it could. The geographically and socially mobile, who had nothing very desirable to look back upon in their past, might be quite ready to do so. This was notably the case with many middle-class Jews in the countries which offered total equality through assimilation – Paris was worth a mass to more than King Henry IV – until they discovered from the end of the century on, that an unlimited readiness to assimilate was not enough, if the receiving nation was not prepared to accept the assimilee fully. On the other hand it must not be forgotten that the USA was by no means the only state freely offering membership of a 'nation' to anybody who wanted to join it, and 'nations' accepted open entry more readily than classes. The generations before 1914 are full of great-nation chauvinists whose fathers, let alone mothers, did not speak the language of their sons' chosen people, and whose names, Slav or Magyarized German or Slav testified to their choice. The rewards of assimilation could be substantial.

---

[62] For a relevant quotation from President Grant's Inaugural, see E. J. Hobsbawm, *The Age of Capital 1848–1875* (London 1975), epigraphs to ch. 3.

But the modern nation was part of liberal ideology in another way. It was linked to the remainder of the great liberal slogans by long association rather than by logical necessity: as liberty and equality are to fraternity. To put it another way, because the nation itself was historically novel, it was opposed by conservatives and traditionalists, and therefore attracted their opponents. The association between the two lines of thought may be illustrated by the example of a typical pan-German from Austria, born in that area of acute national conflict, Moravia. Arnold Pichler,[63] who served the Vienna police with a devotion unbroken by political transformations from 1901 to 1938, was, and to some extent remained, all his life a passionate nationalist German, anti-Czech and anti-Semitic – though he drew the line at putting all Jews into concentration camps, as fellow anti-Semites suggested.[64] At the same time he was a passionate anticlerical and even a liberal in politics; at all events he contributed to the most liberal of Vienna's daily papers in the first republic. In his writings nationalism and eugenical reasoning go together with an enthusiasm for the industrial revolution and, more surprisingly, for its creation of a body of 'citizens of the world' (Weltbürger) ... which ... remote from small-town provincialism and horizons bounded by the church steeple' opened up the entire globe to those previously imprisoned in their regional corners.[65]

Such, then, was the concept of 'nation' and 'nationalism' as seen by liberal thinkers in the heyday of bourgeois liberalism, which was also the era when the 'principle of nationality' first became a major issue in international politics, As we shall see, it differed in one fundamental respect from the Wilsonian principle of national self-determination, which is also, in theory, the Leninist one, and which dominated the debate on these matters from the end of the nineteenth century onwards, and still does. It was not unconditional. In this respect it also differed from the radical-democratic view, as put in the French Revolution's Declaration of Rights cited above, which specifically rejected the 'threshold principle'.

---

[63] Franz Pichler, *Polizeihofrat P. Ein treuer Diener seienes ungetreuen Staates. Wiener Polizeidienst 1901–1938* (Vienna 1984). I thank Clemens Heller for this reference.
[64] *Ibid.*, p. 19.   [65] *Ibid.*, p. 30.

However, in practice the mini-peoples whose right to sovereignty and self-determination were thus guaranteed were not generally permitted by their larger and more rapacious neighbours to exercise either, nor did most of them contain many sympathizers with the principles of 1795. One thinks of the (conservative) free mountain cantons of Switzerland, which could hardly be far from the minds of the readers of Rousseau who drafted Declarations of the Rights of Man in that era. The days of left-wing autonomist or independence movements in such communities had not yet come.

From the point of view of liberalism, and – as the example of Marx and Engels demonstrates, not only of liberalism – the case for 'the nation' was that it represented a stage in the historical development of human society, and the case for the establishment of any particular nation-state, irrespective of the subjective feelings of the members of the nationality concerned, or the personal sympathies of the observer, depended on whether it could be shown to fit in with or to advance historical evolution and progress.[66] The universal bourgeois admiration for Scots highlanders did not, so far as I know, lead a single writer to demand nationhood for them – not even the sentimentalists who mourned the failure of the Stuart restoration under Bonnie Prince Charlie, whose main supporters had been highland clansmen.

But if the only historically justifiable nationalism was that which fitted in with progress, i.e. which enlarged rather than restricted the scale on which human economies, societies and culture operated, what could the defence of small peoples, small languages, small traditions be, in the overwhelming majority of cases, but an expression of conservative resistance to the inevitable advance of history? The small people, language or culture fitted into progress only insofar as it accepted subordinate status to some larger unit or retired from battle to become a repository of nostalgia and other sentiments – in short, accepted the status of old family furniture

---

[66] Cf. Frederick Engels' letter to Bernstein, 22–5 February 1882 (*Werke*, vol. 35, pp. 278ff.) on the Balkan Slavs: 'And even if these chaps were as admirable as the Scots Highlanders celebrated by Walter Scott – another bunch of terrible cattle-thieves – the most we can do is to condemn the *ways* in which society today treats them. If we were in power *we also* would have to deal with the banditry of these fellows, which is part of their heritage.'

which Kautsky assigned to it. And which, of course, so many of the small communities and cultures of the world looked like accepting. Why, so the educated liberal observer might reason, should the speakers of Gaelic behave differently from the speakers of the Northumberland dialect? Nothing prevented them from being bilingual. English dialect writers chose their idiom not *against* the standard national language, but with the consciousness that both had their value and their place. And if, in the course of time, the local idiom would retreat before the national, or even fade away, as had already happened to some marginal Celtic languages (Cornish and Manx ceased to be spoken in the eighteenth century), then, surely, this was regrettable but perhaps inevitable. They would not die unmourned, but a generation that invented the concept and term of 'folklore' could tell the difference between living present and survivals from the past.

To understand the 'nation' of the classical liberal era it is thus essential to bear in mind that 'nation-building', however central to nineteenth-century history, applied only to some nations. And indeed the demand to apply the 'principle of nationality' was not universal either. Both as an international problem and as a domestic political problem it affected only a limited number of peoples or regions, even within multilingual and multiethnic states such as the Habsburg empire, where it clearly dominated politics already. It would not be too much to say that, after 1871 – always excepting the slowly disintegrating Ottoman empire – few people expected any further substantial changes in the map of Europe, and recognized few national problems likely to bring them about, other than the perennial Polish question. And, indeed, outside the Balkans, the only change in the European map between the creation of the German empire and World War I was the separation of Norway from Sweden. What is more, after the national alarums and excursions of the years from 1848 to 1867, it was not too much to suppose that even in Austria–Hungary tempers would cool. That, at all events, is what the officials of the Habsburg empire expected when (rather reluctantly) they decided to accept a resolution of the International Statistical Congress at St Petersburg in 1873 to include a question about language in future censuses, but proposed to postpone its application until after 1880 to allow time for opinion to grow less agitated.[67] They could not have been more spectacularly mistaken in their prognosis.

It also follows that, by and large, in this period nations and nationalism were not major domestic problems for political entities which had reached the status of 'nation-states', however nationally heterogeneous they were by modern standards, though they were acutely troublesome to non-national empires which were not (anachronistically) classifiable as 'multinational'. None of the European states west of the Rhine as yet faced serious complications on this score, except Britain from that permanent anomaly, the Irish. This is not to suggest that politicians were unaware of Catalans or Basques, Bretons or Flemings, Scots and Welsh, but they were mainly seen as adding to or subtracting from the strength of some statewide political force. The Scots and the Welsh functioned as reinforcements to liberalism, the Bretons and Flemings to traditionalist Catholicism. Of course the political systems of nation-states still benefited from the absence of electoral democracy, which was to undermine the liberal theory and practice of the nation, as it was to undermine so much else in nineteenth-century liberalism.

That is perhaps why the serious theoretical literature about nationalism in the liberal era is small and has a somewhat casual air. Observers like Mill and Renan were relaxed enough about the elements which made up 'national sentiment' – ethnicity – in spite of the Victorians' passionate preoccupation with 'race' – language, religion, territory, history, culture and the rest – because politically it did not much matter, as yet, whether one or the other among these was regarded as more important than the rest. But from the 1880s on the debate about 'the national question' becomes serious and intensive, especially among the socialists, because the political appeal of national slogans to masses of potential or actual voters or supporters of mass political movements was now a matter of real

---

[67] Emil Brix, *Die Umgangsprachen in Altösterreich zwischen Agitation und Assimilation. Die Sprachenstatistik in den zisleithanischen Volkszählungen 1880–1910* (Vienna–Cologne–Graz 1982).

practical concern. And the debate on such questions as the theoretical criteria of nationhood became passionate, because any particular answer was now believed to imply a particular form of political strategy, struggle and programme. This was a matter of importance not only for governments confronted with various kinds of national agitation or demand, but for political parties seeking to mobilize constituencies on the basis of national, non-national or alternative national appeals. For socialists in central and eastern Europe it made a great deal of difference on what theoretical basis the nation and its future were defined. Marx and Engels, like Mill and Renan, had regarded such questions as marginal. In the Second International such debates were central, and a constellation of eminent figures, or figures with an eminent future, contributed important writings to them: Kautsky, Luxemburg, Bauer, Lenin and Stalin. But if such questions concerned Marxist theorists, it was also a matter of acute practical importance to, say, Croats and Serbs, Macedonians and Bulgarians, whether the nationality of Southern Slavs was defined in one way or another.[68]

The 'principle of nationality' which diplomats debated and which changed the map of Europe in the period from 1830 to 1878 was thus different from the political phenomenon of nationalism which became increasingly central in the era of European democratization and mass politics. In the days of Mazzini it did not matter that, for the great bulk of Italians, the Risorgimento did not exist so that, as Massimo d'Azeglio admitted in the famous phrase: 'We have made Italy, now we have to make Italians.'[69] It did not even matter to those who considered 'the Polish Question' that probably most Polish-speaking peasants (not to mention the third of the population of the old pre-1772 Rzecspopolita who spoke other idioms) did not yet feel themselves to be nationalist Poles; as the eventual liberator of Poland, Colonal Pilsudski recognized in *his* phrase: 'It is the state which makes the nation and

---

[68] Cf. Ivo Banac, *The National Question in Yugoslavia: Origins, History, Politics* (Ithaca and London 1984), pp. 76–86.

[69] Said at the first meeting of the parliament of the newly united Italian kingdom (E. Latham, *Famous Sayings and Their Authors*, Detroit, 1970).

not the nation the state.'[70] But after 1880 it increasingly did matter
how ordinary common men and women felt about nationality. It is
therefore important to consider the feelings and attitudes among
pre-industrial people of this kind, on which the novel appeal of
political nationalism could build. The next chapter will do this.

[70] H. Roos, *A History of Modern Poland* (London 1966), p. 48.

CHAPTER 2

Popular proto-nationalism

Why and how could a concept so remote from the real experience of most human beings as 'national patriotism' become such a powerful political force so quickly? It is plainly not enough to appeal to the universal experience of human beings who belong to groups recognizing one another as members of collectivities or communities, and therefore recognizing others as strangers. The problem before us derives from the fact that the modern nation, either as a state or as a body of people aspiring to form such a state, differs in size, scale and nature from the actual communities with which human beings have identified over most of history, and makes quite different demands on them. It is, in Benedict Anderson's useful phrase, an 'imagined community', and no doubt this can be made to fill the emotional void left by the retreat or disintegration, or the unavailability of *real* human communities and networks, but the question still remains why, having lost real communities, people should wish to imagine this particular type of replacement. One reason may be that, in many parts of the world, states and national movements could mobilize certain variants of feelings of collective belonging which already existed and which could operate, as it were, potentially on the macro-political scale which could fit in with modern states and nations. I shall call these bonds 'proto-national'.

They are of two kinds. First, there are supra-local forms of popular identification which go beyond those circumscribing the actual spaces in which people passed most of their lives: as the Virgin Mary links believers in Naples to a wider world, even though for most purposes affecting the people of Naples collectively, St Januarius, whose blood must (and, by an eternally guaranteed miracle does) liquefy every year if ill is not to befall the city, is much more directly relevant. Second, there are the political bonds and vocabularies of select groups more directly linked to states and institutions, and which are capable of eventual generalization, extension and popularization. These have a little more in common with the modern 'nation'. Nevertheless, neither can be legitimately identified with the modern nationalism that passes as their lineal extension, because they had or have no *necessary* relation with the unit of territorial political organization which is a crucial criterion of what we understand as a 'nation' today.

To take only two obvious examples. Until 1945, and vestigially to this day, speakers of German dialects whose elites used the standard written German language of culture, have been settled not only in their main region of central Europe, but as classes of rulers, as townsmen and in patches of peasant settlement all over eastern and southeastern Europe, not to mention small colonies forming a generally religious diaspora in the Americas. They were scattered in a series of waves of conquest, migration and colonization from the eleventh to the eighteenth century as far east as the lower Volga. (We omit the rather different phenomenon of nineteenth-century migration.) All of them certainly regarded themselves as in some sense 'German' as distinct from other groups among whom they lived. Now while there was often friction between local Germans and other ethnic groups, notably where the Germans monopolized certain crucial functions, e.g. as a landed ruling class in the Baltic area, I know of no case before the nineteenth century where a major political problem arose because these Germans found themselves living under non-German rulers. Again, while the Jews, scattered throughout the world for some millennia, never ceased to identify themselves, wherever they were, as members of a special people quite distinct from the various brands of non-believers among whom they lived, at no stage, at least since the return from the Babylonian captivity, does this seem to have implied a serious desire for a Jewish political state, let alone a territorial state, until a Jewish nationalism was invented at the very end of the nineteenth century by analogy with the newfangled western nationalism. It is entirely illegitimate to identify the Jewish links with the ancestral land of Israel, the merit deriving from pilgrimages there, or the hope of return there when the Messiah came – as he so obviously had *not* come in the view of the Jews – with the desire to gather all Jews into a modern territorial state situated on the ancient Holy Land. One might as well argue that good Muslims, whose highest ambition is to make the pilgrimage to Mecca, in doing so really intend to declare themselves citizens of what has now become Saudi Arabia.

What precisely constitutes popular proto-nationalism? The question is enormously difficult, since it implies discovering the sentiments of the illiterate who formed the overwhelming majority of the world's population before the twentieth century. We are informed about the ideas of that section of the literate who wrote as well as read – or at least of some of them – but it is clearly illegitimate to extrapolate from the elite to the masses, the literate to the illiterate, even though the two worlds are not entirely separable, and the written word influenced the ideas of those who only spoke.[1] What Herder thought about the *Volk* cannot be used as evidence for the thoughts of the Westphalian peasantry. An example may illustrate the potential width of this gap between literate and non-literate. The Germans who formed the class of feudal lords as well as the townspeople and literates in the Baltic region naturally felt that 'national revenge continued to hang as a Damoclean sword over their heads' since, as Christian Kelch pointed out in his Livonian History of 1695, the Estonian and Latvian peasants had plenty of reasons for hating them ('Selbige zu hassen wohl Ursache gehabt') Yet there is no evidence that the Estonian peasants thought in such national terms. In the first place they do not appear to have seen themselves as an ethnic-linguistic group. The word 'Estonian' came into use only in the 1860s. Before then the peasants had simply called themselves 'maarahvas', i.e. 'country people'. In the second place, the word *saks* (Saxon) had the *dominant* meaning 'lord' or 'master' and only the secondary

<hr/>

[1] See Roger Chartier, *The Cultural Uses of Print in Early Modern France* (Princeton 1987), Introduction; also E. J. Hobsbawm, *Worlds of Labour* (London 1984), pp. 39–42, for the relations of popular and hegemonic culture.

meaning 'German'. It has been plausibly argued (by an eminent Estonian historian) that where (German) literates read references in documents as 'German', the peasants had most probably simply meant 'lord' or 'master':

> From the close of the 18th century the local ministers and clerks could read the works of the enlighteners on the conquest of Estonia (the peasants did not read such books) and were inclined to interpret the words of the peasants in a manner that fitted their own way of thinking.[2]

Let us therefore begin with one of the very few attempts to establish the thinking of those who rarely formulate thoughts on public matters systematically and never write them down, the late Michael Cherniavsky's *Tsar and People*.[3] In that book Cherniavsky discusses, among other matters, the concept of 'Holy Russia' or 'the holy Russian land', a term for which he finds relatively few parallels, the closest being 'Holy Ireland'. He might perhaps have added 'das heil'ge Land Tirol' (The holy land Tyrol) for an interesting comparison and contrast.

If we follow Cherniavsky a land could not become 'holy' until it could put forward a unique claim in the global economy of salvation, i.e. in the case of Russia until the middle of the fifteenth century when the attempted reunion of the churches and the fall of Constantinople which ended the Roman empire, left Russia as the only orthodox land in the world and Moscow as the Third Rome, i.e. as the only source of salvation for mankind. At least this would be the Tsar's view. But such reflections are not strictly germane, for the phrase did not come into wide use until the time of troubles in the early seventeenth century when Tsar and state virtually disappeared. Indeed, even had they not, they would not have contributed to the currency of the phrase since neither Tsar, nor bureaucracy, Church or the ideologists of Muscovite power *ever*

---

[2] Data and citations from Juhan Kahk, 'Peasants' movements and national movements in the history of Europe' (*Acta Universitatis Stockholmensis. Studia Baltica Stockholmensia*, 2, 1985: 'National movements in the Baltic Countries during the 19th century', pp. 15–16.

[3] Michael Cherniavsky, *Tsar and People. Studies in Russian Myths* (New Haven and London 1961). See also Jeffrey Brooks, *When Russia Learned to Read* (Princeton 1985), ch. VI, 'Nationalism and national identity', esp. pp. 213–32.

appear to have used it before or after the time of troubles.[4] In short, Holy Russia was a popular term presumably expressing popular ideas. Its use is illustrated in the mid-seventeenth-century epics of the Don cossacks, such as the 'Poetical tale of the siege of Azov' (by the Turks). Here the besieged cossacks sang:

> We shall never be in Holy Russia again. Our sinful death comes in the deserts. We die for your miracle-working icons, for the Christian faith, for the Tsar's name and for all the Muscovite state.[5]

The holy Russian land is therefore defined by the holy icons, the faith, the Tsar, the state. It is a powerful combination, and not only because icons, i.e. visible symbols such as flags, are still the most widely used methods of envisaging what canot be envisaged. And Holy Russia is unquestionably a popular, an unofficial force, not one created from above. Consider, as Cherniavsky does, with that perceptiveness and delicacy he learned from his teacher Ernst Kantorowicz,[6] the word 'Russia'. The empire of the Tsars, the political unit, was *Rossiya*, a neologism of the sixteenth–seventeenth centuries which became official from Peter the Great on. The holy land of Russia was always the ancient *Rus*. To be a Russian is still to this day to be *Russky*. No word derived from the official Rossiya – and several were tried for size in the eighteenth century – succeeded in getting itself accepted as a description of the Russian *people* or nation, or its members. Being *Russky*, as Cherniavsky reminds us, was interchangeable with being a member of the curious doublet *krestianin–christianin* (peasant–Christian) and with being a 'true believer' or Orthodox. This essential popular and populist sense of Holy Russianness may or may not correspond to the modern nation. In Russia its identification with the head of both Church and state obviously facilitated such identification. In the holy land Tyrol it obviously did not, since the post-tridentine combination of land–icons–faith–emperor–state favoured the Roman Catholic Church and the Habsburg Kaiser (whether as such or as Count of Tyrol) against the newfangled concept of a German or Austrian or any 'nation'. It should be remembered that the

---

[4] Cherniavsky, *Tsar and People*, pp. 107, 114.   [5] *Ibid.* p. 113.
[6] See the pioneering Ernst Kantorowicz, *The King's Two Bodies. A Study in Medieval Political Theology* (Princeton 1957).

Tyrolean peasants in 1809 rose not so much against the French as against the neighbouring Bavarians. However, whether or not 'the people of the holy land' can be identified with the later nation, the concept clearly predates it.

And yet, we observe the omission, from the criteria of Holy Russia, Holy Tyrol and perhaps Holy Ireland, of two elements which today we associate closely, if not crucially, with definitions of the nation: language and ethnicity.

What of language? Is it not the very essence of what distinguishes one people from another, 'us' from 'them', real human beings from the barbarians who cannot talk a genuine language but only make incomprehensible noises? Does not every reader of the Bible learn about the tower of Babel, and how friend was told from foe by the right pronunciation of the word 'shibboleth'? Did not the Greeks define themselves proto-nationally in this way against the remainder of humanity, the 'barbarians'? Does not ignorance of another group's language constitute the most obvious barrier to communication, and therefore the most obvious definer of the lines which separate groups: so that the creation or speaking of a special argot still serves to mark people as members of a subculture which wishes to separate itself from other subcultures or from the community at large?

One can hardly deny that people speaking mutually incomprehensible languages who live side by side will identify themselves as speakers of one, and members of other communities as speakers of other languages or at least as non-speakers of their own (as *barbaroi*, or as *nemci* in the terminology of the Slavs). Yet this is not the issue. The question is, whether such linguistic barriers are believed to separate entities which can be regarded as potential nationalities or nations, and not merely groups which happen to have trouble in understanding each other's words. This question takes us on to the terrain of enquiries into the nature of vernacular languages and their use as criteria of in-group membership. And in investigating both we must, again, beware of confusing the debates of the literate, who happen to be almost our only sources, with those of the illiterate, and of reading twentieth-century usage anachronistically into the past.

Non-literate vernacular languages are always a complex of local variants or dialects intercommunicating with varying degrees of ease or difficulty, depending on geographical closeness or accessibility. Some, notably in mountain areas which facilitate segregation, may be as incomprehensible as if they belonged to a different linguistic family. There are, in the relevant countries, jokes about the difficulties of North Walians understanding the Welsh of those from South Wales, or Gheg Albanians understanding the Tosk dialect. For philologists the fact that Catalan is closer to French than Basque may be crucial, but for a Norman sailor who found himself in Bayonne or Port Bou the local language might, at first hearing, be equally opaque. To this day educated native speakers of German from, say, Kiel, may have the greatest difficulty in understanding even educated Swiss Germans speaking the plainly German dialect which is their usual means of oral communication.

Thus in the era before general primary education there was and could be no spoken 'national' language except such literary or administrative idioms as were written, or devised or adapted for oral use, either as a lingua franca in which speakers of dialects could communicate, or – perhaps more to the point – to address popular audiences across dialectal boundaries, e.g. for preachers or the reciters of songs and poems common to a wider cultural area.[7] The size of this area of common potential communicability might vary considerably. It would almost certainly be larger for elites, whose fields of action and horizons were less localized than for, say, peasants. A genuinely spoken 'national language' evolved on a purely oral basis, other than as a pidgin or lingua franca (which may, of course, eventually turn into an all-purpose language), is difficult to conceive for a region of any substantial geographical size. In other words the actual or literal 'mother tongue', i.e. the

[7] The most useful introduction to this complex of questions is Einar Haugen, 'Dialect, language, nation' (*American Anthropologist*, 68, 1966, pp. 922–35). For the comparatively recent field of sociolinguistics, cf. J. A. Fishman (ed.), *Contributions to the Sociology of Language*, 2 vols. (The Hague–Paris 1972), esp. the editor's 'The sociology of language: an interdisciplinary social science approach to language in society' in vol. 1. For a concrete study of language development/construction by a pioneer, Heinz Kloss, *Die Entwicklung neuer germanischer Kultursprachen von 1800 bis 1950* (Munich 1952).

idiom children learned from illiterate mothers and spoke for everyday use, was certainly not in any sense a 'national language'.

This does not, as I have already hinted, exclude a certain popular *cultural* identification with a language, or a patently related complex of dialects, peculiar to a body of communities and distinguishing them from their neighbours, as in the case of Magyar-speakers. And to the extent that this may be so, the nationalism of a later period may have genuinely popular linguistic proto-national roots. This may well be the case among the Albanians, living under rival cultural influences since classical antiquity, and divided among three or (if we include the locally centred Islamic cult of the Bektashi) even four rival religions: Islam, Orthodoxy and Roman Catholicism. It was natural for the pioneers of Albanian nationalism to seek an Albanian cultural identity in language, since religion, and indeed almost everything else in Albania, seemed divisive rather than unifying.[8] Yet even in so apparently clear a case we should beware of too much reliance on the literate. In what sense, or even how far, ordinary Albanians in the late nineteenth and early twentieth centuries saw themselves as such, or recognized an affinity with one another, is far from clear. Edith Durham's guide, a mountain youth from the north, being told that the Albanians in the south had Orthodox churches, said: 'They are not Christians, but Tosks', which does not suggest a strong sense of collective identity, and 'it is not possible to know the precise number of Albanians who came to the United States, for the early immigrants did not often identify themselves as Albanians'.[9] Moreover, even the pioneers of nationhood in that land of feuding clans and lords appealed to more convincing arguments for solidarity before they appealed to language. As Naïm Frashëri (1846–1900) put it: 'All of us are only a single tribe, a single family; we are

---

8 'Les grands noms de cette littérature ... ne célèbrent jamais la réligion dans leurs oeuvres; bien au contraire ils ne manquent aucune occasion pour stigmatiser l'action hostile à l'unité nationale des différents clergés ... Il semble que [la recherche de l'identité culturelle] ... se soit faite essentiellement autour du problème de la langue.' Christian Gut in *Groupe de Travail sur l'Europe Centrale et Orientale. Bulletin d'Information*, no. 2, June 1978, p. 40 (Maison des Sciences de l'Homme, Paris).

9 Edith Durham, *High Albania* (1909, new edn, London 1985), p. 17; S. Thernstrom *et al.*, *Harvard Encyclopedia of American Ethnic Groups* (Cambridge and London 1980), p. 24.

of one blood and one language.'[10] Language, while not absent, came last.

National languages are therefore almost always semi-artificial constructs and occasionally, like modern Hebrew, virtually invented. They are the opposite of what nationalist mythology supposes them to be, namely the primordial foundations of national culture and the matrices of the national mind. They are usually attempts to devise a standardized idiom out of a multiplicity of actually spoken idioms, which are thereafter downgraded to dialects, the main problem in their construction being usually, which dialect to choose as the base of the standardized and homogenized language. The subsequent problems of standardizing and homogenizing national grammar and orthography, and adding new elements to the vocabulary, are secondary.[11] The histories of practically every European language insist on this regional base: literary Bulgarian is based on the West Bulgarian idiom, literary Ukrainian on its southeastern dialects, literary Hungarian emerges in the sixteenth century by combining various dialects, literary Latvian is based on the middle one of three variants, Lithuanian on one of two, and so on. Where, as is usually the case in languages achieving literary status in the eighteenth or nineteenth–twentieth century, the names of the language-architects are known, this choice may be arbitrary (though justified by argument).

Sometimes this choice is political or has obvious political implications. Thus the Croats spoke three dialects (*čakavian*, *kajkavian*, *štokavian*, one of which was also the major dialect of the Serbs. Two of them (*kajkavian* and *štokavian*) developed literary versions. The great Croat apostle of Illyrianism, Ljudevit Gaj

[10] Cited in *Groupe de Travail*, p. 52.

[11] For a convenient survey of the field, acutely aware of the 'artificiality' of most culture-languages, Marinella Lörinczi Angioni, 'Appunti per una macrostoria delle lingue scritte de l'Europa moderna' (*Quaderni Sardi di Storia*, 3, July 1981–June 1983, pp. 133–56). It is particularly useful on the lesser languages. For the difference between the traditional Flemish and the modern language, developed since 1841, see the remarks of E. Coornaert in *Bulletin de la Société d'Histoire Moderne*, 67e année, 8, 1968, p. 5, in the discussion on R. Devleeshouwer, 'Données historiques des problèmes linguistiques belges'. See also Jonathan Steinberg, 'The historian and the *Questione della lingua*' in P. Burke and Roy Porter (eds.), *The Social History of Language* (Cambridge 1987), pp. 198–209).

(1809–72), though a native speaker and writer of *kajkavian* Croat switched his own writings from this dialect to *štokavian* in 1838, in order to underline the basic unity of southern Slavs, thus ensuring (a) that Serbo-Croat developed more or less as one literary language (though written in Roman characters by the Catholic Croats, in Cyrillic ones by the Orthodox Serbs), (b) depriving Croat nationalism of the convenient linguistic justification, and (c) providing both Serbs, and later Croats, with an excuse for expansionism.[12] On the other hand sometimes they guess wrong. Bernolák picked one dialect as the basis of what he intended to be literary Slovak around 1790, which failed to establish itself, but a few decades later Ludovit Štur chose what proved to be a more viable base. In Norway the nationalist Wergeland (1808–45) demanded a more purely Norwegian Norwegian, as distinct from the excessively Danicized written language, and such a language was promptly constructed (Landsmål, known today as Nynorsk). In spite of official support after Norway became independent, it has never established itself as more than a minority language of the country, which, since 1947 is *de facto* bilingual in writing, Nynorsk being confined to 20% of Norwegians, especially those living in western and central Norway.[13] Of course in several of the older literary languages history made the required choice, as when dialects associated with the area of royal administration became the foundation of the literary idiom in France and England, or when the combination of commercial-maritime usage, cultural prestige and Macedonian support helped Attic to become the foundation of the Hellenistic *koiné* or common Greek idiom.

We may leave aside, for the time being, the lesser, but also urgent problem, of how to modernize even such old 'national' literary idioms as exist in order to suit them for a contemporary life not envisaged by the French Academy or Dr Johnson. The problem is

---

[12] The matter is well put by Ivo Banac, *The National Question in Yugoslavia: Origins, History, Politics* (Ithaca and London 1984) (whence these data come): 'The unique Croatian dialectal situation, that is the use of three dialects ... could not be reconciled with the romantic belief that language was the most profound expression of national spirit. Obviously one nation could not have three spirits, nor could one dialect be shared by two nationalities' (p. 81).

[13] Einar Haugen, *The Scandinavian languages: An Introduction* (London 1976).

universal, though complicated in many cases – notably among the Dutch, the Germans, the Czechs, the Icelanders and several others – by what one might call philological nationalism, i.e. the insistence on the linguistic purity of the national vocabulary, which obliged German scientists to translate 'oxygen' into 'Sauerstoff', and is today inspiring a desperate French rearguard action against the ravages of *franglais*. However, inevitably the problem is more acute in languages which have not been the major carriers of culture, but wish to become suitable vehicles for, say, higher education and modern techno-economic communication. Let us not underestimate the seriousness of such problems. Thus Welsh claims, possibly with some justification, to be the most ancient living literary language, dating back to the sixth century or thereabouts. Yet in 1847 it was observed that it

> would be impossible to express in Welsh many an ordinary proposition in politics and science in such a way as completely to convey the sense to even an intelligent Welsh reader unacquainted with English.[14]

It is thus clear that, except for the rulers and the literate, language could hardly be a criterion of nationhood, and even for these it was first necessary to choose a national vernacular (in a standardized literary form) over the more prestigious languages, holy or classical or both, which were, for small elites, perfectly practicable means of administrative or intellectual communication, public debate, or even – one thinks of classical Persian in the Mughal Empire, classical Chinese in Heian Japan – of literary composition. That choice, admittedly, was made everywhere sooner or later, except perhaps in China where the lingua franca of the classically educated became the only means of communication between otherwise mutually incomprehensible dialects in the vast empire, and is in the process of becoming something like a spoken language.

Why, indeed, should language be such a criterion of group membership, except perhaps where language differentiation coincided with some other reason to mark oneself off from some other community? Marriage itself, as an institution, does not assume

[14] Reports of the Commissioners of Inquiry into the State of Education in Wales (*Parliamentary Papers* XXVII of 1847, part III, p. 853n.).

community of language, otherwise there could hardly be institutionalized exogamy. One sees no reason to dissent from the learned historian of opinions on the multiplicity of languages and peoples, who holds that 'only late generalization establishes human beings of the same language as friends, foreign languages as foes'.[15] Where there are no other languages within earshot, one's own idiom is not so much a group criterion as something that all people have, like legs. Where several languages coexist, multilingualism may be so normal as to make an exclusive identification with any one idiom quite arbitrary. (This makes censuses requiring such an exclusive choice unreliable sources of linguistic information.)[16] In such areas linguistic statistics may swing wildly from one census to another, since identification with an idiom depends not on knowledge but on some other changing factor, as in some areas of Slovenia and Moravia under the Habsburgs; or else people may speak both their own language and an officially unrecognized lingua franca, as in parts of Istria.[17] Moreover, these languages are not interchangeable. People in Mauritius do not arbitrarily choose between speaking creole and whatever their own domestic language is, because they use each for different purposes as do the German Swiss who write High German and speak Schwyzerdütsch, or the Slovene father in Josef Roth's moving novel *Radetzkymarsch*, who addresses his promoted officer son, not in their native language, as the young man expects, but in 'the ordinary harsh German of army Slavs'[18] out of respect for the status of a Habsburg officer. In fact, the mystical identification of nationality with a sort of platonic idea of the language, existing behind and above all its variant and imperfect versions, is much more characteristic of the ideological construction of nationalist intellectuals, of whom Herder is the prophet, than of the actual grassroots users of the idiom. It is a literary and not an existential concept.

[15] Arno Borst, *Der Turmbau von Babel: Geschichte der Meinungen über Ursprung und Vielfalt der Sprachen der Völker*, 4 vols. in 6 (Stuttgart 1957–63) vol. IV, p. 1913.

[16] Paul M. G. Lévy, 'La Statistique des langues en Belgique' (*Revue de l'Institut de Sociologie* (Bruxelles), 18, 1938, pp. 507–70).

[17] Emil Brix, *Die Umgangsprachen in Altösterreich zwischen Agitation und Assimilation. Die Sprachstatistik in den zisleithanischen Volkszählungen 1880–1910* (Vienna–Cologne–Graz 1982), e.g. pp. 182, 214, 332.

[18] Josef Roth, *The Radetzkymarch* (Harmondsworth 1974), p. 5.

This is not to deny that languages, or even linguistic families, are not part of popular reality. For most peoples of Germanic languages most foreigners to their west and south – mainly Romance speakers, but also Celts – are *Welsh*, whereas most people of Finnish and later Slavonic speech to their east and southeast were *Wends*; and conversely, to most Slavs all German speakers are *nemci*. However, it was always evident to all that language and people (however each was defined) did not coincide. In the Sudan the settled Fur live in symbiosis with the nomadic Baggara, but a neighbouring camp of Fur nomads speaking Fur is treated as though they were Baggara, since the crucial distinction between the two peoples is not one of language but function. That these nomads speak Fur 'simply makes the standard transactions of buying milk, allocating camp sites, or obtaining manure, which one would have with other Baggara, flow a bit more smoothly.'[19]

In more 'theoretical' terms, the famous seventy-two languages into which the human race was split after the tower of Babel (at least by medieval commentators on the Book of Genesis) each covered several *nationes* or tribes, according to Anselm of Laon, pupil of the great Anselm of Canterbury. William of Alton, an English Dominican, speculating further along these lines in the mid-thirteenth century, distinguished among men between language groups (according to the idiom spoken), between *generationes* (according to origin), between the inhabitants of particular territories, and between *gentes* who were defined by differences in customs and conversations. These classifications did not necessarily coincide, and were not to be confused with a *populus* or people, which was defined by the will to obey a common law, and which was therefore a historico-political rather than a 'natural' community.[20] In this analysis William of Alton showed an admirable, but, until the late nineteenth century, not uncommon perspicacity and realism.

For language was merely one, and not necessarily the primary, way of distinguishing between cultural communities. Herodotus held that the Greeks formed one people, in spite of their geo-

[19] Frederik Barth (ed.), *Ethnic Groups and Boundaries* (Boston 1969), p. 30.
[20] Borst, *Der Turmbau von Babel*, pp. 752–3.

graphical and political fragmentation, because they were of common descent, had a common language, common gods and sacred places, sacrificial festivals and customs, mores or ways of life.[21] Surely language would be of crucial importance to literates like Herodotus. Would it have been an equally important criterion of Greekness to run-of-the-mill Boeotians or Thessalians? We do not know. What we do know is that nationalist struggles have sometimes been complicated in modern times by the refusal of fractions of linguistic groups to accept political unity with their co-speakers. Such cases (the so-called *Wasserpolacken* in Silesia during its German period, the so-called *Windische* in the border zone between what became Austria and the Slovene part of Yugoslavia) led to embittered accusations by Poles and Slovenes that such categories had been invented by great-German chauvinists to justify their territorial expansionism, and no doubt these accusations had some truth. Nevertheless the existence of groups of linguistic Poles and Slovenes who, for whatever reason, preferred to consider themselves politically German or Austrian, cannot be entirely denied.

Language in the Herderian sense of the language spoken by the *Volk* was therefore plainly not a central element in the formation of proto-nationalism directly, though it was not necessarily irrelevant to it. However, indirectly it was to become central to the modern definition of nationality, and therefore also to the popular perception of it. For where an elite literary or administrative language exists, however small the number of its actual users, it can become an important element of proto-national cohesion for three reasons which are well set out by B. Anderson.[22]

First, it creates a community of this intercommunicating elite which, if it coincides with or can be made to coincide with a particular territorial state area and vernacular zone, can be a sort of model or pilot project for the as yet non-existent larger intercom-

---

[21] Herodotus, *Histories*, VIII, 144. Borst, who discusses the question, points out that, while the Greeks certainly thought 'language' was tied to 'people' and both could be numbered, Euripides thought language was irrelevant, and Zeno the Stoic was bilingual in Phoenician and Greek (*ibid.* 137, 160).

[22] Benedict Anderson, *Imagined Communities: Reflections on the Origins and Spread of Nationalism* (London 1983), pp. 46–9; more generally on language, chapter 5.

municating community of 'the nation'. To this extent the spoken idioms are not irrelevant to the future nationality. Dead 'classical' or ritual languages, however prestigious, are ill-suited to become national languages, as was discovered in Greece, where there was actual linguistic continuity between ancient and modern spoken Greek. Vuk Karadzić (1787–1864), the great reformer, and indeed virtual founder, of modern literary Serbo-Croat, was undoubtedly right in resisting the early attempts to create such a literary language out of Church Slavonic by those who anticipated the later creation of modern Hebrew out of an adapted ancient Hebrew, and in building it on the dialects spoken by the Serbian people.[23] Both the impulse which led to the creation of modern spoken Hebrew, and the circumstances which led to its successful establishment, are too unusual to set a general example.

However, given that the dialect which forms the basis of a national language is actually spoken, it does not matter that those who speak it are a minority, so long as it is a minority of sufficient political weight. In this sense French was essential to the concept of France, even though in 1789 50% of Frenchmen did not speak it at all, only 12–13% spoke it 'correctly' – and indeed outside a central region it was not usually habitually spoken even in the area of the *langue d'oui*, except in towns, and then not always in their suburbs. In northern and southern France virtually nobody talked French.[24] If French had at least a state whose 'national language' it could be, the only basis for Italian unification was the Italian language, which united the educated elite of the peninsula as readers and writers, even though it has calculated that at the moment of unification (1860) only 2½% of the population used the language for everyday

---

[23] For a similar debate in connection with the Slovak language, see Hugh Seton-Watson, *Nations and States: An Enquiry into the Origins of Nations and the Politics of Nationalism* (London 1977), pp. 170–1.

[24] The basic source in these matters is Ferdinand Brunot (ed.) *Histoire de la langue française* (13 vols., Paris 1927–43), esp. vol. IX; and M. de Certeau, D. Julia, J. Revel, *Une politique de la langue: La Révolution Française et les patois: l'enquête de l'Abbé Grégoire* (Paris 1975). For the problem of extending a minority official language into a mass national language during and after the French Revolution, see the excellent Renée Balibar, *L'Institution du français: essai sur le co-linguisme des Carolingiens à la République* (Paris 1985); see also R. Balibar and D. Laporte, *Le Français national: politique et pratique de la langue nationale sous la Révolution* (Paris 1974).

purposes.[25] For this tiny group was, in a real sense *a* and therefore potentially *the* Italian people. Nobody else was.

Just so the Germany of the eighteenth century was a purely cultural concept, and yet, because it was the only one in which 'Germany' had a being, as distinct from the multiplicity of principalities and states, large and small, administered and divided by religion and political horizons, which were administered by means of the German language. It consisted of at most 3–500,000 readers[26] of works in the literary vernacular, and the almost certainly much smaller number who actually spoke the 'Hochsprache' or culture-language for everyday purposes,[27] notably the actors who performed the (new) works which became the vernacular classics. For in the absence of a state standard of what was correct (the 'King's English') in Germany the standard of correctness was established in the theatres.

The second reason is that a common language, just because it is not naturally evolved but constructed, and especially when forced into print, acquired a new fixity which made it appear more permanent and hence (by an optical illusion) more 'eternal' than it really was. Hence the importance not only of the invention of printing, especially where a vernacular version of a holy book provided the foundation of the literary language, as has often been the case, but also of the great correctors and standardizers who appear in the literary history of every culture-language, at all events after the emergence of the printed book. Essentially this era occurs

---

[25] Tullio de Mauro, *Storia linguistica dell'Italia unita* (Bari 1963), p. 41.

[26] Until the 'early nineteenth century' *all* works by Goethe and Schiller, jointly and severally, appear to have sold less than 100,000 copies, i.e. over 30–40 years. H. U. Wehler, *Deutsche Gesellschaftsgeschichte 1700–1815* (Munich 1987), p. 305.

[27] Except for Switzerland it is probably a slight exaggeration to maintain that 'anche oggi il tedesco (*Hochdeutsch*), ancor più che l'italiano, è una vera e propria lingua artificiale di cultura, sovradialettale, "sotto" o insieme con la quale la maggior parte degli utenti si servono anche di una *Umgangsprache* locale' (Lörinczi Angioni, 'Appunti', p. 139n.), but it was certainly true in the early nineteenth century. Thus Manzoni, whose *I Promessi sposi* created Italian as a national language of prose fiction, did not speak it in everyday life, communicating with his French wife in her language (which he may have spoken better than Italian) and with others in his native Milanese. Indeed, the first edition of his great novel still showed many traces of Milanese, a defect he systematically attempted to remove in the second edition. I am indebted to Professor Conor Fahy for this information.

between the late eighteenth and the early twentieth century for all except a handful of European languages.

Thirdly, the official or culture-language of rulers and elite usually came to be the actual language of modern states *via* public education and other administrative mechanisms.

However, all these are later developments. They hardly affect the language of the common people in the pre-nationalist and certainly in the pre-literate era. No doubt Mandarin tied together a vast Chinese empire many of whose peoples could not understand each other's language, but it did not do so directly through language, but through the administration of a centralized empire which happened to operate through a common set of ideographs and a means of elite communication. For most Chinese it would not have mattered if the mandarins had communicated in Latin, just as it did not matter for most inhabitants of India that the East India Company in the 1830s replaced the Persian language, which had been the administrative idiom of the Mughal empire, with English. Both were equally foreign to them, and, since they did not write or even read, irrelevant. To the grief of subsequent nationalist historians, the Flemish inhabitants of what later became Belgium were not mobilized against the French by the ruthless Gallicization of public and official life in the revolutionary and Napoleonic years, nor did Waterloo lead to any 'pronounced movement in Flanders in favour of the Flemish language or of Flemish culture'.[28] Why should they? For those who could understand no French practical administrative concessions had to be made even by a regime of linguistic zealots. It is much less surprising that the influx of francophone foreigners into the rural communes of Flanders was resented more for their refusal to attend mass on Sundays than on linguistic grounds.[29] In short, special cases aside, there is no reason to suppose that language was more than one among several criteria by which people indicated belonging to a human collectivity. And it

28 Shepard B. Clough, *A History of the Flemish Movement in Belgium: A Study in Nationalism* (New York 1930, repr. 1968), p. 25. For the slowness of the growth of linguistic consciousness, see also Val R. Lorwin, 'Belgium: religion, class and language in national politics' in Robert A. Dahl, *Political Opposition in Western Democracies* (New Haven 1966), p. 158ff.

29 S. B. Clough, *A History of the Flemish Movement in Belgium*, pp. 21-2.

is absolutely certain that language had as yet no political potential. As a French commentator on the tower of Babel observed in 1536:

> There are now more than LXXII languages, because there are now more different nations on earth than there were in those days.[30]

Languages multiply with states; not the other way round.

What of ethnicity? In ordinary usage this is almost always connected in some unspecified way with common origin and descent, from which the common characteristics of the members of an ethnic group are allegedly derived. 'Kinship' and 'blood' have obvious advantages in bonding together members of a group and excluding outsiders, and are therefore central to ethnic nationalism. 'Culture (Kultur) can't be acquired by education. Culture is in the blood. The best proof of this today is the Jews, who cannot do more than appropriate our civilization (Zivilisation) but never our culture.' Thus the National Socialist Kreisleiter of Innsbruck in 1938, Hans Hanak – ironically, the name demonstrates Slavonic origin – congratulating the Nazi women of Innsbruck because the Jewish attempt to destroy their 'high and respected status' by preaching the equality of men and women, had only had a fleeting moment of success.[31] Yet the genetic approach to ethnicity is plainly irrelevant, since the crucial base of an ethnic group as a form of social organization is cultural rather than biological.[32]

Moreover, the populations of large territorial nation-states are almost invariably too heterogeneous to claim a common ethnicity, even if we leave aside modern immigration, and in any case the demographic history of large parts of Europe has been such that we *know* how multifarious the origin of ethnic groups can be, especially when areas have been depopulated and resettled in the course of time, as in vast areas of central, eastern and south-eastern Europe, or even in parts of France.[33] The precise mixture of pre-Roman Illyrians, Romans, Greeks, immigrant Slavs of various kinds and various waves of central Asian invaders from the Avars

---

[30] Borst, *Der Turmbau von Babel*.
[31] Cited in Leopold Spira, 'Bemerkungen zu Jörg Haider' (*Wiener Tagebuch*, October 1988, p. 6).
[32] I follow the convincing argument of Fredrik Barth, *Ethnic Groups and Boundaries*.
[33] Theodore Zeldin, *France 1848–1945* (Oxford 1977), vol. I, pp. 46–7.

to the Ottoman Turks, which make up the ethnicity of any people in southeastern Europe, is an eternal matter of debate (especially in Romania). Thus the Montenegrins, originally considered Serbs but now a 'nationality' and federated republic of their own, appear to be a combination of Serb peasants, relics of the Old Serb kingdom and of Vlach herdsmen moving into the area depopulated by the Turkish conquest.[34] Of course it is not to be denied that, say, thirteenth-century Magyars would see themselves as an ethnic community, since they were, or could claim to be, descended from waves of central Asian nomadic invaders, spoke variants of a language utterly unlike any which surrounded them, lived, by and large, in a specific ecological environment, in their own kingdom and doubtless shared various ancestral practices. But such cases are not particularly common.

Nevertheless, ethnicity in the Herodotean sense was, is and can be something that binds together populations living on large territories or even in dispersion, and lacking a common polity, into something which can be called proto-nations. This may well be the case of the Kurds, the Somalis, the Jews, the Basques and others. However, such ethnicity has no historic relation to what is the crux of the modern nation, namely the formation of a nation-state, or for that matter any state, as the case of the ancient Greeks demonstrates. One might even argue that the peoples with the most powerful and lasting sense of what may be called 'tribal' ethnicity, not merely resisted the imposition of the modern state, national or otherwise, but very commonly *any* state: as witness the Pushtu speakers in and around Afghanistan, the pre-1745 Scots highlanders, the Atlas Berbers, and others who will come readily to mind.

Conversely, insofar as 'the people' was identified with a particular polity, even when seen from below it cut across ethnic (and linguistic) divides within it, obvious though these were. The men of the holy land Tyrol who rose against the French in 1809 under

---

[34] Ivo Banac, *The National Question in Yugoslavia*, p. 44. However, since these facts are taken from an ample and erudite *Istorija Crne Gore*, published in 1970 in the capital of a republic based on the assumption that Montenegrins are not the same as Serbs, the reader should, as always in Balkan historiography, keep an ear open for the sound of grinding axes.

Andreas Hofer, included both the Germans and the Italians as well as, no doubt, the Ladinsch speakers.[35] Swiss nationalism is, as we know, pluri-ethnic. For that matter, if we were to suppose that the Greek mountaineers who rose against the Turks in Byron's day were nationalists, which is admittedly improbable, we cannot fail to note that some of their most formidable fighters were not Hellenes but Albanians (the Suliotes). Moreover, very few modern national movements are actually based on a strong ethnic consciousness, though they often invent one once they have got going, in the form of racism. To sum up, we need not therefore be surprised that the Don cossacks left out ethnicity or common ancestry from their definition of what made them sons of the holy Russian land. As a matter of fact they were wise to do so, since – like so many bodies of free peasant fighters – their origins were extremely mixed. Many of them were Ukrainians, Tatars, Poles, Lithuanians as well as Great Russians. What united them was not blood but belief.

Is ethnicity or 'race' therefore irrelevant to modern nationalism? Plainly this is not the case, since visible differences in physique are too obvious to be overlooked and have too often been used to mark or reinforce distinctions between 'us' and 'them', including national ones. Only three things need be said about such differences. First, they have, historically, functioned as horizontal dividers as well as vertical ones, and, before the era of modern nationalism, probably more commonly served to separate social strata than entire communities. The commonest use of colour discrimination in history appears, unfortunately, to be the one which assigned a higher social position to lighter colours within the same society (as e.g. in India), though both mass migration and social mobility have tended to complicate matters, or even to reverse the relationship, so that the 'right' kind of racial classification goes with the 'right' kind of social position, irrespective of physical appearance; as in Andean countries where Indians who

---

[35] John W. Cole and Eric R. Wolf, *The Hidden Frontier: Ecology and Ethnicity in an Alpine Valley* (New York and London 1974), pp. 112–13.

join the lower middle class are automatically reclassified as 'mesti-zos' or *cholos*, irrespective of appearance.[36]

Second, 'visible' ethnicity tends to be negative, inasmuch as it is much more usually applied to define 'the other' than one's own group. Hence the proverbial role of racial stereotypes (the 'Jewish nose'), the relative colour-blindness of colonizers to colour differences among those classified as globally 'black', and the claim that 'they all look alike to me' which is probably based on selective social vision of what 'the other' is believed to have in common, such as slant eyes and yellow skin. The ethnic-racial homogeneity of one's own 'nationality' is taken for granted, where it is asserted – which is by no means in all cases – even when the most superficial inspection might throw doubt on it. For to 'us' it seems obvious that the members of our 'nationality' cover a wide range of sizes, shapes and appearances, even when all of them share certain physical characteristics, such as a certain type of black hair. It is only to 'them' that we all look alike.

Third, such negative ethnicity is virtually always irrelevant to proto-nationalism, unless it can be or has been fused with something like a state tradition, as perhaps in China, Korea and Japan, which are indeed among the extremely rare examples of historic states composed of a population that is ethnically almost or entirely homogeneous.[37] In such cases it is quite possible that ethnicity and political loyalty are linked. I am informed that the special role of the Ming dynasty in Chinese rebellions since its overthrow in 1644 – its restoration was, and perhaps still is, on the programme of important secret societies – is due to the fact that, unlike its predecessor, the Mongol, and its successor, the Manchu dynasty, it was purely Chinese or Han dynasty. For this reason the most

---

[36] Conversely, those who do not know the person's social position – perhaps because he or she has migrated to the big city – judge it purely by colour and therefore declass him or her. Resentment at this appears to have been a common cause for the political radicalization of students in Lima in the 1960s and 1970s, when masses of children of upwardly mobile provincial *cholo* families flooded into the rapidly expanding universities. I am grateful to Nicolas Lynch whose unpublished study of the Maoist student leaders at San Marcos University makes the point.

[37] Thus of the (non-Arab) Asian states today Japan and the two Koreas are 99% homogeneous, and 94% of the People's Republic of China are Han. These countries exist, more or less, within their historic frontiers.

obvious ethnic differences have played a rather small part in the genesis of modern nationalism. Indians in Latin America since the Spanish conquest have had a deep sense of ethnic difference from whites and mestizos, especially as this was reinforced and institutionalized by the Spanish colonial system of dividing the population into racial castes.[38] However, I know of no case where this has as yet led to a nationalist movement. It has rarely even inspired pan-Indian sentiment among Indians, as distinct from *indigenista* intellectuals.[39] Again, what the inhabitants of sub-Saharan Africa have in common as against their light-skinned conquerors, is a relatively dark colour. *Négritude* is a feeling which really exists, not only among black intellectuals and elites, but whenever an assembly of the more dark-skinned confront those of lighter sk.n. It may be a political factor, but mere colour-consciousness has not produced a single African state, not even Ghana and Senegal whose founders were inspired by pan-African ideas. Nor has it resisted the pull of the actual African states which were formed out of former European colonies whose only internal cohesion came from a few decades of colonial administration.

We are therefore left with the criteria of Holy Russia as the seventeenth-century Cossacks saw them: that is to say religion and kingship or empire.

The links between religion and national consciousness can be very close, as the examples of Poland and Ireland demonstrate. In fact, the relation seems to grow closer where nationalism becomes a mass force than in its phase as a minority ideology and activists'

[38] The standard work is Magnus Mörner, *El mestizaje en la historia de Ibero-América* (Mexico City 1961); see also Alejandro Lipschutz, *El problema racial en la conquista de América y el mestizaje* (Santiago de Chile 1963), esp. chapter v. 'However, while the Leyes de Indias frequently refer to *castes*, the concepts and terminology are shifting and contradictory' (Sergio Bagú, *Estructura social de la Colonia* (Buenos Aires 1952), p. 122.

[39] The major exception, which confirms the analysis of this chapter – see below p. 162 – is the memory of the Inca empire in Peru, which has inspired both myths and (localized) movements envisaging its restoration. See the anthology *Ideología mesiánica del mundo andino*, ed. Juan M. Ossio A. (Lima 1973) and Alberto Flores Galindo, *Buscando un Inca: identidad y Utopia en los Andes* (Havana 1986). However, it seems clear from Flores' excellent treatment of the Indian movements and their supporters (a) that Indian movements against the *mistis* were essentially social, (b) that they had no 'national' implications, if only because until after World War II Andean Indians did not know themselves to be living in Peru (p. 321), and (c) that the *indigenista* intellectuals of the period knew virtually nothing about the Indians (e.g. p. 292).

movement. Zionist militants in the heroic days of the Palestine
Yishuv were more likely to eat ham sandwiches demonstratively
than to wear ritual caps, as Israeli zealots are apt to do today. The
nationalism of Arab countries is today so identified with Islam that
friends and enemies find it hard to fit into it the various Arab
Christian minorities, Copts, Maronites and Greek Catholics, who
were its main pioneers in Egypt and Turkish Syria.[40] Indeed, this
growing identification of nationalism with religion is characteristic
of the Irish movement also. Nor is this surprising. Religion is an
ancient and well-tried method of establishing communion through
common practice and a sort of brotherhood between people who
otherwise have nothing much in common.[41] Some versions of it,
such as Judaism, are specifically designed as membership badges
for particular human communities.

Yet religion is a paradoxical cement for proto-nationalism, and
indeed for modern nationalism, which has usually (at least in its
more crusading phases) treated it with considerable reserve as a
force which could challenge the 'nation's' monopoly claim to its
members' loyalty. In any case genuinely tribal religions normally
operate on too small a scale for modern nationalities, and resist
much broadening out. On the other hand the world religions which
were invented at various times between the sixth century BC and the
seventh century AD, are universal by definition, and therefore
designed to fudge ethnic, linguistic, political and other differences.
Spaniards and Indians in the empire, Paraguayans, Brazilians and
Argentines since independence, were equally faithful children of
Rome, and could not distinguish themselves as communities by
their religion. Fortunately universal truths are often in competition,
and peoples on the borders of one can sometimes choose another as
an ethnic badge, as Russians, Ukrainians and Poles could differen-
tiate themselves as Orthodox, Uniate and Roman Catholic
believers (Christianity having proved itself the most convenient

[40] George Antonius, *The Arab Awakening* (London 1938) is, by and large, supported by
Maxime Rodinson, 'Développement et structure de l'arabisme' in his *Marxisme et monde
musulman* (Paris 1972), pp. 587–602.
[41] Fred R. Van der Mehden, *Religion and Nationalism in Southeast Asia: Burma,
Indonesia, the Philippines* (Madison 1963) is useful in considering countries of very
different religions.

breeder of rival universal truths). Perhaps the fact that the great Confucian empire of China is surrounded on the land side by a vast semi-circle of small peoples who are loyal to other religions (mainly Buddhism but also Islam) is part of the same phenomenon. Nevertheless, it is worth noting that the prevalence of transnational religions, at all events in the regions of the world in which modern nationalism developed, imposed limits on religio-ethnic identification. It is far from universal, and even where it is found, it usually distinguishes the people in question not from all its neighbours, but only from some, as, e.g. Lithuanians are separated from Lutheran Germans and Latvians and from Orthodox Russians and Byelorussians by their Roman Catholicism, but not from Poles who are equally fervent Catholics. In Europe only the nationalist Irish, who have no neighbours other than Protestants, are exclusively defined by their religion.[42]

But what exactly does religio-ethnic identification mean, where it occurs? Clearly in some cases an ethnic religion is chosen because a people feels different from neighbouring peoples or states in the first place. Iran, it would appear, has gone its own divine way both as a Zoroastrian country and, since its conversion to Islam, or at any rate since the Safavids, as a Shiite one. The Irish only came to be identified with Catholicism when they failed, or perhaps refused, to follow the English into the Reformation, and massive colonization of part of their country by Protestant settlers who took away their best land was not likely to convert them.[43] The Churches of England and Scotland are politically defined, even though the latter represents orthodox Calvinism. Perhaps the people of Wales, not till then much given to going a separate religious way, converted *en masse* to Protestant dissent in the first half of the nineteenth century as part of that acquisition of a national consciousness which has recently been the subject of some perceptive research.[44] On the

[42] However, in the nineteenth century the distinction between fervent believers and the lukewarm or godless introduced additional possibilities for wearing national-religious badges. This inclined the Catholic Church to sympathize with such movements as the Bretons, Basques and Flemings.

[43] In a county like Antrim it is said that the feel of a handful of soil will tell a man whether the land from which it came is inhabited by Catholic or Protestant.

[44] Cf. Gwyn Alfred Williams, *The Welsh in their History* (London and Canberra 1982); 'When was Wales?' (London 1985).

other hand it is equally clear that conversion to different religions can help to create two different nationalities, for it is certainly Roman Catholicism (and its by-product, the Latin script) and Orthodoxy (with its by-product, the Cyrillic script) which has most obviously divided Croats from Serbs, with whom they share a single language of culture. But, then again, there are peoples which clearly possessed some proto-national consciousness, such as the Albanians, while divided by more religious differences than are usually found in a territory the size of Wales (various forms of Islam, Orthodoxy, Roman Catholicism). And finally, it is far from clear whether separate religious identity, however powerful, is, taken by itself, similar to nationalism. The modern tendency is to assimilate the two, since we are no longer familiar with the model of the multi-corporate state, in which various religious communities coexist under a supreme authority as in some senses autonomous and self-administering entities; as under the Ottoman empire.[45] It is by no means evident that Pakistan was the product of a national movement among the Muslim of the then Indian Empire, though it may well be regarded as a reaction against an all-Indian national movement which failed to give adequate recognition to the special feelings or requirements of Muslims, and though, in an era of the modern nation-state, territorial partition seemed to be the only available formula, it is far from clear that a separate territorial state is what even the Muslim League had in mind until very late, or would have insisted on but for the intransigence of Jinnah (who was indeed something like a Muslim nationalist, for he was certainly not a religious believer). And it is quite certain that the bulk of ordinary Muslims thought in communal and not in national terms, and would not have understood the concept of national self-determination as something which could apply to belief in Allah and His Prophet.

No doubt Pakistanis now see themselves as members of a separate (Islamic) nation, as do Bangladeshis, having lived under separate states for varying periods of time. No doubt Bosnian and Chinese Muslims will eventually consider themselves a nationality,

---

[45] On the *millet* system in the Ottoman empire, see H. A. R. Gibb and H. A. Bowen, *Islamic Society in the West* (Oxford 1957), vol. I, pt. 2, pp. 219–26.

since their governments treat them as one. However, like so many national phenomena, this will be or has been an *ex post facto* development. Indeed, powerful as the religious identification of Muslims is with Islam, within the vast area where Islam borders on other religions there seem to be few if any proto-national or national movements unambiguously characterized by the Islamic badge, except the Iranian. That they may be developing today against Israel or perhaps in the Soviet central Asian republics, is another matter. In short, the relations between religion and proto-national or national identification remain complex and extremely opaque. They certainly resist simple generalization.

However, as Gellner points out,[46] a people's junction with larger cultures, especially literate cultures, which is often mediated by a conversion to a variant of a world religion, does allow ethnic groups to acquire assets which may later help to turn them into nations and to structure them as such. African groups so linked, he has persuasively argued, are in a better position than others to develop nationalism – as in the Horn of Africa where both the Christian Amhara and the Muslim Somali have found it easier to become 'state peoples' because they are 'people of the book', though, in Gellner's phrase, in different and rival editions. This seems plausible enough, though one would like to know how much bearing conversion to variants of Christianity has on the only other sub-Saharan political phenomena that look like modern mass nationalism, namely the Biafra secession of 1967 and the South African National Congress.

If religion is not a necessary mark of proto-nationality (though one can see why it was for seventeenth-century Russians, pressed both by Catholic Poland and the Muslim Turks and Tatars), the holy icons, on the other hand, are a crucial component of it, as they are of modern nationalism. They represent the symbols and rituals or common collective practices which alone give a palpable reality to otherwise imaginary community. They may be shared images (as the icons were) or practices like the Muslim's five daily prayers, or even ritual words like the Muslims' Allah Akbar or the Jews Shema Yisroel. They may be named images identified with territories

[46] Gellner, *Nations and Nationalism* (Oxford 1983).

sufficiently large to constitute a nation such as the Virgin of
Guadalupe in Mexico or the Virgin of Montserrat in Catalonia.
They may be periodic festivals or contests which bring scattered
groups together such as the Greek Olympics and more recent
nationalist inventions along the same lines such as the Catalan Jocs
Florals, the Welsh Eisteddfodau and others. The significance of the
holy icons is demonstrated by the universal use of simple pieces of
coloured fabric – namely flags – as the symbol of modern nations,
and their association with highly charged ritual occasions or acts of
worship.

However, as in the case of religion, 'holy icons' whatever their
form and nature, may be either too wide or too narrow to serve as
symbols of a proto-nation. The Virgin Mary alone is difficult to
confine to any limited sector of the Catholic world, and for every
localized Virgin who becomes a proto-national symbol, there are
scores or hundreds who remain patronesses of restricted communities or are otherwise irrelevant for our purpose. The most satisfactory icons from a proto-national point of view are obviously those
specifically associated with a state, i.e. in the pre-national phase,
with a divine or divinely imbued king or emperor whose realm
happens to coincide with a future nation. Rulers who are ex officio
heads of their churches (as in Russia) naturally lend themselves to
this association, but the magical kingships of England and France
demonstrate its potential even where Church and state are disso-
ciated.[47] Since there are comparatively few theocracies which have
nation-making possibilities, it is difficult to judge how far purely
divine authority is enough. The question must be left to experts in
the history of Mongols and Tibetans or, nearer to the west, of the
medieval Armenians. It was certainly not enough in nineteenth-
century Europe, as the Neo-Guelphs discovered in Italy when they
tried to build an Italian nationalism round the Papacy. They failed,
even though the Papacy was *de facto* an Italian institution and
indeed before 1860 the *only* properly all-Italian institution.
However, the Holy Church could hardly be expected to turn itself
into a localized national, let alone nationalist, establishment, least

[47] The classical treatment of this theme is still Marc Bloch's *Les Rois thaumaturges* (Paris
1924).

of all under Pius IX. What Italy unified under the papal banner would have been like in the nineteenth century is not even worth speculating about.

This brings us to the last and almost certainly the most decisive criterion of proto-nationalism, the consciousness of belonging or having belonged to a lasting political entity.[48] The strongest proto-national cement known is undoubtedly to be what nineteenth-century jargon called a 'historical nation', especially if the state which formed the framework of the later 'nation' was associated with a special *Staatsvolk* or state-people such as the Great Russians, the English or the Castilians. However, here a clear distinction must be made between the direct and indirect effects of national historicity.

For in most cases the 'political nation' which originally formulates the vocabulary of what later becomes the nation-people is not understood to include more than a small fraction of the inhabitants of a state, namely the privileged elite, or the nobility and gentry. When the French nobles described the Crusades as *gesta Dei per francos* they had no intention of associating the triumph of the cross with the bulk of the inhabitants of France, or even of that small part of the hexagon which bore that name in the late eleventh century, if only because most of those who saw themselves as the descendants of the Franks would consider the populace over which they ruled as the descendants of people conquered by the Franks. (This view was turned upside down for democratic purposes by the Republic which insisted through its schools textbooks that 'our ancestors' were the Gauls and not the Franks, and was reaffirmed for reactionary and eugenic purposes by post-revolutionary reactionaries like Count Gobineau.) This 'nationalism of the nobility' may certainly be regarded as proto-national, inso far as 'the three elements *natio*, political *fidelitas* and *communitas*, that is to say the categories of 'nationality', political 'loyalty' and 'political commonwelath' were ... already united in the socio-political

---

[48] However, it must not be assumed that this consciousness affected all groups of the population in the same way, or covered anything like the territory of the modern 'nation', or implied modern nationality. Popular Greek consciousness, presumably based on the Byzantine heritage, was of being parts of the Roman empire (*romaiosyne*).

consciousness and the emotions of a group within society (*einer gesellschaftlichen Gruppe*)'.[49] It is the direct ancestor of certain later nationalisms in countries like Poland and Hungary, where the idea of a nation of Magyars and Poles could accommodate, without the slightest difficulty, the fact that a large part of the inhabitants of the lands under the crown of St Stephen or of the Polish Commonwealth were not Magyars or Poles by any modern national definition. For these plebeians counted no more than the plebeians who happened to be Magyars and Poles. They were by definition outside the enclosure of the 'political nation'. And in any case that 'nation' must not be confused with modern nationality.[50]

Obviously the concept and vocabulary of 'the political nation' could eventually be extended to a nation assumed to consist of the mass of a country's inhabitants, though almost certainly this happened much later than retrospective nationalism would have it. Moreover the links between the two were almost certainly indirect, for while there is plenty of evidence that the common people in a kingdom could identify themselves with country and people through the supreme ruler, king or tsar – as Joan of Arc did – there is not much likelihood that peasants would identify with a 'country' that consisted of the community of the lords who were, inevitably, the chief targets of their discontents. If they happened to be attached and loyal to their particular lord, this would imply neither identification with the interests of the rest of the gentry, nor any attachment to any country larger than his and their home territory.

Indeed when in the pre-national era we encounter what would today be classified as an autonomous popular movement of

---

[49] Jenö Szücs, *Nation und Geschichte* (Budapest 1981), pp. 84–5.

[50] 'The nobility maintained systematic communications – the only class to do so – through their administrative disctricts and the Diet of estates where they, as "the Croatian political nation" debated issues and took decisions. It was a nation without "nationality" … i.e. without national consciousness … because the nobility could not identify with other members of the Croatian ethnic community, the peasants and townsmen. The feudal "patriot" loved his "fatherland" but his fatherland embraced the estates and possessions of his peers and the "Kingdom." To him "the political nation" of which he was a member meant the territory and traditions of the former state.' Mirjana Gross, 'On the integration of the Croatian nation: a case study in nation-building', *East European Quarterly*, xv, 2, June 1981, p. 212.

national defence against foreign invaders, as in fifteenth- and sixteenth-century central Europe, its ideology seems to have been social and religious but *not* national. Peasants appear to have argued that they had been betrayed by the nobles whose duty as *bellatores* should have been to defend them against the Turks. Perhaps they had a secret agreement with the invaders? It was thus left to the common people to defend the true faith against paganism by means of a crusade.[51] Such movements might under certain circumstances create the basis of a broader popular national patriotism, as in Hussite Bohemia – the original Hussite ideology was not Czech-national – or on the military frontiers of Christian states among a peasantry armed and set relatively free for the purpose. The cossacks, as we have seen, are a case in point. However, where state tradition did not provide it with a firm and permanent framework, such popular grassroots patriotism cannot usually be seen as growing over continuously into modern national patriotism.[52] But of course it was rarely expected to by governments of the old regime. The duty of the subject in such regimes, other than those specifically charged with military duties, was obedience and tranquillity, not loyalty or zeal. Frederick the Great indignantly refused the offer of his loyal Berliners to help him defeat the Russians who were about to occupy his capital, on the ground that wars were the business of soldiers, not civilians. And we all remember the reaction of emperor Francis II to the guerrilla rising of his faithful Tyroleans: 'Today they are patriots for me, tomorrow they may be patriots against me.'

Nevertheless, in one way or another membership of a historic (or actual) state present or past, can act directly upon the consciousness of the common people to produce proto-nationalism – or perhaps even, as in the case of Tudor England, something close to modern patriotism. (It would be pedantic to refuse this label to Shakespeare's propagandist plays about English history; but of course we are not entitled to assume that the groundlings read into them what we do.) There is no reason to deny proto-national feelings to pre-nineteenth-century Serbs, not because they were Orthodox as against neighbouring Catholics and Muslims – this

[51] Szücs, *Nation und Geschichte*, pp. 112–25.   [52] *Ibid.* pp. 125–30.

would not have distinguished them from Bulgars – but because the memory of the old kingdom defeated by the Turks was preserved in song and heroic story, and, perhaps more to the point, in the daily liturgy of the Serbian church which had canonized most of its kings. That there was a Tsar in Russia undoubtedly helped Russians to see themselves as something like a nation. The potential popular appeal of a state tradition for modern nationalism, whose object it is to establish the nation as a territorial state, is obvious. It has led some such movements to reach far back beyond the real memory of their peoples in the search for a suitable (and suitably impressive) national state in the past, as in the case of the Armenians, whose last sufficiently important kingdom is to be found not later than the first century BC, or the Croats, whose nationalists saw themselves (implausibly) as the heirs of the noble 'Croatian political nation'. As always, the content of nineteenth-century national propaganda is an unreliable guide to what the rank and file of the common people actually thought before they began to adhere to the national cause.[53] This is not, of course, to deny that proto-national identification, on which later nationalism could build, existed among Armenians or, though probably to a distinctly smaller extent, pre-nineteenth-century Croat peasants.

Nevertheless, where there are, or appear to be continuities between proto-nationalism, they may well be quite factitious. There is no historical continuity whatever between Jewish proto-nationalism and modern Zionism. The German inhabitants of the holy land Tyrol became a sub-variety of German nationalists in our century, and indeed enthusiastic supporters of Adolf Hitler. But this process, which has been excellently analysed in the literature, has no intrinsic connexion with the Tyrolean popular rising of 1809 under the (ethnic and linguistic German) inn-keeper Andreas Hofer, even though pan-German nationalists think otherwise.[54] Sometimes indeed we can see the total non-congruence of proto-nationalism and nationalism even when the two exist simultaneously and in combination. The literate champions and organizers

---

[53] Failure to allow for this adequately makes I. Banac's otherwise excellent discussion less persuasive on the Croatian aspect of the problem.

[54] Cole and Wolf, *The Hidden Frontier*, pp. 53, 112–13.

of Greek nationalism in the early nineteenth century were undoubtedly inspired by the thought of ancient Hellenic glories, which also aroused the enthusiasm of educated, i.e. classically educated, philhellenes abroad. And the national literary language constructed by and for them, the Katharevousa, was and is a high-flown neo-classical idiom seeking to bring the language of the descendants of Themistocles and Pericles back to their true heritage from the two millennia of slavery which had corrupted it. Yet the real Greeks who took up arms for what turned out to be the formation of a new independent nation-state, did not talk ancient Greek any more than Italians talk Latin. They talked and wrote Demotic. Pericles, Aeschylus, Euripides and the glories of ancient Sparta and Athens meant little if anything to them, and insofar as they had heard of them, they did not think of them as relevant. Paradoxically, they stood for Rome rather than Greece (*romaiosyne*), that is to say they saw themselves as heirs of the Christianized Roman Empire (i.e. Byzantium). They fought as Christians against Muslim unbelievers, as Romans against the Turkish dogs.

Nevertheless it is evident – if only from the Greek example just cited – that proto-nationalism, where it existed, made the task of nationalism easier, however great the differences between the two, insofar as existing symbols and sentiments of proto-national community could be mobilized behind a modern cause or a modern state. But this is far from saying that the two were the same, or even that one must logically or inevitably lead into the other.

For it is evident that proto-nationalism alone is clearly not enough to form nationalities, nations, let alone states. The number of national movements, with or without states, is patently much smaller than the number of human groups capable of forming such movements by current criteria of potential nationhood, and certainly smaller than the number of communities with a sense of belonging together in a manner which is hard to distinguish from the proto-national. And this despite the fact that (even if we leave aside the question of self-determination for the 1,800 inhabitants of the Falkland Islands or Malvinas) serious claims to independent statehood have been made by populations as small as the 70,000 who fight for an independent Saharan nation or the 120,000 or so who have virtually declared independence for the Turkish part of Cyprus. One must agree with Gellner that the apparent universal ideological domination of nationalism today is a sort of optical illusion. A world of nations cannot exist, only a world where some potentially national groups, in claiming this status, exclude others from making similar claims, which, as it happens, not many of them do. If proto-nationalism were enough, a serious national movement of the Mapuche or Aymara would have appeared by now. If such movements were to appear tomorrow it would be because other factors had intervened.

In the second place, while a proto-national base may be desirable, perhaps even essential, for the formation of serious state-aspiring national movements – though in itself not sufficient to create them – it is *not* essential for the formation of national patriotism and loyalty once a state has been founded. As has been often observed, nations are more often the consequence of setting up a state than they are its foundation. The USA and Australia are obvious examples of nation-states *all* of whose specific national characteristics and criteria of nationhood have been established since the late eighteenth century, and indeed could not have existed before the foundation of the respective state and country. However, we need hardly remind ourselves that the mere setting up of a state is not sufficient in itself to create a nation.

Finally, and as always, a word of warning is in order. We know too little about what went on, or for that matter what still goes on, in the minds of most relatively inarticulate men and women, to speak with any confidence about their thoughts and feelings towards the nationalities and nation-states which claim their loyalties. The real relations between proto-national identification and subsequent national or state patriotism must often remain obscure for this reason. We know what Nelson meant when he signalled his fleet on the eve of the battle of Trafalgar that England expected every man to do his duty, but not what passed through the minds of Nelson's sailors on that day, even if it would be quite unreasonable to doubt that some of it could be described as patriotic. We know what national parties and movements read into the support of such members of the nation as give them their backing, but not what these customers are after as they purchase the collection of very miscellaneous goods presented to them as a package by the salesmen of national politics. Sometimes we can be fairly clear about what parts of the content they do not want – e.g. in the case of the Irish people, the universal use of the Gaelic language – but such silent selective referenda are rarely possible. We are constantly running the risk of giving the people marks in terms of a syllabus they have not studied and an examination they are not taking.

Suppose, for instance, we take the readiness to die for the fatherland as an index of patriotism, as seems plausible enough and as nationalists and national governments have naturally been inclined to do. We would then expect to find that William II's and Hitler's soldiers, who were presumably more open to the national appeal, fought more bravely than the eighteenth-century Hessians, hired out as mercenaries by their prince, who presumably were not so motivated. But did they? And did they fight better than, say, the Turks in World War I, who can hardly yet be regarded as national patriots? Or the Gurkhas who, fairly evidently, have not been motivated by either British or Nepalese patriotism? One formulates such fairly absurd questions not to elicit answers or stimulate research theses, but to indicate the denseness of the fog which surrounds questions about the national consciousness of common men and women, especially in the period before modern nationalism unquestionably became a mass political force. For most nations even in western Europe this did not happen until rather late in the nineteenth century. Then, at least, the choice became clear even though, as we shall see, its content was not.

CHAPTER 3

The government perspective

Let us now turn from the grassroots to the high peaks from which those who governed states and societies after the French Revolution surveyed the problems of nation and nationality.

The characteristic modern state, receiving its systematic shape in the era of the French revolutions, though in many ways anticipated by the evolving European principalities of the sixteenth–seventeenth centuries, was novel in a number of respects. It was defined as a (preferably continuous and unbroken) territory over all of whose inhabitants it ruled, and separated by clearly distinct frontiers or borders from other such territories. Politically it ruled over and administered these inhabitants directly, and not through intermediate systems of rulers and autonomous corporations. It sought, if at all possible, to impose the same institutional and administrative arrangements and laws all over its territory, though after the Age of Revolution, no longer the same religious or secular-ideological ones. And increasingly it found itself having to take notice of the opinions of its subjects or citizens, because its political arrangements gave them a voice – generally through various kinds of elected representatives – and/or because the state needed their practical consent or activity in other ways, e.g. as tax-payers or as potential conscript soldiers. In short, the state ruled over a territorially defined 'people' and did so as the supreme 'national' agency of rule over its territory, its agents increasingly reaching down to the humblest inhabitant of the least of its villages.

In the course of the nineteenth century these interventions became so universal and so routinized in 'modern' states that a family would have to live in some very inaccessible place if some member or other were not to come into regular contact with the national state and its agents: through the postman, the policeman or gendarme, and eventually through the schoolteacher; through the men employed on the railways, where these were publicly owned; not to mention the garrisons of soldiers and the even more widely audible military bands. Increasingly the state kept records of each of its subjects and citizens through the device of regular periodic censuses (which did not become general until the middle of the nineteenth century), through theoretically compulsory attendance at primary school and, where applicable, military conscription. In bureaucratic and well-policed states a system of personal documentation and registration brought the inhabitant into even more direct contact with the machinery of rule and administration, especially if he or she moved from one place to another. In states which provided a civil alternative to the ecclesiastical celebration of the great human rites, as most did, inhabitants might encounter the representatives of the state on these emotionally charged occasions; and always they would be recorded by the machinery for registering births, marriages and deaths, which supplemented the machinery of censuses. Government and subject or citizen were inevitably linked by daily bonds, as never before. And the nineteenth-century revolutions in transport and communications typified by the railway and the telegraph tightened and routinized the links between central authority and its remotest outposts.

From the point of view of states and ruling classes this transformation posed two major kinds of political problems, if we leave aside the changing relationship between central government and local elites, which – in Europe, where federalism was extremely untypical and getting rarer – shifted steadily in favour of the national centre.[1] First, it raised technical-administrative questions about the best way of implementing the new form of government in

---

[1] The abolition of a separate Irish parliament, the revocation of the autonomy of 'Congress Poland', the domination of formerly federal Germany by a hegemonic member (Prussia) and a single all-national Parliament, and the transformation of Italy into a centralized state and the formation of a single national police force in Spain, independent of local interests, are so many examples of this trend. Central governments might, as in Britain, leave much room for local initiative by central permission, but the only federal government in Europe before 1914 was the Swiss.

which every adult (male) inhabitant, and indeed as a subject of administration every inhabitant irrespective of sex and age, was directly linked with state government. These concern us here only insofar as they implied the construction of a machine of administration and agency, composed of a very numerous body of agents, and which automatically raised the question of the written or even the spoken language or languages of communication within the state, which the aspiration to universal literacy could make politically sensitive. While the percentage of these government agents was modest enough by our standards – around 1910 it was, at most, of the order of 1 in 20 of the national occupied population – it was growing, sometimes quite rapidly, and represented a substantial number of employees: c.700,000 in Cisleithanian Austria (1910), over half a million in France (1906), c.1.5 millions in Germany (1907), 700,000 in Italy (1907), to cite but some examples.[2] We note in passing that in the respective countries it probably constituted the largest single body of employment requiring literacy.

Second, it raised the politically much more sensitive issues of citizen loyalty to, and identification with, the state and ruling system. In the days before citizen and secularized national rulers confronted each other directly, state loyalty and identification had either not been required of the common man – not to mention the common woman – or they had been ensured by means of all those autonomous or intermediate instances which the Age of Revolution dismantled or demoted: through religion and social hierarchy ('God bless the squire and his relations/and keep us in our proper stations'), or even through the autonomous constituted authorities inferior to the ultimate ruler or the self-governing communities and corporations which stood like a screen between subject and emperor or king, leaving monarchy free to represent virtue and justice. Just as children's loyalty was to parents, women's to their menfolk who acted 'on their behalf'. Alternatively, the classical liberalism which found expression in the regimes of the French and Belgian revolutions of 1830 and the

---

[2] Peter Flora, *State, Economy and Society in Western Europe 1815–1975*, vol. I, chapter 5 (Frankfurt, London and Chicago 1983).

Reform Era after 1832 in Britain, side-stepped the problem of the citizen's politics by limiting political rights to men of property and education.

Yet in the last third of the nineteenth century it became increasingly manifest that the democratization, or at least the increasingly unlimited electoralization of politics, were unavoidable. It became equally obvious, at least from the 1880s, that wherever the common man was given even the most nominal participation in politics as a citizen – with the rarest exception the common woman remained excluded – he could no longer be relied on to give automatic loyalty and support to his betters or to the state. Especially not when the classes to which he belonged were historically novel, and hence lacked a traditional place in the scheme of things. The need for state and ruling classes to compete with rivals for the loyalty of the lower orders therefore became acute.

And simultaneously, as modern war illustrates, state interests now depended on the participation of the ordinary citizen to an extent not previously envisaged. Whether the armies were composed of conscripts or volunteers, the willingness of men to serve was now an essential variable in government calculations; and so indeed was their actual physical and mental capacity to do so, which governments therefore began systematically to investigate – as in the famous inquiry into 'Physical deterioration' in Britain after the Boer War. The degree of sacrifice which could be imposed on civilians had to enter the plans of strategists: the British ones before 1914 were reluctant, on these grounds, to weaken the Navy, guardian of Britain's imported food supplies, by strengthening the country's participation in mass warfare on land. The political attitudes of citizens, and particularly workers, were matters of vital interest, given the rise of labour and socialist movements. Obviously the democratization of politics, i.e. on the one hand the growing extension of the (male) franchise, on the other the creation of the modern, administrative, citizen-mobilizing and citizen-influencing state, both placed the question of the 'nation', and the citizen's feelings towards whatever he regarded as his 'nation', 'nationality' or other centre of loyalty, at the top of the political agenda.

For rulers the problem was thus not simply that of acquiring a new legitimacy, though where states were new or novel this had also to be solved, and identification with a 'people' or 'nation', however defined, was a convenient and fashionable way of solving it, and in states which insisted on popular sovereignty, by definition the only way. What else could legitimize the monarchies of states which had never previously existed as such, like Greece, Italy, or Belgium, or whose existence broke with all historical precedents, like the German empire of 1871? The need to adapt arose even in long-established regimes, for three reasons. Between 1789 and 1815 few of them had not been transformed – even post-Napoleonic Switzerland was in important respects a new political entity. Such traditional guarantors of loyalty as dynastic legitimacy, divine ordination, historic right and continuity of rule, or religious cohesion, were severely weakened. Last, but not least, all these traditional legitimations of state authority were, since 1789, under permanent challenge.

This is clear in the case of monarchy. The need to provide a new, or at least a supplementary, 'national' foundation for this institution was felt in states as secure from revolution as George III's Britain and Nicholas I's Russia.[3] And monarchies certainly tried to adapt themselves.

However, if the adjustments of monarch to 'the nation' are a useful indicator of the extent to which traditional institutions after the Age of Revolution had to adapt or die, the institution of hereditary rule by princes itself, as developed in sixteenth–seventeenth century Europe, had no necessary relation whatever with it. In fact, most of the monarchs of Europe in 1914 – when monarchy was still almost universal in that continent – were supplied from an inter-related set of families whose personal nationality (if they felt themselves to have one) was entirely irrelevant to their function as heads of state. Prince Albert, Victoria's consort, wrote to the King of Prussia as a German, with a sense

---

[3] Linda Colley, 'The apotheosis of George III: loyalty, royalty and the British nation' (*Past & Present*, 102 (1984), pp. 94–129); for Count Uvarov's proposal (1832) that the Tsar's government should base itself not only on the principles of autocracy and orthodoxy, but also on that of 'natsionalnost' cf. Hugh Seton-Watson, *Nations and States* (London 1977), p. 84.

of Germany as his personal fatherland, yet the policy he firmly represented was, even more unambiguously, that of Great Britain.[4] Transnational corporations in the late twentieth century are far more apt to choose their chief executives from members of the nation in which they originated, or where their headquarters are situated, than nineteenth-century nation-states were to choose kings with local connections.

On the other hand the post-revolutionary state, whether headed by a hereditary ruler or not, had a necessary organic relationship to 'the nation', i.e. to the inhabitants of its territory considered as, in some sense, a collectivity, a 'people', both as we have seen by virtue of its structure, and by virtue of the political transformations that were turning it into a body of variously mobilizable citizens with political rights or claims. Even when the state as yet faced no serious challenge to its legitimacy or cohesion, and no really powerful forces of subversion, the mere decline of the older socio-political bonds would have made it imperative to formulate and inculcate new forms of civic loyalty (a 'civic religion' to use Rousseau's phrase), since other potential loyalties were now capable of political expression. For what state, in the era of revolutions, liberalism, nationalism, democratization and the rise of working-class movements, could feel itself absolutely secure? The sociology which sprang up in the last twenty years of the century was primarily a political sociology, and the problem of socio-political cohesion in states was at its core. But states required a civic religion ('patriotism') all the more because they increasingly required more than passivity from their citizens. 'England', as Nelson told his sailors in the patriotic song as they prepared for the battle of Trafalgar, 'expects that every man this day will do his duty.'

And if, by any chance, the state did not succeed in converting its citizens to the new religion before they listened to rival evangelists, it might well be lost. Ireland, as Gladstone realized, was lost to the United Kingdom as soon as the democratization of the vote in 1884–5 demonstrated that the virtual totality of the Catholic

---

[4] Cf. *Revolutionsbriefe 1848: Ungedrucktes aus dem Nachlass König Friedrich Wilhelms IV von Preussen* (Leipzig 1930).

parliamentary seats in that island would henceforth belong to an Irish (i.e. nationalist) party; however, it remained a United Kingdom because its other national components accepted the state-centred nationalism of 'Great Britain', which had been evolved, largely for their own benefit, in the eighteenth century, and which still puzzles theorists representing a more orthodox nationalism.[5] The Habsburg empire, an assembly of Irelands, was not so lucky. Here lies a crucial difference between what the Austrian novelist Robert Musil called Kakania (after the letters k and k, abbreviations of the German 'imperial and royal'), and what Tom Nairn, following him, calls Ukania (from the initials of the United Kingdom).

A purely state-based patriotism is not necessarily ineffective, since the very existence and functions of the modern territorial citizen-state constantly involve its inhabitants in its affairs, and, inevitably, provide an institutional or procedural 'landscape' which is unlike any other such landscape and is the setting for their lives, which it largely determines. The mere fact of existing for a few decades, less than the length of a single human lifetime, may be enough to establish at least a passive identification with a new nation-state in this manner. If this were not so, we should have expected the rise of revolutionary Shia fundamentalism in Iran to have had as significant repercussions in Iraq as among the Shia of divided Lebanon, for most of the non-Kurdish Muslim population of that state, which incidentally contains the major holy places of the sect, belong to the same faith as the Iranians.[6] Yet the very idea of a sovereign secular nation-state in Mesopotamia is even more recent than that of a territorial Jewish state. An extreme example of the potential effectiveness of pure state-patriotism is the Finnish

---

[5] For the evolution of British consciousness, see in general Raphael Samuel (ed.), *Patriotism: The Making and Unmaking of British National Identity* (3 vols., London 1989), but esp. Linda Colley, 'Whose nation? Class and national consciousness in Britain 1750–1830' (*Past & Present*, 113, November 1986, pp. 97–117) and 'Imperial South Wales' in Gwyn A. Williams, *The Welsh in their History* (London and Canberra 1982). For the puzzlement, Tom Nairn, *The Enchanted Glass: Britain and its Monarchy* (London 1988), part 2.

[6] Repression no doubt discouraged the expression of such sympathies in Iraq; on the other hand the considerable temporary successes of the invading Iranian revolutionary armies do not seem to have succeeded in encouraging it.

loyalty to the Tsarist empire for so much of the nineteenth century, indeed until the policy of Russification after the 1880s produced an anti-Russian reaction. In fact, while memorials to the House of Romanov are not easily found in Russia itself, a statue of Tsar Alexander II, the Liberator, still stands proudly in the main square of Helsinki.

One might well go further. The original, revolutionary-popular, idea of patriotism was state-based rather than nationalist, since it related to the sovereign people itself, i.e. to the state exercising power in its name. Ethnicity or other elements of historic continuity were irrelevant to 'the nation' in this sense, and language relevant only or chiefly on pragmatic grounds. 'Patriots', in the original sense of the word, were the opposite of those who believed in 'my country, right or wrong', namely – as Dr Johnson, citing the ironical use of the word put it – 'factious disturbers of government'.[7] More seriously, the French Revolution, which appears to have used the term in the manner pioneered by Americans and more especially the Dutch revolution of 1783,[8] thought of patriots as those who showed the love of their country by wishing to renew it by reform or revolution. And the *patrie* to which their loyalty lay, was the opposite of an existential, pre-existing unit, but a nation created by the political choice of its members who, in doing so, broke with or at least demoted their former loyalties. The 1,200 National Guards from Languedoc, Dauphiné and Provence who met near Valence on 19 November 1789 took an oath of loyalty to Nation, Law and King, and declared that henceforth they were no longer Dauphinois, Provençaux or Languedociens, but only Frenchmen; as, even more to the point, did the National Guards of Alsace, Lorraine and Franche Comté at a similar meeting in 1790, thus transforming the inhabitants of provinces annexed by France a bare century ago into genuine Frenchmen.[9] As Lavisse put it:[10] 'La Nation consentie, voulue par elle-même' was France's contribution

---

[7] Cf. Hugh Cunningham, 'The language of patriotism, 1750–1914' (*History Workshop Journal*, 12, 1981, pp. 8–33).

[8] J. Godechot, *La Grande Nation: l'expansion révolutionnaire de la France dans le monde 1789–1799* (Paris 1956), vol. I, p. 254.

[9] *Ibid.* I, p. 73.

[10] Cited in Pierre Nora (ed.), *Les Lieux de Mémoire II* La Nation*, p. 363 (Paris 1986).

to history. The revolutionary concept of the nation as constituted by the deliberate political option of its potential citizens is, of course, still preserved in a pure form in the USA. Americans are those who wish to be. Nor did the French concept of the 'nation' as analogous to a plebiscite ('un plébiscite de tous les jours' as Renan phrased it) lose its essentially political character. French nationality was French citizenship: ethnicity, history, the language or patois spoken at home, were irrelevant to the definition of 'the nation'.

Moreover, the nation in this sense – as the body of citizens, whose rights as such gave them a stake in the country and thereby made the state to some extent 'our own' – was not only a phenomenon of revolutionary and democratic regimes, although anti-revolutionary and reluctantly democratizing regimes were extremely slow to recognize this. That is why belligerent governments in 1914 were so surprised to find their peoples rushing to arms, however briefly, in an access of patriotism.[11]

The very act of democratizing politics, i.e. of turning subjects into citizens, tends to produce a populist consciousness which, seen in some lights, is hard to distinguish from a national, even a chauvinist, patriotism – for if 'the country' is in some way 'mine', then it is more readily seen as preferable to those of foreigners, especially if these lack the rights and freedom of the true citizen. E. P. Thompson's 'free-born Englishman', the eighteenth-century Britons who never shall be slaves, readily contrasted themselves with the French. This did not necessarily imply any sympathy with ruling classes or their governments, and these in turn might well suspect the loyalty of lower-class militants to whom the rich and the aristocrats who exploited the common people were more immediately and constantly present than the most hated foreigners. The class-consciousness which working classes in numerous countries were aquiring in the last decades before 1914 implied, nay asserted, a claim to the Rights of Man and Citizen, and thus a potential patriotism. Mass political consciousness or class consciousness implied a concept of the 'patrie' or 'fatherland', as

11 Marc Ferro, *La Grande Guerre 1914–1918* (Paris 1969), p. 23; A. Offner, 'The working classes, British naval plans and the coming of the Great War' (*Past & Present*, 107, May 1985, pp. 225–26).

the history both of Jacobinism and of movements like Chartism demonstrates. For most Chartists were both against the rich and the French.

What made this populist-democratic and Jacobin patriotism extremely vulnerable, was the subalternity, both objective and – among the working classes – subjective, of these citizen-masses. For in the states in which it developed, the political agenda of patriotism was formulated by governments and ruling classes. The unfolding of political and class consciousness among the workers taught them to demand and to exercise citizen rights. Its tragic paradox was that, where they had learned to assert them, it helped to plunge them willingly into the mutual massacre of World War I. But it is significant that the belligerent governments appealed for support for this war, not simply on the grounds of blind patriotism, and even less on the grounds of macho glory and heroism, but by a propaganda addressed fundamentally to civilians and citizens. All the major belligerents presented the war as defensive. All presented it as a threat from abroad to civic advantages peculiar to their own country or side; all learned to present their war aims (somewhat inconsistently) not only as the elimination of such threats, but as, in some way, the social transformation of the country in the interest of its poorer citizens ('homes for heroes').

Democratization might thus automatically help to solve the problems of how states and regimes could acquire legitimacy in the eyes of their citizens, even if these were disaffected. It reinforced, it could even create, state patriotism. Yet it had its limits, especially when confronted with alternative, and now more easily mobilized, forces attracting the loyalty of which the state claimed to be the only legitimate repository. Nationalisms independent of the state were the most formidable of these. As we shall see, they were increasing in both numbers and the scale of their appeal, and, in the last third of the nineteenth century, formulating ambitions which increased their potential threat to states. It has often been suggested that the very modernization of states itself stimulated, if it did not create, these forces. Indeed, theories of nationalism as a function of modernization have become extremely prominent in the recent literature.[12] Yet, whatever the relation of nationalism to the modernizing of nineteenth-century states, the state confronted nationalism as a political force separate from it, quite distinct from 'state patriotism', and with which it had to come to terms. However, it could become an enormously powerful asset of government, if it could be integrated into state patriotism, to become its central emotional component.

This, of course, was often possible, by the mere projection of the sentiments of genuine, existential, identification with one's 'little' homeland on to the big one, which is recorded in the philological expansion of the scope of such words as 'pays', 'paese', 'pueblo', or indeed 'patrie', a word which as late as 1776 had been defined in local terms by the French Academy. 'A Frenchman's country was merely that part of it in which he happened to be born.'[13] Merely by dint of becoming a 'people', the citizens of a country became a sort of community, though an imagined one, and its members therefore found themselves seeking for, and consequently finding, things in common, places, practices, personages, memories, signs and symbols. Alternatively, the heritage of sections, regions and localities of what had become 'the nation' could be combined into an all-national heritage, so that even ancient conflicts came to symbolize their reconciliation on a higher, more comprehensive plane. Walter Scott thus built a single Scotland on the territory soaked in the blood of warring Highlanders and Lowlanders, kings and Covenanters, and he did so by emphasizing their ancient divisions. In a more general sense, the theoretical problem, so well summarized in Vidal de la Blache's great *Tableau de la géographie de la France* of 1903,[14] had to be solved for practically every nation-state, namely 'how a fragment of the earth's surface that is neither island nor peninsula, and which cannot properly be considered as a

---

12 Since Karl Deutsch, *Nationalism and Social Communication. An Enquiry into the Foundations of Nationality* (Cambridge MA 1953), Ernest Gellner, *Nations and Nationalism* (Oxford 1983) is a good example. Cf. John Breuilly, 'Reflections on nationalism' (*Philosophy and Social Sciences*, 15/1 March 1985, pp. 65–75).

13 J. M. Thompson, *The French Revolution* (Oxford 1944), p. 121.

14 It was designed as the initial volume of the famous multi-volume *Histoire de la France* edited by Ernest Lavisse, a monument to positivist science and Republican ideology. See J.-Y. Guiomar, 'Le Tableau de la géographie de la France de Vidal de la Blache' in Pierre Nora (ed.), *Les Lieux de Mémoire II*, p. 569ff.

single unit by physical geography, has risen to the state of a political country, and finally became a fatherland (*patrie*)'. For any nation of even middling size had to construct its unity on the basis of evident disparity.

States and regimes had every reason to reinforce, if they could, state patriotism with the sentiments and symbols of 'imagined community', wherever and however they originated, and to concentrate them upon themselves. As it happened, the time when the democratization of politics made it essential to 'educate our masters', to 'make Italians', to turn 'peasants into Frenchmen' and attach all to nation and flag, was also the time when popular nationalist, or at all events xenophobic sentiments and those of national superiority preached by the new pseudo-science of racism, became easier to mobilize. For the period from 1880 to 1914 was also that of the greatest mass migrations yet known, within and between states, of imperialism and of growing international rivalries ending in world war. All these underlined the differences between 'us' and 'them'. And there is no more effective way of bonding together the disparate sections of restless peoples than to unite them against outsiders. One does not have to accept the absolute *Primat der Innenpolitik* to recognize that governments had a considerable domestic interest in mobilizing nationalism among their citizens. Conversely, nothing stimulated nationalism on both sides as much as international conflict. The role of the 1840 dispute over the Rhine in the development of both French and German nationalist clichés is familiar.[15]

Naturally states would use the increasingly powerful machinery for communicating with their inhabitants, above all the primary schools, to spread the image and heritage of the 'nation' and to inculcate attachment to it and to attach all to country and flag,

---

[15] On the French side it gave universal currency to the theme of the nation's 'natural frontiers', a term which, contrary to historical myth, belongs essentially to the nineteenth century. (Cf. D. Nordmann, 'Des Limites d'état aux frontières nationales' in P. Nora (ed.) *Les Lieux de Mémoire*, vol. II**, pp. 35–62 *passim*, but esp. p. 52). On the German side the public campaign of the autumn of 1840 produced 'the breakthrough of modern German nationalism as a mass phenomenon' which was almost immediately – and for the first time – recognized by princes and governments. Cf. H.-U. Wehler, *Deutsche Gesellschaftsgeschichte 1815–1845/49* (vol. II, Munich 1987), p. 399. It also produced a future quasi-national anthem.

often 'inventing traditions' or even nations for this purpose.[16] The present writer recalls being submitted to such a piece of (unsuccessful) political invention in an Austrian primary school of the middle 1920s, in the form of a new national anthem desperately attempting to convince children that a few provinces left over when the rest of a large Habsburg empire seceded or was torn from them, formed a coherent whole, deserving love and patriotic devotion; a task not made any easier by the fact that the only thing they had in common was what made the overwhelming majority of their inhabitants want to join Germany. 'German Austria', this curious and short-lived anthem began, 'thou magnificent (*herrliches*) land, we love thee', continuing, as one might expect, with a travelogue or geography lesson following the alpine streams down from glaciers to the Danube valley and Vienna, and concluding with the assertion that this new rump-Austria was 'my homeland' (*mein Heimatland*).[17]

While governments were plainly engaged in conscious and deliberate ideological engineering, it would be a mistake to see these exercises as pure manipulation from above. They were, indeed, most successful when they could build on already present unofficial nationalist sentiments, whether of demotic xenophobia or *chauvinism* – the root word itself, like 'jingoism' appears first in the demagogic music-hall or vaudeville[18] – or, more likely, in nationalism among the middle and lower middle classes. To the extent that such sentiments were not created but only borrowed and fostered by governments, those who did so became a kind of sorcerer's apprentice. At best they could not entirely control the forces they had released; at worst they became their prisoners. Thus it is not conceivable that the British government of 1914, or indeed

16 E. J. Hobsbawm, 'Mass-producing traditions: Europe 1870–1914' in E. J. Hobsbawm and T. Ranger (eds.) *The Invention of Tradition* (Cambridge 1983) chs 7. Guy Vincent, *L'Ecole primaire française: Etude sociologique* (Lyons 1980), ch. 8: 'L'École et la nation', esp. pp. 188–93.

17 This anthem was later replaced by another, geographically in more general terms, but – since few Austrians believed in Austria – stressing its Germanness more emphatically, as well as bringing in God – incidentally, to the Haydn tune which both Habsburg anthem and 'Deutschland über alles' also shared.

18 See Gérard de Puymège, 'Le Soldat Chauvin' in P. Nora *Les Lieux de Mémoire*, II***, esp. pp. 51ff. The original Chauvin seems to have taken pride in the conquest of Algiers.

the British ruling class, would have wished to organize the orgy of anti-German xenophobia which swept the country after the declaration of war, incidentally forcing the British royal family to change the venerable dynastic name of Guelph for the less German-sounding Windsor. For, as we shall see, the type of nationalism which emerged towards the end of the nineteenth century had no fundamental similarity to state-patriotism, even when it attached itself to it. Its basic loyalty was, paradoxically, not to 'the country', but only to its particular version of that country: to an ideological construct.

The merger of state patriotism with non-state nationalism was politically risky, since the criteria of the one were comprehensive e.g. all citizens of the French Republic – whereas the criteria of the other were exclusive – e.g. only those citizens of the French Republic speaking the French language and, in extreme cases, blonde and long-headed.[19] The potential cost of infusing one with the other was therefore high, where identification with one nationality alienated others who refused to be assimilated to or eliminated by it. There were, in Europe, few enough genuinely homogeneous nation-states like, say, Portugal, though in the middle and even late nineteenth century still a very large number of groups potentially classifiable as 'nationalities', which did not compete with the claims of the officially dominant 'nation' and an immense number of individuals, who actively sought assimilation to one or other of dominant nationalities and languages of culture.

Yet if the identification of the state with one nation risked creating a counter-nationalism, the very process of its modernization made this far more probable, because it implied a homogenization and standardization of its inhabitants, essentially by means of a written 'national language'. Both the direct administration of vast numbers of citizens by modern governments, and the technical and economic development require this, for they make universal literacy desirable and the mass development of secondary edu-

19 For the strong racist element in the debates on French nationalism, see Pierre André Taguieff, La Force du préjugé: Essai sur le racisme et ses doubles (Paris 1987), pp. 126–8). For the novelty of this social-darwinist racism, see Günter Nagel, Georges Vacher de Lapouge (1854–1936). Ein Beitrag zur Geschichte des Sozialdarwinismus in Frankreich (Freiburg im Breisgau 1975).

cation almost mandatory. It is the scale on which the state operates as well as its need for *direct* contacts with its citizens which create the problem. Thus mass education must, for practical purposes, be conducted in a vernacular, whereas education for a limited elite can be conducted in a language not understood or spoken by the body of the population or, in the case of 'classical' languages like Latin, classical Persian or classical written Chinese, by anyone at all. Administrative or political transactions at the apex can be conducted in a language incomprehensible to the mass of the people, as the Hungarian nobility conducted its parliamentary business before 1840 in Latin, or – still – English in India, but an electoral campaign under a democratic suffrage must be conducted in the vernacular. Indeed, economics, technology and politics increasingly make a language of mass *spoken* communication essential – a necessity intensified by the rise of film, radio and television – so that languages originally designed as, or functioning as, lingua-francas for speakers of mutually incomprehensible vernaculars or as cultural idioms for the educated, are pressed into service as media for national speech: Mandarin Chinese, Bahasa Indonesia, Pilipino.[20]

If the choice of the 'official' national language were merely one of pragmatic convenience, it would be relatively simple. One would merely have to choose the idiom most likely to be spoken and/or understood by the largest number of citizens, or that which would most facilitate communication between them. Joseph II's choice of German as the administrative language of his multinational empire was quite pragmatic in this sense, as was Gandhi's choice of Hindi for the future independent India – he himself was a native speaker of Gujarati – and, since 1947, the choice of English as the medium of national communication which was least unacceptable to Indians. In multinational states the problem could be solved in theory, as the Habsburgs sought to solve it from 1848 on, by the device of giving the 'language of common use' (*Umgangsprache*) some official recognition at an appropriate administrative level.

---

[20] Cf. e.g. on the Philippines: 'Land of 100 tongues but not a single language' (*New York Times*, 2 December 1987). For the problem in general, see J. Fishman, 'The sociology of language: an interdisciplinary social science approach to language in society' in T. Sebeok (ed.), *Current Trends in Linguistics*, vol. 12*** (The Hague–Paris 1974).

The more localized and illiterate, i.e. the closer to traditional rural life, the smaller the occasions for conflict between one linguistic level, one geographical entity and another. Even at the peak of the conflict between Germans and Czechs in the Habsburg empire it was still possible to write:

> In a multinational state we may take it for granted that even those who occupy no official position are under the stimulus, indeed, the obligation, to learn the second language – e.g. traders, artisans, workers. The peasants are least affected by this *de facto* constraint. For the self-segregation (*Abgeschlossenheit*) and self-sufficiency of village life, which persist to this day, mean that they are rarely conscious of the proximity of a settlement speaking a different language, at least in Bohemia and Moravia, where the country people of both nations enjoy the same economic and social status. In such areas the linguistic frontier may remain unchanged for centuries, especially since village endogamy and what is in practice the priority right to purchase [holdings] by members of the community limit the recruitment of outsiders into the village. What few strangers come in, are soon assimilated and incorporated.[21]

Yet the 'national language' is rarely a pragmatic matter, and still less a dispassionate one, as is shown by the reluctance to recognize them as constructs, by historicizing, and inventing traditions for, them.[22] Least of all was it to be pragmatic and dispassionate for the ideologists of nationalism as it evolved after 1830 and was transformed towards the end of the century. For them, language was the soul of a nation, and, as we shall see, increasingly the crucial criterion of nationality. What language or languages were to be used in the secondary schools of Celje (Cilli) where speakers of German and Slovene coexisted was far from a matter of administrative convenience. (Indeed this particular issue convulsed Aus-

---

[21] Karl Renner, *Das Selbstbestimmungsrecht der Nationen in besonderer Anwendung auf Oesterreich* (Leipzig and Vienna 1918), p. 65. This is the second, rewritten, edition of *Der Kampf der österreichischen Nationen um den Staat* (1902) by the Austro-Marxist author, who was himself a German peasant's son from Moravia.

[22] 'Many speech communities create and cultivate myths and genealogies concerning the origin and development of the standard varieties [of their language] in order to de-emphasize the numerous components of more recent vintage that they contain... A variety achieves historicity by coming to be associated with some great ideological or national movement or tradition.' J. Fishman, 'The Sociology of Language', p. 164.

trian politics in 1895.)[23] All, except the most fortunate governments in multilingual countries, were aware of the explosiveness of the language problem.

What made it even more explosive was that, under the circumstances, all nationalism not already identified with a state necessarily became *political*. For the state was the machine which had to be manipulated if a 'nationality' was to turn into a 'nation', or even if its existing status was to be safeguarded against historical erosion or assimilation. As we shall see, linguistic nationalism was and is essentially about the language of public education and official use. It is about 'office and school' as Poles, Czechs and Slovenes never tired of repeating as early as 1848.[24] It is about whether schools in Wales should give their instruction in Welsh as well as English, or even *only* in Welsh; about the necessity to give Welsh names to places in the principality which, not having been settled by Welsh-speakers, never had any; about the language of road signs and street names; about public subsidies for a television channel in Welsh; about the language in which debates in district councils are conducted and their minutes drawn up; about the language on the application form for driving licences or electricity bills, or even about whether bilingual forms should be distributed or separate forms in each language, or perhaps, one day, only forms in Welsh. For, as a nationalist author puts it:

> At a time when Welsh was still reasonably secure, Emrys ap Iwan saw the necessity of making it once more an official language and the language of education if it was to survive.[25]

States thus found themselves, in one way or another, forced to come to terms with the new 'principle of nationality' and its symptoms, whether or not they were able to use it for their own purposes. The best way to conclude this chapter is to look briefly at the evolution of their attitudes in the mid-nineteenth century to the problem of nation and language. The question may be pursued

23 W. A. Macartney, *The Habsburg Empire* (London 1971), p. 661.
24 P. Burian, 'The state language problem in Old Austria' (*Austrian History Yearbook*, 6–7, 1970–1, p. 87.
25 Ned Thomas, *The Welsh Extremist: Welsh Politics, Literature and Society Today* (Talybont 1973), p. 83.

through the debates of technical experts, namely the government statisticians who attempted to co-ordinate and standardize the periodic national censuses which, from the middle of the century, became a normal part of the machinery of documentation needed by all 'advanced' or modern states. The problem which appeared at the First International Statistical Congress in 1853 was whether a question on the 'spoken language' should be included in such censuses, and what bearing, if any, it had on nation and nationality.

The matter was originally raised, not surprisingly, by the Belgian Quetelet, who was not only the founder of social statistics, but came from a state where the relationship between French and Flemish was already a matter of some political moment. The International Statistical Congress of 1860 decided that a question on language should be optional in censuses, each state deciding whether it had or had not any 'national' significance. The Congress of 1873, however, recommended that such a question should henceforth be included in all censuses.

The initial view of the experts was that the 'nationality' of an individual would not be established by census questions, except in the sense in which the French gave to the word, namely the person's state citizenship. In this sense language was irrelevant to 'nationality', though in practice this meant simply that the French, and anyone else who accepted this definition such as the Magyars, officially recognized only one language within their borders. The French simply neglected the others, the Magyars, who could hardly do so, since less than half the inhabitants of their kingdom spoke that language, found themselves obliged to describe them juridically as 'Magyars not speaking Magyar',[26] much as the Greeks later described the inhabitants of the parts of Macedonia they annexed as 'slavophone Greeks'. In short, a linguistic monopoly masqueraded as a non-linguistic definition of the nation.

Nationality, it seemed evident, was too complex to be seized by language alone. The Habsburg statisticians, who had more experience of it than anyone else, took the view (a) that it was not an attribute of individuals but of communities, and (b) that it required study of 'the situation, demarcation and climatic conditions, as

[26] K. Renner, *Staat und Nation*, p. 13.

well as anthropological and ethnological studies of the physical and intellectual, external and internal characteristics of a people, of its customs, mores, etc.'[27] Dr Glatter, ex-director of the Vienna Statistical Institute, went even further and, in the proper nineteenth-century spirit, decided that it was not language but *race* which determined nationality.

However, nationality was too big a political issue for census-takers to overlook. It clearly had *some* relation to spoken language, if only because language had begun since the 1840s to play a significant role in international territorial conflicts – very notably so in the matter of Schleswig-Holstein, disputed between Danes and Germans,[28] even though before the nineteenth century linguistic arguments had not been used to back the territorial claims of states.[29] But in 1842 the *Revue des Deux Mondes* already observed that 'the true natural frontiers were not determined by mountains and river, but rather by the language, the customs, the memories, all that distinguishes one nation from another', an argument admittedly used to explain why France should *not* necessarily aspire to the Rhine frontier; just as the argument that 'the idiom spoken in Nice has only a remote similarity to Italian' gave Cavour an official excuse for ceding that part of the kingdom of Savoy to Napoleon III.[30] The fact remains that language had now become a factor in international diplomacy. It patently was already a factor in the domestic politics of some states. Moreover, as the Petersburg Congress noted, it was the only aspect of nationality which could be at least objectively counted and tabulated.[31]

In accepting language as an indication of nationality, the Congress not only took an administrative view, but also followed the arguments of a German statistician who argued, in influential publications of 1866 and 1869, that language was the only

[27] Emil Brix, *Die Umgangsprachen in Altösterreich zwischen Agitation und Assimilation. Die Sprachenstatistik in den zisleithanischen Volkszählungen, 1880–1910* (Vienna–Cologne–Graz 1982), p. 76. The account of the statistical debates given here is based on this work.
[28] Cf. Sarah Wambaugh, *A Monograph on Plebiscites, With a Collection of Official Documents* (Carnegie Endowment for Peace, New York 1920), esp. p.138.
[29] Nordmann in P. Nora (ed.), *Les Lieux de mémoire*, vol. II**, p. 52.
[30] *Ibid.*, pp. 55–6.
[31] Brix, *Die Ungangsprachen*, p. 90.

adequate indicator of nationality.[32] This had long been the view of nationality held among German intellectuals and nationalists, given the absence of a single German nation-state and the wide distribution across Europe of communities speaking German dialects, and whose educated members wrote and read standard German. This did not necessarily imply the demand for a single German nation-state including all these Germans – such a demand was and remained entirely unrealistic[33] – and in Böckh's purely philological version it is not at all clear how much common consciousness and culture it implied; for, as we have seen, on linguistic grounds he logically included among Germans the speakers of Yiddish, the medieval German dialect modified into the universal language of Eastern Jews. Nevertheless, as we have also seen, territorial claims on linguistic grounds were now possible – the German campaign of 1840 had rejected the French demand of a Rhine frontier precisely on this ground – and, whatever exactly the implications of language, they could no longer be politically overlooked.

But what exactly was to be counted? At this point the apparent census analogy of language with birthplace, age or marital status dissolved. Language implied a political choice. Ficker, the Austrian statistician, as a scholar rejected choosing the language of public life, which might be imposed on individuals by state or party, though this was entirely acceptable to his French and Hungarian colleagues. For the same reason he rejected the language of church and school. However, the Habsburg statisticians, in the spirit of nineteenth-century liberalism, tried to make room for the flux and change of language, and above all for linguistic assimilation, by asking the citizens not for their *Muttersprache* or (in the literal sense) the tongue first learned from their mothers, but for the

---

32 Richard Böckh, 'Die statistische Bedeutung der Volkssprache als Kennzeichen der Nationalität' (*Zeitschrift für Völkerpsychologie und Sprachwissenschaft*, 4, 1866, pp. 259–402; the same, *Der Deutschen Volkszahl und Sprachgebiet in den europäischen Staaten* (Berlin 1869).

33 Even Hitler distinguished between the Germans of the Reich and the 'national Germans' (*Volksdeutsche*) living outside its frontiers, but who might be given the option of coming 'home' to the Reich.

'family tongue', i.e. the language usually spoken in the home, which might be different.[34]

Nobody was satisfied with this equation of language and nationality: the nationalists, because it precluded individuals speaking one language at home from opting for another nationality, governments – certainly the Habsburg government – because they could recognize a hot potato without having to taste it. All the same, they underestimated its self-heating capacity. The Habsburgs put off the language question until after national tempers, so visibly overheated in the 1860s, had, as they thought, cooled down. They would start counting in 1880. What nobody quite appreciated was that asking such a question would in itself generate linguistic nationalism. Each census was to become a battlefield between nationalities, and the increasingly elaborate attempts of the authorities to satisfy the contending parties failed to do so. They only produced monuments of disinterested scholarship, like the Austrian and Belgian censuses of 1910, which satisfy historians. In truth, by asking the language question censuses for the first time *forced* everyone to choose not only a nationality, but a linguistic nationality.[35] The technical requirements of the modern administrative state once again helped to foster the emergence of nationalism, whose transformations we are about to trace.

[34] Brix, *Die Umgangsprachen*, p. 94.   [35] *Ibid.* p. 114.

CHAPTER 4

The transformation of nationalism, 1870–1918

Once a certain degree of European development has been reached, the linguistic and cultural communities of peoples, having silently matured throughout the centuries, emerge from the world of passive existence as peoples (*passiver Volkheit*). They become conscious of themselves as a force with a historical destiny. They demand control over the state, as the highest available instrument of power, and strive for their political self-determination. The birthday of the political idea of the nation and the birth-year of this new consciousness, is 1789, the year of the French Revolution.[1]

Two hundred years after the French Revolution no serious historian and, it is hoped, no one who has read up to this point in the present book, will regard statements like the one quoted above as other than exercises in programmatic mythology. Yet the quotation seems a representative statement of that 'principle of nationality' which convulsed the international politics of Europe after 1830, creating a number of new states which corresponded, so far as practicable, with one half of Mazzini's call 'Every nation a state', though less so with the other half, 'only one state for the entire nation'.[2] It is representative, in particular, in five ways: in stressing linguistic and cultural community, which was a nineteenth-century innovation,[3] in stressing the nationalism that aspired to form or capture states rather than the 'nations' of already existing states, in its historicism and sense of historic mission, in claiming the

---

[1] K. Renner, *Staat und Nation*, p. 89.   [2] *Ibid.* p. 9.
[3] Cf. Th. Schieder, 'Typologie und Erscheinungsformen des Nationalstaats' in H. A. Winkler (ed.), *Nationalismus* (Königstein im Taunus 1985), p. 128.

paternity of 1789, and not least in its terminological ambiguity and rhetoric.

Yet while the quotation at first sight reads like something that might have been written by Mazzini himself, in fact it was written seventy years after the 1830 revolutions, and by a Marxian socialist of Moravian origin in a book about the specific problems of the Habsburg empire. In short, while it might be confused with the 'principle of nationality' which transformed the political map of Europe between 1830 and the 1870s, in fact it belongs to a later, and different, phase of nationalist development in European history.

The nationalism of 1880–1914 differed in three major respects from the Mazzinian phase of nationalism. First, it abandoned the 'threshold principle' which, as we have seen, was central to nationalism in the Liberal era. Henceforth *any* body of people considering themselves a 'nation' claimed the right to self-determination which, in the last analysis, meant the right to a separate sovereign independent state for their territory. Second, and in consequence of this multiplication of potential 'unhistorical' nations, ethnicity and language became the central, increasingly the decisive or even the only criteria of potential nationhood. Yet there was a third change which affected not so much the non-state national movements, which now became increasingly numerous and ambitious, but national sentiments within the established nation-states: a sharp shift to the political right of nation and flag, for which the term 'nationalism' was actually invented in the last decade(s) of the nineteenth century. Renner's quotation represents the first two, but (coming from the left) very distinctly not the third of these changes.

There are three reasons why it has not often been recognized how late the ethnic-linguistic criterion for defining a nation actually became dominant. First, the two most prominent non-state national movements of the first half of the nineteenth century were essentially based on communities of the educated, united across political and geographical borders by the use of an established language of high culture and its literature. For Germans and Italians, their national language was not merely an administrative convenience or a means of unifying state-wide communication, as French had been in France since the ordinance of Villers-Cotterets in 1539, or even a revolutionary device for bringing the truths of liberty, science and progress to all, ensuring the permanence of citizen equality and preventing the revival of *ancien régime* hierarchy, as it was for the Jacobins.[4] It was more even than the vehicle of a distinguished literature and of universal intellectual expression. It was the *only* thing that made them Germans or Italians, and consequently carried a far heavier charge of national identity than, say, English did for those who wrote and read that language. However, while for the German and Italian liberal middle classes language thus provided a central argument for the creation of a unified national state – in the first half of the nineteenth century this was not yet the case anywhere else. The political claims to independence of Poland or Belgium were not language-based, nor indeed were the rebellions of various Balkan peoples against the Ottoman Empire, which produced some independent states. Nor was the Irish movement in Britain. Alternatively, where linguistic movements already had a significant political base, as in the Czech lands, national self-determination (as opposed to cultural recognition) was not yet an issue, and the establishment of a separate state was not seriously thought of.

However, since the later eighteenth century (and largely under German intellectual influence) Europe had been swept by the romantic passion for the pure, simple and uncorrupted peasantry, and for this folkloric rediscovery of 'the people', the vernacular

---

4 'All members of the sovereign (people) may occupy all (public) posts; it is desirable that all should fill them in rotation, before returning to their agricultural or mechanical occupations. This state of affairs confronts us with the following alternative. If these posts are occupied by men incapable of expressing themselves in, or writing, the national language, how can the rights of the citizens be safeguarded by documents whose texts contain terminological errors, ideas lacking precision – in a word, all the symptoms of ignorance? If, on the other hand, such ignorance were to exclude men from public posts, we would soon see the rebirth of that aristocracy which once used *patois* as a sign of protective affability when speaking to those it insolently called 'the lower orders' (*les petits gens*). Soon society would once again be infected by 'the right sort of people' (*de gens comme il faut*) ... Between two separated classes a sort of hierarchy will establish itself. Thus ignorance of the language would put at risk social welfare, or it would destroy equality.' (From Abbé Grégoire's *Rapport*, cited in Fernand Brunot, *Histoire de la langue française* (Paris 1930–48), vol. IX, 1, pp. 207–8.

languages it spoke were crucial. Yet while this populist cultural renaissance provided the foundation for many a subsequent nationalist movement, and has therefore been justifiably counted as the first phase ('phase A') of their development, Hroch himself makes it clear that in no sense was it yet a political movement of the people concerned, nor did it imply any political aspiration or programme. Indeed, more often than not the discovery of popular tradition and its transformation into the 'national tradition' of some peasant people forgotten by history, was the work of enthusiasts from the (foreign) ruling class or elite, such as the Baltic Germans or the Finnish Swedes. The Finnish Literature Society (founded 1831) was established by Swedes, its records were kept in Swedish, and all the writings of the chief ideologue of Finnish cultural nationalism, Snellman, appear to have been in Swedish.[5] While nobody could possibly deny the widespread European cultural and linguistic revival movements in the period from the 1780s to the 1840s, it is a mistake to confuse Hroch's phase A with his phase B, when a body of activists devoted to the political agitation in favour of the 'national idea' has come into existence, and still less his 'phase C', when mass support for 'the national idea' can be counted on. As the case of the British Isles shows, there is, incidentally, no necessary connection between cultural revival movements of this kind and subsequent national agitations or movements of political nationalism, and, conversely, such nationalist movements may originally have little or nothing to do with cultural revivalism. The Folklore Society (1878) and the folksong revival in England were no more nationalist than the Gypsy Lore Society.

The third reason concerns ethnic rather than linguistic identification. It lies in the absence – until quite late in the century – of influential theories or pseudo-theories identifying nations with genetic descent. We shall return to this point below.

The growing significance of 'the national question' in the forty years preceding 1914 is not measured simply by its intensification within the old multinational empires of Austro-Hungary and Turkey. It was now a significant issue in the domestic politics of

---

[5] E. Juttikala and K. Pirinen, *A History of Finland* (Helsinki 1975), p. 176.

virtually all European states. Thus even in the United Kingdom it was no longer confined to the Irish problem, even though Irish nationalism, under that name, also grew – the number of newspapers describing themselves as 'national' or 'nationalist' rose from 1 in 1871 through 13 in 1881 to 33 in 1891[6] – and became politically explosive in British politics. However, it is often overlooked that this was also the period when the first official recognition of Welsh national interests as such was made (the Welsh Sunday Closing Act of 1881 has been described as 'the first distinctively Welsh Act of Parliament')[7] and when Scotland acquired both a modest Home Rule movement, a Scottish Office in government and, via the so-called 'Goschen Formula', a guaranteed national share of the public expenditure of the United Kingdom. Domestic nationalism could also – as in France, Italy and Germany – take the form of the rise of those right-wing movements for which the term 'nationalism' was in fact coined in this period, or, more generally, of the political xenophobia which found its most deplorable, but not its only, expression in anti-Semitism. That so relatively tranquil a state as Sweden should in this era have been shaken by the national secession of Norway (1907) (which was not proposed by anyone until the 1890s) is at least as significant as the paralysis of Habsburg politics by rival nationalist agitations.

Moreover, it is during this period that we find nationalist movements multiplying in regions where they had been previously unknown, or among peoples hitherto only of interest to folklorists, and even for the first time, notionally, in the non-western world. How far the new anti-imperialist movements can be regarded as nationalist is far from clear, though the influence of western nationalist ideology on their spokesmen and activists is undeniable – as in the case of the Irish influence on Indian nationalism. However, even if we confine ourselves to Europe and its environs, we find plenty of movements in 1914 that had existed hardly or not

---

[6] I owe these data, extracted from the Newspaper Press Directory of those years, to the unpublished researches into the Irish provincial press, 1852–1892, of Mary Lou Legg of Birkbeck College.

[7] See 'Report of the Commissioners appointed to inquire into the operation of the Sunday Closing (Wales) Act, 1881' (Parliamentary Papers, H.o.C., vol. XL of 1890); K. O. Morgan, Wales, Rebirth of a Nation 1880–1980 (Oxford 1982), p. 36.

at all in 1870: among the Armenians, Georgians, Lithuanians and other Baltic peoples and the Jews (both in Zionist and non-Zionist versions), among the Macedonians and Albanians in the Balkans, the Ruthenians and the Croats in the Habsburg empire – Croat nationalism must not be confused with the earlier Croat support for Yugoslav or 'Illyrian' nationalism – among the Basques and Catalans, the Welsh, and in Belgium a distinctly radicalized Flemish movement, as well as hitherto unexpected touches of local nationalism in places like Sardinia. We may even detect the first hints of Arab nationalism in the Ottoman empire.

As already suggested most of these movements now stressed the linguistic and/or ethnic element. That this was often new can be readily demonstrated. Before the foundation of the Gaelic League (1893), which initially had no political aims, the Irish language was not an issue in the Irish national movement. It figured neither in O'Connell's Repeal agitation – though the Liberator was a Gaelic-speaking Kerryman – nor in the Fenian programme. Even serious attempts to create a uniform Irish language out of the usual complex of dialects were not made until after 1900. Finnish nationalism was about the defence of the Grand Duchy's autonomy under the Tsars, and the Finnish Liberals who emerged after 1848 took the view that they represented a single bi-lingual nation. Finnish nationalism did not become essentially linguistic until, roughly, the 1860s (when an Imperial Rescript improved the public position of the Finnish language against the Swedish), but until the 1880s the language struggle remained largely an internal class struggle between the lower class Finns (represented by the 'Fennomen' who stood for a single nation with Finnish as its language) and the upper-class Swedish minority, represented by the 'Svecomen' who argued that the country contained two nations and therefore two languages). Only after 1880, as Tsarism shifted into its own russifying nationalist mode, did the struggle for autonomy and for language and culture come to coincide.[8]

Again, Catalanism as a (conservative) cultural-linguistic move-ment can hardly be traced back further than the 1850s, the festival of the Jocs Florals (analogous to the Welsh Eisteddfodau) being

[8] Juttikala and Pirinen A History of Finland, pp. 176–86.

revived not before 1859. The language itself was not authoritatively standardized until the twentieth century,[9] and Catalan regionalism was not concerned with the linguistic question until the middle or later 1880s.[10] The development of Basque nationalism, it has been suggested, lagged some thirty years behind that of the Catalan movement, although the ideological shift of Basque autonomism from the defence or restoration of ancient feudal privileges to a linguistic-racial argument was sudden: in 1894, less than twenty years after the end of the Second Carlist War, Sabino Arana founded his Basque National Party (PNV), incidentally inventing the Basque name for the country ('Euskadi') which had hitherto not existed.[11]

At the other end of Europe the national movements of the Baltic peoples had hardly left their first (cultural) phases by the last third of the century, and in the remote Balkans, where the Macedonian question raised its bloodstained head after 1870, the idea that the various nationalities living on this territory should be distinguished by their *language*, was the last of many to strike the states of Serbia, Greece, Bulgaria and the Sublime Porte which contended for it.[12] The inhabitants of Macedonia had been distinguished by their religion, or else claims to this or that part of it had been based on history ranging from the medieval to the ancient, or else on ethnographic arguments about common customs and ritual practices. Macedonia did not become a battlefield for Slav philologists until the twentieth century, when the Greeks, who could not compete on this terrain, compensated by stressing an imaginary ethnicity.

At the same time – roughly, in the second half of the century – ethnic nationalism received enormous reinforcements, in practice from the increasingly massive geographical migrations of peoples, and in theory by the transformation of that central concept of

[9] Carles Riba, 'Cent anys de defensa il.lustració de l'idioma a Catalunya' (*L'Avenç*, 71, May 1984, pp. 54–62). This is the text of a lecture originally given in 1939.
[10] Francesc Vallverdú, 'El català al segle XIX' (*L'Avenç*, 27, May 1980), pp. 30–6.
[11] H.-J. Puhle, 'Baskischer Nationalismus im spanischen Kontext' in H. A. Winkler (ed.), *Nationalismus in der Welt von Heute* (Göttingen 1982), p. 61.
[12] Carnegie Endowment for International Peace: *Report of the International Commission to Enquire into the Cause and Conduct of the Balkan Wars* (Washington 1914), p. 27.

nineteenth-century social science, 'race'. On the one hand the old-established division of mankind into a few 'races' distinguished by skin colour was now elaborated into a set of 'racial' distinctions separating peoples of approximately the same pale skin, such as 'Aryans' and 'Semites', or, among the 'Aryans', Nordics, Alpines and Mediterraneans. On the other hand Darwinian evolutionism, supplemented later by what came to be known as genetics, provided racism with what looked like a powerful set of 'scientific' reasons for keeping out or even, as it turned out, expelling and murdering strangers. All this was comparatively late. Anti-Semitism did not acquire a 'racial' (as distinct from a religio-cultural) character until about 1880, the major prophets of German and French racism (Vacher de Lapouge, Houston Stewart Chamberlain) belong to the 1890s, and 'Nordics' do not enter the racist or any discourse until about 1900.[13]

The links between racism and nationalism are obvious. 'Race' and language were easily confused as in the case of 'Aryans' and 'Semites', to the indignation of scrupulous scholars like Max Muller who pointed out that 'race', a genetic concept, could not be inferred from language, which was not inherited. Moreover, there is an evident analogy between the insistence of racists on the importance of racial purity and the horrors of miscegenation, and the insistence of so many – one is tempted to say of most – forms of linguistic nationalism on the need to purify the national language from foreign elements. In the nineteenth century the English were quite exceptional in boasting of their mongrel origins (Britons, Anglo-Saxons, Scandinavians, Normans, Scots, Irish, etc.) and glorying in the philological mixture of their language. However, what brought 'race' and 'nation' even closer was the practice of using both as virtual synonyms, generalizing equally wildly about 'racial'/'national' character, as was then the fashion. Thus before the Anglo-French Entente Cordiale of 1904, a French writer observed, agreement between the two countries had been dismissed

---

[13] J. Romein, *The Watershed of Two Eras: Europe in 1900* (Middletown 1978), p. 108. A 'Nordic' race under that name first appears in the classificatory literature of anthropology in 1898 (*OED Supplement*: 'nordic'). The term seems to belong to J. Deniker, *Races et peuples de la terre* (Paris 1900), but was taken up by racists who found it convenient to describe the blonde, long-headed race they associated with superiority.

as impossible because of the 'hereditary enmity' between the two races.[14] Linguistic and ethnic nationalism thus reinforced each other.

It is hardly surprising that nationalism gained ground so rapidly from the 1870s to 1914. It was a function of both social and political changes, not to mention an international situation that provided plenty of pegs on which to hang manifestos of hostility to foreigners. Socially three developments gave considerably increased scope for the development of novel forms of inventing 'imagined' or even actual communities as nationalities: the resistance of traditional groups threatened by the onrush of modernity, the novel and quite non-traditional classes and strata now rapidly growing in the urbanizing societies of developed countries, and the unprecedented migrations which distributed a multiple diaspora of peoples across the globe, each strangers to both natives and other migrant groups, none, as yet, with the habits and conventions of coexistence. The sheer weight and pace of change in this period would be enough to explain why under such circumstances occasions for friction between groups multiplied, even if we were to overlook the tremors of the 'Great Depression' which so often, in these years, shook the lives of the poor and the economically modest or insecure. All that was required for the entry of nationalism into politics was that groups of men and women who saw themselves, in whatever manner, as Ruritanians, or were so seen by others, should become ready to listen to the argument that their discontents were in some way caused by the inferior treatment (often undeniable) of Ruritanians by, or compared with, other nationalities, or by a non-Ruritanian state or ruling class. At all events by 1914 observers were apt to be surprised at European populations which still seemed completely unreceptive to any appeal on the grounds of nationality, though this did not necessarily imply adherence to a nationalist programme. US citizens of immigrant origins did not demand any linguistic or other concessions to their nationality by the Federal Government, but nevertheless every Democratic city politician knew perfectly well that appeals to the Irish as Irish, to Poles as Poles, paid off.

[14] Jean Finot, *Race Prejudice* (London 1906), pp. v–vi.

As we have seen, the major political changes which turned a potential receptivity to national appeals into actual reception, were the democratization of politics in a growing number of states, and the creation of the modern administrative, citizen-mobilizing and citizen-influencing state. And yet, the rise of mass politics helps us to reformulate the question of popular support for nationalism rather than to answer it. What we need to discover is what precisely national slogans meant in politics, and whether they meant the same to different social constituencies, how they changed, and under what circumstances they combined or were incompatible with other slogans that might mobilize the citizenry, how they prevailed over them or failed to do so.

The identification of nation with language helps us to answer such questions, since linguistic nationalism essentially requires control of a state or at least the winning of official recognition for the language. This is plainly not equally important for all strata or groups within a state or nationality, or to every state or nationality. At all events problems of power, status, politics and ideology and not of communication or even culture, lie at the heart of the nationalism of language. If communication or culture had been the crucial issue, the Jewish nationalist (Zionist) movement would not have opted for a modern Hebrew which nobody as yet spoke, and in a pronunciation unlike that used in European synagogues. It rejected Yiddish, spoken by 95% of the Ashkenazic Jews from the European East and their emigrants to the west – i.e. by a substantial majority of all the world's Jews. By 1935, it has been said, given the large, varied and distinguished literature developed for its ten million speakers, Yiddish was 'one of the leading "literate" languages of the time'.[15] Nor would the Irish national movement have launched itself after 1900 into the doomed campaign to reconvert the Irish to a language most of them no longer understood, and which those who set about teaching it to their countrymen had only themselves begun to learn very incompletely.[16]

Conversely, as the example of Yiddish shows, and that golden

---

[15] Lewis Glinert, 'Viewpoint: the recovery of Hebrew' (Times Literary Supplement, 17, June 1983, p. 634).

[16] Cf. Declan Kiberd, Synge and the Irish Language (London 1979), e.g. p. 223.

age of dialect literatures, the nineteenth century, confirms, the existence of a widely spoken or even written idiom did not necessarily generate language-based nationalism. Such languages or literatures could see themselves and be seen quite consciously as supplementing rather than competing with some hegemonic language of general culture and communication.

The politico-ideological element is evident in the process of language-construction which can range from the mere 'correction' and standardization of existing literary and culture-languages, through the formation of such languages out of the usual complex of overlapping dialects, to the resuscitation of dead or almost extinct languages which amounts to virtual invention of new ones. For, contrary to nationalist myth, a people's language is not the basis of national consciousness but, in the phrase of Einar Haugen, a 'cultural artifact'.[17] The development of modern Indian vernaculars illustrates this clearly.

The deliberate Sanskritization of the literary Bengali which emerged in the nineteenth century as a culture-language, not only separated the literate upper classes from the popular masses, but also Hinduized Bengali high culture, thus demoting the Bengali Muslim masses; in return a certain de-Sanskritization has been noted in the language of Bangladesh (East Bengal) since partition. Even more instructive is the attempt by Gandhi to develop and maintain a single Hindi language based on the unity of the national movement, i.e. to prevent the Hindu and Muslim variants of the common lingua franca of North India from drifting too far apart, while simultaneously providing a national alternative to English. However, the ecumenically minded champions of Hindi were opposed by a strongly pro-Hindu and anti-Muslim (hence anti-Urdu) group which in the 1930s gained control of the organization formed by the National Congress to propagate the language, leading to the resignation from this organization (the Hindi Sahitya Samuelan or HSS) of Gandhi, Nehru and other Congress leaders. In

[17] Einar Haugen, *Language Conflicts and Language Planning: The Case of Modern Norwegian* (The Hague 1966); by the same author, 'The Scandinavian languages as cultural artifacts' in Joshua A. Fishman, Charles A. Ferguson, Jyotindra Das Gupta (eds.), *Language Problems of Developing Nations* (New York–London–Sydney–Toronto 1968), pp. 267–84.

1942 Gandhi unsuccessfully returned to the project of creating a
'broad Hindi'. The HSS meanwhile created a standardized Hindi in
its own image eventually building up examination centres for
secondary and college diplomas and degrees in the language, which
was therefore standardized for teaching purposes, given a 'Board of
Scientific Terminology' for the extension of its vocabulary in 1950,
and crowned by a Hindi Encyclopaedia, initiated in 1956.[18]

Indeed, languages become more conscious exercises in social
engineering in proportion as their symbolic significance prevails
over their actual use, as witness the various movements to 'indige-
nize' or make more truly 'national' their vocabulary, of which the
struggle of French governments against 'franglais' is the best-
known recent example. The passions behind them are easy to
understand, but they have nothing to do with speaking, writing,
understanding, or even the spirit of literature. Danish-influenced
Norwegian was and remains the main medium of Norwegian
literature. The reaction against it in the nineteenth century was
nationalist. As its tone shows, the German Casino in Prague which,
in the 1890s, declared that learning Czech – by then the language of
93% of the city's population – was *treason*,[19] was not making a
statement about communications. The Welsh language enthusiasts
who are even now devising Cymric place-names for places which
never had any until today, know quite well that Welsh-speakers
need no more cymricize the name of Birmingham than they do that
of Bamako or any other foreign town. Nevertheless, whatever the
motivation of planned language construction and manipulation,
and whatever the degree of transformation envisaged, state power
is essential to it.

How, except by state power, could Romanian nationalism insist
(in 1863) on its Latin origins (as distinct from the surrounding
Slavs and Magyars) by writing and printing the language in Roman

[18] J. Bhattacharyya, 'Language, class and community in Bengal' (*South Asia Bulletin*, VII, 1
and 2, Fall 1987, pp. 56–63); S. N. Mukherjee, Bhadralok in Bengali Language and
Literature: an essay on the language of class and status' (*Bengal Past And Present*, 95,
part II, July–December 1976, pp. 225–37); J. Das Gupta and John Gumperz, 'Language,
communication and control in North India', in Fishman, Ferguson, Das Gupta (eds.),
Language Problems, pp. 151–66.
[19] B. Suttner, *Die Badenischen Sprachenverordnungen von 1897*, 2 vols. (Graz–Cologne
1960, 1965), vol. II, pp. 86–8.

letters instead of the hitherto usual Cyrillic? (Count Sedlnitzky, the Habsburg police chief under Metternich, had practised a similar form of cultural-linguistic politics by subsidizing the printing of Orthodox religious works in Roman as against Cyrillic, in order to discourage pan-Slav tendencies among the Habsburg empire's Slavs.)[20] How, except through support by the public authorities and recognition in education and administration, were domestic or rural idioms to be transformed into languages capable of competing with the prevailing languages of national or world culture, let alone virtually non-existent languages to be given reality? What would the future of Hebrew have been, had not the British Mandate in 1919 accepted it as one of the three official languages of Palestine, at a time when the number of people speaking Hebrew as an everyday language was less than 20,000? What, other than a system of secondary or even tertiary education in Finnish, could remedy the observed fact that, as linguistic lines congealed in Finland towards the end of the nineteenth century, 'the proportion of intellectuals speaking Swedish was many times greater than that of the common people speaking it', i.e. that educated Finns continued to find Swedish more useful than their mother-tongue?[21]

Yet, however symbolic of national aspirations, languages have a considerable number of practical and socially differentiated uses, and attitudes towards the language(s) chosen as the official one(s) for administrative, educational or other purposes, differ in consequence. Let us remind ourselves, once again, that the controversial element is the *written* language, or the language spoken for *public purposes*. The language(s) spoken within the private sphere of communication raise no serious problems even when it or they coexist with public languages, since each occupies its own space, as every child knows when it switches from the idiom appropriate for talking to parents to the one suited to teachers or friends.

Moreover, while the extraordinary social and geographical mobility of the period forced, or encouraged, unprecedented numbers of men – and even, in spite of their confinement to the

[20] J. Fishman, 'The sociology of language: an interdisciplinary approach' in T. E. Sebeok (ed.), *Current Trends in Linguistics*, vol. 12*** (The Hague–Paris 1974), p. 1755.
[21] Juttikala and Pirinen, *A History of Finland*, p. 176.

private sphere, of women – to learn new languages, this process in itself did not necessarily raise ideological issues, unless one language was deliberately *rejected* and another *substituted*, generally – indeed almost universally – as a means of entering a wider culture or a higher social class identified with a different language. This was certainly often the case, as with assimilated middle-class Ashkenazic Jews in central and western Europe who took pride in not speaking or even understanding Yiddish, or, presumably at some time in the family history of the numerous impassioned German nationalists or national socialists in central Europe whose surnames indicate an obviously Slavonic origin. Nevertheless, more often than not old and new languages lived in symbiosis, each in its own sphere. For the educated middle class of Venice speaking Italian no more implied giving up speaking Venetian at home or in the market than bilingualism suggested a betrayal of his native Welsh language to Lloyd George.

The spoken language thus presented no major political problems either for the upper strata of society or for the mass of the labouring people. Top people spoke one of the languages of wider culture, and if their own national vernacular or family language was not one of these, their men – and by the early 1900s sometimes even their women – learned one or more of them. They would naturally speak the standard national language in the 'educated' mode, with or without regional accent or a touch of regional vocabulary, but usually in a manner which identified them as members of their social stratum.[22] They might or might not speak the patois, dialect or vernacular of the lower orders with whom they came into contact, depending on their own family origins, place of residence, upbringing, the conventions of their class and, of course, the extent to which communication with these lower orders required a knowledge of their language(s) or of some creole or pidgin. The official status of any of these languages was unimportant since, whatever the language of official use and culture, it was at their disposal.

For the illiterate among the common people the world of words

[22] No Viennese cabdriver, hearing the dialect of Ochs von Lerchenau, even without seeing the speaker, would be in the slightest doubt about his social status.

was entirely oral, and consequently the language of official or any other writing was of no significance except, increasingly, as a reminder of their lack of knowledge and power. The demand of Albanian nationalists that their language should be written neither in Arabic nor in Greek script, but in the Latin alphabet, which implied inferiority to neither Greeks nor Turks, was obviously irrelevant to people who could read no script. As people from different homelands increasingly came into contact with each other, and the self-sufficiency of the village was eroded, the problem of finding a common language for communication became serious – less so for women, confined to a restricted milieu, least so for those raising crops or livestock – and the easiest way of solving it was by learning enough of the (or a) national language to get by. All the more so as the two great institutions of mass education, primary school and army, brought some knowledge of the official language into every home.[23] That languages of purely local or socially restricted use should lose ground to languages of wider use, is not surprising. Nor is there any evidence that such linguistic change and adaptation met with any resistance from below. As between two languages, the one which was more widely used, had overwhelming and patent advantages, and no apparent disadvantages, inasmuch as there was nothing at all to prevent the use of the mother tongue among monoglots. However, the monoglot Breton was helpless outside his or her native area and its traditional occupations. Elsewhere he or she was little better than a dumb animal: a mute bundle of muscles. From the point of view of poor men looking for work and to better themselves in a modern world there was nothing wrong with peasants being turned into Frenchmen or Poles and Italians in Chicago learning English and wishing to become Americans.

If the advantages of knowing a non-local language were obvious, those of literacy in a language of wider circulation, and especially a world language, were even more undeniable. Such pressure as exists in Latin America for schooling in vernacular Indian lan-

---

[23] As early as 1794 the Abbé Grégoire noted, with satisfaction, that 'in general French is spoken in our batallions', presumably because men of different regional origins were often mixed.

guages lacking a written language has not come from Indians but from *indigenista* intellectuals. To be monolingual is to be shackled, unless your local language happens to be a *de facto* world language. The advantages of knowing French were such that in Belgium, between 1846 and 1910, far more native Flemish speakers became bilingual than French-speakers bothered to learn Flemish.[24] The decline of localized or small-circulation languages existing by the side of major languages, does not need to be explained by the hypothesis of national linguistic oppression. On the contrary, admirable and systematic efforts to maintain them, often at great expense, have not done more than slow down the retreat of Sorbian, Rhaetoroman (Romansch/Ladinsch) or Scots Gaelic. In spite of the embittered memories of vernacular intellectuals forbidden, by unimaginative pedagogues, to use their patois or language in the schoolrooms where lessons were conducted in English or French, there is no evidence that the pupils' parents *en masse* would have preferred an exclusive education in their own language. Of course the obligation to be educated exclusively in another language of *limited* circulation – e.g. In Romanian rather than Bulgarian – might have met with more resistance.

Hence there was no special enthusiasm for linguistic nationalism from either the aristocracy or big bourgeoisie on one hand, the workers and peasants on the other. The 'grande bourgeoisie' as such was not necessarily committed to either of the two variants of nationalism which came to the fore towards the end of the nineteenth century, imperialist chauvinism or small-people nationalism, and still less to small-nation linguistic zeal. The Flemish bourgeoisie in Ghent and Antwerp was, and perhaps still in part remains, deliberately francophone and anti-*Flamingant*. The Polish industrialists, most of whom saw themselves as Germans or Jews rather than Poles,[25] clearly saw their economic interests best served by supplying the all-Russian or other super-national market, to an extent which misled Rosa Luxemburg into underestimating the

---

[24] A. Zolberg, 'The making of Flemings and Walloons: Belgium 1830–1914' (*Journal of Interdisciplinary History*, V/2, 1974, pp. 210–15.

[25] Waclaw Długoborski, 'Das polnische Bürgertum vor 1918 in vergleichender Perspektive' in J. Kocka (ed.), *Bürgertum im 19. Jahrhundert: Deutschland im europäischen Vergleich* (Munich 1988), vol. I, pp. 266–89.

force of Polish nationalism. The Scottish business classes, however proud of their Scottishness, would have regarded any suggestion that the Union of 1707 should be abrogated as sentimental idiocy.

The working classes, as we have seen, were rarely apt to get excited about language as such, though it might well serve as a symbol for other kinds of friction between groups. That most Ghent and Antwerp workers could not even communicate without translation with their comrades in Liège and Charleroi did not prevent both from forming a single labour movement, in which language caused so little trouble that a standard work on socialism in Belgium in 1903 did not so much as refer to the Flemish question: a situation inconceivable today.[26] In fact, in South Wales both bourgeois and working-class liberal interests joined to resist the attempts by the young Lloyd George's nationalist North Wales Liberalism, to identify Welshness with linguistic Welshness and the Liberal Party – the national part of the Principality – with its defence. They were successful in the 1890s.

The classes which stood or fell by the official use of the written vernacular were the socially modest but educated middle strata, which included those who acquired lower middle-class status precisely by virtue of occupying non-manual jobs that required schooling. The socialists of the period who rarely used the word 'nationalism' without the prefix 'petty-bourgeois', knew what they were talking about. The battle-lines of linguistic nationalism were manned by provincial journalists, schoolteachers and aspiring subaltern officials. The battles of Habsburg politics, when national strife made the Austrian half of the empire virtually ungovernable, were fought about the language of instruction in secondary schools or the nationality of station-masters' jobs. Just so the ultra-nationalist pan-German activists in William II's empire recruited heavily among the educated – but the *Oberlehrer* rather than the Professors – and the half-educated of an expanding and socially mobile society.

I do not wish to reduce linguistic nationalism to a question of

[26] Jules Destrée and Emile Vandervelde, *Le Socialisme en Belgique* (Paris 1903, originally 1898). To be precise the 48-page bibliography contains a *single* title on the Flemish problem – an election pamphlet.

jobs, as vulgar-materialist liberals used to reduce wars to a question of the profits of armaments firms. Nevertheless it cannot be fully understood, and the opposition to it even less, unless we see the vernacular language as, among other things, a vested interest of the lesser examination-passing classes. Moreover, each step giving the vernacular greater official standing, especially as a teaching language, multiplied the number of men and women who could have a share in this vested interest. The creation of essentially linguistic provinces in post-independence India, and the resistance to the imposition of one vernacular (Hindi) as the national language, both reflect this situation: within Tamilnadu literacy in Tamil opens state-wide public careers, while the maintenance of English does not put the Tamil-educated person at a national disadvantage with respect to those educated in any other vernacular. Hence the crucial moment in the creation of language as a potential asset is not its admission as a medium of primary education (though this automatically creates a large body of primary teachers and language-indoctrinators) but its admission as a medium of secondary education, such as was achieved in Flanders and Finland in the 1880s. For it is this which, as the Finnish nationalists were clearly aware, linked social mobility to the vernacular, and in turn to linguistic nationalism. 'It was to a large extent in Antwerp and Ghent that a new secular-minded generation, educated in Flemish in public secondary schools ... produced many of the individuals and groups who formed and sustained a new *Flamingant* ideology.'[27]

Yet in creating vernacular middle strata, linguistic progress underlined the inferiority, the status insecurity and resentment which were so characteristic of the lower middle strata and made the new nationalism so attractive to them. Thus the new Flemish-educated class found itself poised between the Flemish masses, whose most dynamic elements were drawn to French because of the practical advantages of knowing that language, and the upper levels of the Belgian administration, culture and affairs, which remained unshakeably francophone.[28] The very fact that, for the same post, a Fleming had to be bilingual whereas a native French speaker needed only the barest nod to the other language, if that,

[27] Zolberg, 'The making of Flemings and Walloons', p. 227.   [28] *ibid.* pp. 209ff.

underlined the inferiority of the lesser language, as it was later to do in Quebec. (For jobs in which bilingualism was a genuine asset, and bilingual speakers of the lesser vernacular were therefore at an actual advantage, were normally subaltern.)

One might have expected the Flemings, like the Québécois, with demography in their favour, to look to the future with confidence. After all, in this respect they were more favoured than the speakers of ancient and declining rural idioms like Irish, Breton, Basque, Frisian, Romansch or even Welsh which, left to themselves, plainly did not look like effective competitors in a purely Darwinian interlingual struggle for existence. Flemish and Canadian French were in no sense threatened as languages, but their speakers did not require a socio-linguistic elite, and conversely, the speakers of the dominant language did not need to recognize the educated users of the vernacular as an elite either. What was under threat was not their language but the status and social position of the *Flamingant* or Québécois middle strata. Only political protection could raise these.

Essentially the situation was no different where the linguistic issue was the defence of a declining idiom – often one which, like Basque and Welsh, was virtually on the point of extinction in the new industrial-urban centres of the country. Certainly defence of the old language signified defence of an entire society's old ways and traditions against the subversions of modernity: hence the support which such movements as Bretons, Flemings, Basques and others received from the Roman Catholic clergy. To this extent they were not simply middle-class movements. Yet Basque linguistic nationalism was not a movement of the traditional countryside, where people still spoke the language which the hispanophone founder of the Basque National Party (PNV), like so many later linguistic militants, had to learn as an adult. The Basque peasantry showed little interest in the new nationalism. Its roots were in the (urban and coastal) 'conservative, Catholic and petty-bourgeois milieu'[29] reacting against the threat of industrialization and the godless immigrant proletarian socialism it brought with it, while rejecting the big Basque bourgeoisie whose interests bound it to the

---

[29] Puhle, 'Baskischer Nationalismus', pp. 62–5.

all-Spanish monarchy. Unlike Catalan autonomism, the PNV had only fleeting support from the bourgeoisie. And the claim to linguistic and racial uniqueness on which Basque nationalism based itself, is one which rings familiar to every connoisseur of the petty-bourgeois radical right: Basques were superior to other peoples because of their racial *purity*, demonstrated by the uniqueness of the language which indicated refusal to mix with other peoples, above all with Arabs and Jews. Much the same can be said of the movements of an exclusively Croatian nationalism which first emerged on a small scale in the 1860s ('supported by the petite bourgeoisie, primarily by the small-scale retailers and tradesmen') and gained some foothold – again among the same kind of economically hard-pressed lower middle classes – during the Great Depression of the late nineteenth century. It 'mirrored the opposition of the petite bourgeoisie to Yugoslavism as an ideology of the wealthier bourgeoisie'. In this instance, since neither language nor race were available to mark the chosen people off from the rest, a historic mission of the Croat nation to defend Christianity against invasion from the east served to provide strata lacking in self-confidence with the required sense of superiority.[30]

The same social strata formed the core of that sub-variety of nationalism, the movements of political anti-Semitism which appear in the last two decades of the century, notably in Germany (Stöcker), Austria (Schönerer, Lueger), and France (Drumont, the Dreyfus affair). Uncertainty about their status and definition, the insecurity of large strata situated between the unquestionable sons and daughters of manual toil and the unquestioned members of the upper and upper middle classes, overcompensation by claims to uniqueness and superiority threatened by someone or other – these provided links between the modest middle strata and a militant nationalism, which may almost be definable as a response to such threats – from workers, from foreign states and individuals, from immigrants, from the capitalists and financiers so readily identifiable with the Jews, who were also seen as the revolutionary

[30] Mirjana Gross, 'Croatian national-integrational ideologies from the end of Illyrism to the creation of Yugoslavia' (*Austrian History Yearbook*, 15–16, 1979–80, pp. 3–44, esp. 18, 20–1, 34 (discussion by A. Suppan).

agitators. For these middle strata saw themselves as embattled and endangered. The key word in the political vocabulary of the French Right in the 1880s was not 'family', 'order', 'tradition', 'religion', 'morality' or any similar term. It was, according to the analysts, 'menace'.[31]

Among the lesser middle strata nationalism thus mutated from a concept associated with liberalism and the left, into a chauvinist, imperialist and xenophobic movement of the right, or more precisely, the radical right, a move already observable in the ambiguous usage of such terms as 'patrie' and 'patriotism' round 1870 in France.[32] The term 'nationalism' itself was coined to reflect the emergence of this tendency, notably in France and a little later in Italy, where Romance language lent itself to this formation.[33] At the end of the century it seemed quite novel. However, even where there was continuity, as in the 'Turner', the mass gymnastic organisations of German nationalism, the shift to the right of the 1890s can be measured by tracking the spread of anti-Semitism from Austria into the German branches, and the substitution of the imperial (black–white–red) tricolour for the Liberal–national (black–red–gold) tricolour of 1848, and the new enthusiasm for imperial expansionism.[34] How high up in the middle-class scale we find the centre of gravity of such movements – e.g. of 'that rebellion of groups of the lower and middle urban bourgeoisie against what they saw as a hostile and rising proletariat',[35] which drove Italy into World War I, may be a matter of debate. But work on the social composition of Italian and German fascism leaves no doubt that

[31] Antoine Prost, *Vocabulaire des proclamations électorales de 1881, 1885 et 1889* (Paris 1974), p. 37.

[32] Jean Dubois, *Le Vocabulaire politique et social en France de 1869 à 1872* (Paris n.d. – 1962), p. 65, item 3665. The term 'nationalisme' is not yet recorded, and remains absent from A. Prost *Vocabulaire des proclamations électorales*, which discusses the rightward shift of the 'national' vocabulary in this period, esp. pp. 52–3, 64–5.

[33] For France, Zeev Sternhell, *Maurice Barrès et le nationalisme français* (Paris 1972); for Italy the chapters by S. Valtutti and F. Perfetti in R. Lill and F. Valsecchi (eds.), *Il nazionalismo in Italia e in Germania fino alla Prima Guerra Mondiale* (Bologna 1983).

[34] Hans-Georg John, *Politik und Turnen: die deutsche Turnerschaft als nationale Bewegung im deutschen Kaiserreich von 1871 bis 1914* (Ahrensberg bei Hamburg 1976), pp. 41ff.

[35] Jens Petersen in W. Schieder (ed.), *Faschismus als soziale Bewegung* (Göttingen 1983), p. 122, citing a source from 1923.

these movements drew their strength essentially from the middle strata.[36]

Moreover, while in established nation-states and powers the patriotic zeal of these intermediate strata was more than welcome to governments engaged in imperial expansion and national rivalry against other such states, we have seen that such sentiments were autochthonous, and therefore not entirely manipulable from above. Few governments, even before 1914, were as chauvinist as the nationalist ultras who urged them on. And, as yet, there were no governments which had been created by the ultras.

Nevertheless, if governments could not entirely control the new nationalism, and it could not yet control governments, identification with the state was essential to the nationalist petty-bourgeoisie and lesser middle classes. If they had no state as yet, national independence would given them the position they felt they deserved. To preach the return of Ireland to its ancient language would no longer be a propagandist slogan for men and women studying elementary Gaelic in Dublin evening classes and teaching what they had just learned to other militants. As the history of the Irish Free State was to demonstrate, it would become the qualification for all but the most subaltern civil service jobs and passing examinations in Irish would therefore be the criterion of belonging to the professional and intellectual classes. If they already lived in a nation-state, nationalism gave them the social identity which proletarians got from their class movement. One might suggest that the self-definition of the lower middle classes – both that section which was helpless as artisans and small shop-keepers and social strata which were largely as novel as the workers, given the unprecedented expansion of higher education white-collar and professional occupations – was not so much as a class, but as the body of the most zealous and loyal, as well as the most 'respectable' sons and daughters of the fatherland.

Whatever the nature of the nationalism which came to the fore in the fifty years before 1914, all versions of it appeared to have

[36] Michael Kater, *The Nazi Party: a social profile of members and leaders 1919–1945* (Cambridge MA 1983), esp. p. 236; Jens Petersen, 'Elettorato e base sociale del fascismo negli anni venti' (*Studi Storici*, XVI/3, 1975), pp. 627–69.

something in common: a rejection of the new proletarian socialist movements, not only because they were proletarian but also because they were, consciously and militantly *internationalist*, or at the very least non-nationalist.[37] Nothing seems more logical, therefore, than to see the appeals of nationalism and socialism as mutually exclusive, and the advance of one as equivalent to the retreat of the other. And the canonical view among historians is indeed that in this period mass nationalism triumphed against rival ideologies, notably class-based socialism, as demonstrated by the outbreak of war in 1914 which revealed the hollowness of socialist internationalism, and by the overwhelming triumph of the 'principle of nationality' in the post-1918 peace settlements.

Yet, contrary to common assumptions, the various principles on which the political appeal to the masses were based – notably the class appeal of the socialists, the confessional appeal of religious denominations and the appeal of nationality were not mutually exclusive. There was not even a sharp line distinguishing one from the other, even in the one case when both sides tended to insist on an, as it were, ex-officio incompatibility: religion and godless socialism. Men and women did not choose collective identification as they chose shoes, knowing that one could only put on one pair at a time. They had, and still have, several attachments and loyalties simultaneously, including nationality, and are simultaneously concerned with various aspects of life, any of which may at any one time be foremost in their minds, as occasion suggests. For long periods of time these different attachments would not make incompatible demands on a person, so that a man might have no problem about feeling himself to be the son of an Irishman, the husband of a German woman, a member of the mining community, a worker, a supporter of Barnsley Football Club, a Liberal, a Primitive Methodist, a patriotic Englishman, possibly a Republican, and a supporter of the British empire.

It was only when one of these loyalties conflicted directly with

[37] This is considered in chapter 4 of E. J. Hobsbawm, *Worlds of Labour* (London 1984) and by the same author, 'Working-class internationalism' in F. van Holthoon and Marcel van der Linden (eds.), *Internationalism in the Labour Movement* (Leiden–New York–Copenhagen–Cologne 1988), pp. 3–16.

another or others that a problem of choosing between them arose. The minority of committed political militants would naturally be far more sensitive to such incompatibilities, so that it is safe to say that August 1914 was a far less traumatic experience for most British, French and German workers than it was for the leaders of their socialist parties, simply because – for reasons partly discussed above (see chapter 3, pp. 88–9) – supporting their own government in war seemed to ordinary workers quite compatible with demonstrating class consciousness and hostility to employers. The South Wales miners who shocked their revolutionary syndicalist, and internationalist, leaders by rushing to the colours equally readily brought the coalfield out in a general strike less than a year later, deaf to the accusation that they were unpatriotic. However, even militants might happily combine what theorists regarded as incompatible: for instance, French nationalism and total loyalty to the USSR, as many a militant of the French Communist Party has shown.

Indeed, the very fact that the new mass political movements, nationalist, socialist, confessional or whatever, were often in competition for the same masses, suggests that their potential constituency was prepared to entertain all their various appeals. The alliance of nationalism and religion is obvious enough, especially in Ireland and Poland. Which is primary? The answer is far from clear. Much more surprising and unnoticed is the vast overlap between the appeals of national and social discontent, which Lenin, with his usual piercing eye for political realities, was to make into one of the foundations of communist policy in the colonial world. The well-known international Marxist debates on 'the national question' are not merely about the appeal of nationalist slogans to workers who ought to listen only to the call of internationalism and class. They were also, and perhaps more immediately, about how to treat working-class parties which simultaneously supported nationalist and socialist demands.[38] What is more – though this did not then figure much in the debates

38 For a brief summary, G. Haupt in Haupt, Lowy and Weill, *Les Marxistes et la question nationale* (Paris 1974), pp. 39–43. The Polish question was the chief, but not the only one of the kind.

– it is now evident that there were initially socialist parties which were or became *the main vehicles of their people's national movement*, just as there were essentially socially minded peasant parties which (as in Croatia) naturally developed a nationalist dimension. In short, the unity of socialist and national liberation of which Connolly dreamed in Ireland – and which he failed to lead – was actually achieved elsewhere.

One might go further. The combination of social and national demands, on the whole, proved very much more effective as a mobilizer of independence than the pure appeal of nationalism, whose appeal was limited to the discontented lower middle classes, for whom alone it *replaced* – or appeared to replace – both a social and a political programme.

Poland is an instructive case in point. The restoration of the country after a century and a half of partition was achieved not under the banner of any of the political movements devoted exclusively to this object, but under that of the Polish Socialist Party, whose leader, Colonel Pilsudski, became his country's liberator. In Finland it was the Socialist Party which, *de facto*, became the national party of the Finns, scoring 47% of the vote in the last (free) elections before the Russian Revolution of 1917. In Georgia it was another socialist party that acquired this function, the Mensheviks; in Armenia, the Dashnaks, who were affiliated to the Socialist International.[39] Among the Jews of eastern Europe socialist ideology dominated national organization both in the non-Zionist (Bundist) and the Zionist versions. Nor was this phenomenon confined to the Tsarist empire, where indeed almost any organization and ideology envisaging change had to see itself in the first place as representing social and political revolution. The national feelings of the Welsh and Scots in the United Kingdom did not find expression through special nationalist parties, but through the major all-UK opposition parties – first Liberals, then Labour. In the Netherlands (but not in Germany) the modest but real national

[39] On the failure of Finnish nationalism to compete with the Socialist Party, see David Kirby, 'Rank-and-file attitudes in the Finnish Social Democratic Party (1905–1918)', (*Past & Present*, 111, May 1986), esp. p. 164. On the Georgians and Armenians see Ronald G. Suny (ed.), *Transcaucasia: Nationalism and Social Change* (Ann Arbor 1983), esp. part II, the essays of R. G. Suny, Anahide Ter Minassian and Gerard J. Libaradian.

feelings of a small people were translated mainly into left-wing radicalism. The Frisians are consequently as over-represented in the history of the Netherlands left as the Scots and Welsh are in that of the British left. The most eminent leader of the early Dutch Socialist Party, Troelstra (1860–1930) had begun his career as a Frisian-language poet and leader of 'Young Friesland', a Frisian revival group.[40] In recent decades the phenomenon has also been observable, though it has been to some extent concealed by the tendency of old petty-bourgeois nationalist movements and parties, originally associated with pre-1914 right-wing ideologies (as in Wales, Euskadi, Flanders and elsewhere) to put on the fashionable costume of social revolution and Marxism. Nevertheless, the DMK, which has become the main vehicle of Tamil nationality demands in India, began life as a regional socialist party in Madras, and similar shifts towards Sinhalese chauvinism may unfortunately be detected in the left in Sri Lanka.[41]

The point of these illustrations is not to assess the relationship of the nationalist and socialist elements within such movements which, justifiably enough, preoccupied and troubled the Socialist International. It is to demonstrate that mass movements could simultaneously express aspirations which we regard as mutually exclusive, and, indeed, that movements making a primarily social-revolutionary appeal could form the matrix of what were eventually to become the mass national movements of their peoples.

Indeed, the very case which has been so often cited as the decisive proof of the supremacy of national over class appeal, actually illustrates the complexity of the relations between the two. Thanks to some excellent research, we are today quite well informed about a crucial case for judging such a conflict of ideas, namely the multinational Habsburg empire.[42] In what follows I summarize an

---

[40] A. Fejtsma, 'Histoire et situation actuelle de la langue frisonne' (*Pluriel*, 29, 1982, pp. 21–34).

[41] For a brief account of the shift from ultra-leftism to Sinhala chauvinism in the JVP movement (Janatha Vimukti Peramuna) which led the rural left 'youth' uprising of 1971, see Kumari Jayawardene, *Ethnic and Class Conflicts in Sri Lanka* (Dehiwala 1985), pp. 84–90.

[42] See Z. A. Zeman, *The Break-up of the Habsburg Empire, 1914–1918* (London 1961); and the collection of studies *Die Auflösung des Habsburgerreiches. Zusammenbruch und*

interesting exploration of opinion by Peter Hanák, based on the analysis of a large body of letters between soldiers and their families censored or confiscated during World War I in Vienna and Budapest.[43] In the first years there was not much nationalism or anti-monarchism among the correspondents, except for those belonging to an *irredenta*, such as the *Serbs* (notably those from Bosnia and Voivodina) who overwhelmingly sympathize as Serbs with the Serbian kingdom and as Slavs and Orthodox with Holy Russia; among the *Italians*, and – after the entry of Romania into the war – among the Romanians. The social base of Serbian hostility to Austria was clearly popular, but the bulk of the nationalist letters from Italians and Romanians came from the middle class or intelligentsia. The only other major national dissidence was to be found among the Czechs (to judge by the letters of war-prisoners, which admittedly included a large body of patriotic deserters). However, more than half the active enemies of the Habsburgs, and volunteers for the Czech forces in Russia, came from the middle class and intelligentsia. (The letters from Bohemia to prisoners were much more cautious and hence less instructive.)

The years of war, but especially the first Russian Revolution, raised the political content of the intercepted correspondence dramatically. Indeed, the censors' reports on public opinion unanimously observed that the Russian Revolution was the first political event since the outbreak of war whose shock-waves penetrated to the lowest levels of the people. Among the activists of some of the oppressed nationalities such as the Poles and Ukrainians, the event raised hopes of reform – perhaps even of independence. However, the dominant mood was a desire for peace and *social* transformation.

The political opinions which now begin to appear even in the letters of labourers, peasant and working-class women, is best analysed in terms of three interlocking binary opposites: rich–poor (or lord–peasant, boss–worker), war–peace, and order–disorder.

Neuorientierung im Donauraum (Schriftenreihe des österreichischen Ost- und Südosteuropainstituts, vol. III, Vienna 1970).

[43] Péter Hanák, 'Die Volksmeinung während des letzten Kriegsjahres in Österreich–Ungarn' in, *Die Auflösung*, pp. 58–66.

The links, at least in the letters, are obvious: the rich live well and don't serve in the army, the poor people are at the mercy of the rich and powerful, the authorities of state and army and so on. The novelty lies not only in the greater frequency of complaints, in the sense that in different ways the poor in uniform and on the home front were being equally mistreated, but in the sense that a revolutionary expectation of fundamental changes was now available as an alternative to the passive acceptance of destiny.

The fundamental theme in the correspondence of the poor was war as a disruption and destruction of the *order of life and labour*. Consequently the desire to return to a decent orderly life increasingly implied hostility to war, to military service, to the war economy, etc. and the wish for peace. But once again we now find complaint transformed into resistance. 'If only the good Lord would bring us peace again' turns into 'we've had enough', or 'they say the socialists are going to make peace'.

National feeling comes into these arguments only indirectly, chiefly because, to cite Hanák 'until 1918 national sentiment had not yet crystallized out, among broad masses of the people, into a stable component of consciousness, or because people were not yet conscious of the discrepancy between loyalty to the state and to the nation, or had not yet made a clear choice between the two'.[44] Nationality appears most often as an aspect of the conflict between rich and poor, especially where the two belong to different nationalities. But even where we find the strongest national tone – as among the Czech, Serbian and Italian letters, we also find an overwhelming wish for social transformation.

I will not follow the censors' detailed monitoring of changing moods in the year 1917. But Hanák's analysis of a sample of about 1,500 letters written between mid-November 1917 and mid-March 1918 – i.e. after the October revolution – is instructive. Two-thirds were written by workers and peasants, a third by intellectuals, roughly in the national proportions corresponding to the national composition of the monarchy. 18% of these letters represent primarily the social theme, 10% the desire for peace, 16% the national question and attitude to the monarchy, and 56% a

[44] *Ibid.* p. 62.

combination of these, namely: bread and peace – if I may simplify the issue – 29%, bread and the nation 9%, peace and the nation 18%. The social theme thus appears in 56% of the letters, the peace theme in 57% and the national theme in 43%. The social and in effect revolutionary note is particularly struck in letters from Czechs, Hungarians, Slovaks, Germans and Croats. Peace, which a third of the letters hope to receive from Russia, a third from the revolution, and another 20% from a combination of both, naturally appealed to correspondents of all nationalities, with a qualification I will note. Of the letters on the national theme 60% represent hostility to the empire and the more or less open wish for independence, 40% are loyal – or rather, if we omit the Germans and Hungarians, 28% are loyal. 35% of the 'national' letters expect independence as a result of an Allied victory, but 12% still believe what they want to be achievable within the frame of the monarchy.

As one might expect, the wish for peace and social revolution went together, especially among Germans, Czechs and Hungarians. But peace and national aspirations were not so readily compatible, just because national independence seemed to depend so much on an Allied victory. Indeed, during the Brest-Litowsk negotiations, many nationalist letters disapproved of an immediate conclusion of peace for this very reason. This is notable among the Czech, Polish, Italian and Serbian elite letters. The period when the October revolution made its first impact was one in which the social element in the public mood was at its strongest, but at the same time a moment when – as both Zeman and Hanák agree – the national and social elements in the desire for revolution began to diverge and conflict. The great January strikes of 1918 marked a sort of turning-point. In a sense, as Zeman observes, in deciding to suppress revolutionary agitation and continue a lost war, the authorities of the Habsburg monarchy made sure that there would be a Wilsonian rather than a Soviet Europe. But even when, in the course of 1918, the national theme finally became dominant in popular consciousness, it was not separate from or opposed to the social theme. For most poor people the two went together, as the monarchy crashed.

What can we conclude from this brief survey? *First*, that we still know very little about what national consciousness meant to the mass of the nationalities concerned. To find out we need not only a great deal of the sort of research of which Hanák's plunges into the censored letters are one example, but, before this can be useful, a cold and demystifying eye cast at the terminology and ideology surrounding 'the national question' in this period, particularly its nationalist variant. *Second*, that the acquisition of national consciousness cannot be separated from the acquisition of other forms of social and political consciousness during this period: they all go together. *Third*, that the progress of national consciousness (outside the classes and cases identified with integralist or extreme right-wing nationalism) is neither linear nor necessarily at the expense of other elements of social consciousness. Seen from the perspective of August 1914, one might have concluded that nation and nation-state had triumphed over all rival social and political loyalties. Could one have said so in the perspective of 1917? Nationalism was victorious in the formerly independent nationalities of belligerent Europe, to the extent that the movements which reflected the real concerns of the poor people of Europe, failed in 1918. When this happened, the middle and lower middle strata of the oppressed nationalities were in a position to become the ruling elites of the new independent Wilsonian petty states. National independence without social revolution was, under the umbrella of Allied victory, a feasible fall-back position for those who had dreamed of a combination of both. In the major defeated or semi-defeated belligerent states there was no such fall-back position. There collapse led to social revolution. The soviets, even short-lived soviet republics, were to be found not among the Czechs and Croats, but in Germany, German Austria, Hungary – and their shadow rested on Italy. Nationalism there re-emerged not as a milder substitute for social revolution, but as the mobilization of ex-officers, lower middle and middle-class civilians for counter-revolution. It emerged as the matrix of fascism.

CHAPTER 5

The apogee of nationalism, 1918–1950

If there was a moment when the nineteenth-century 'principle of nationality' triumphed it was at the end of World War I, even though this was neither predictable, nor the intention of the future victors. In fact, it was the result of two unintended developments: the collapse of the great multinational empires of central and eastern Europe and the Russian Revolution which made it desirable for the Allies to play the Wilsonian card against the Bolshevik card. For, as we have seen, what looked like mobilizing the masses in 1917–18 was social revolution rather than national self-determination. One might speculate on what effect a victorious all-European revolution might have had on the nationalities of the continent, but such speculation is idle. Except for Soviet Russia, Europe was not reconstructed on the basis of the Bolshevik policy on the 'national question'. Essentially the continent became, for the first and last time in its history, a jigsaw puzzle of states defined, with rare exceptions, both as nation-states and as some kind of bourgeois parliamentary democracies. This state of affairs was extremely short-lived.

Inter-war Europe also happened to see the triumph of that other aspect of the 'bourgeois' nation which was discussed in an earlier chapter: the nation as a 'national economy'. Though most economists, businessmen and western governments dreamed of a return to the world economy of 1913, this proved to be impossible. Indeed, even had it been, there could have been no return to the economy of freely competitive private enterprise and free trade which was the ideal, and even part of the reality of the world economy in the heyday of British global supremacy.

By 1913 capitalist economies were already moving rapidly in the direction of large blocks of concentrated enterprise, supported, protected, and even to some extent guided by governments. The war itself had greatly accelerated this shift towards a state-managed, even a state-planned capitalism. When Lenin envisaged the planned socialist economy of the future, to which socialists before 1914 had given practically no thought at all, his model was the German planned war-economy of 1914–17. Of course, even a return to such a big-business-cum-state economy would not have re-established the international pattern of 1913, given the dramatic redistribution of economic and political power in the western world that the war brought about. However, any kind of return to 1913 proved to be a utopian hope. The inter-war economic crises reinforced the self-contained 'national economy' in the most spectacular manner. For a few years the world economy itself appeared to be on the verge of collapse, as the great rivers of international migration dried to trickles, high walls of exchange controls inhibited international payments, international commerce contracted, and even international investment showed momentary signs of collapse. As even the British abandoned Free Trade in 1931, it seemed clear that states were retreating as far as they could into a protectionism so defensive that it came close to a policy of autarchy, mitigated by bilateral agreements. In short, as the economic blizzard swept across the global economy, world capitalism retreated into the igloos of its nation-state economies and their associated empires. Did it have to? In theory it did not. After all, there has – so far – been no comparable retreat in response to the global economic storms of the 1970s and 1980s. However, between the wars it unquestionably did.

The inter-war situation thus provides us with an exceptionally good opportunity for assessing the limitations and the potential of nationalism and nation-states. However, before considering these, let us look briefly at the actual pattern of nation-states imposed on Europe by the peace settlement of Versailles and the associated treaties, including, for the sake of both reason and convenience, the Anglo-Irish treaty of 1921. This brief glance immediately reveals the utter impracticability of the Wilsonian principle to make state frontiers coincide with the frontiers of nationality and language. For the peace settlement after 1918 actually translated this principle into practice as far as was feasible, except for some politico-strategic decisions about the frontiers of Germany, and a few reluctant concessions to the expansionism of Italy and Poland. At all events, no equally systematic attempt has been made before or since, in Europe or anywhere else, to redraw the political map on national lines.

It simply did not work. Inevitably, given the actual distribution of peoples, most of the new states built on the ruins of the old empires, were quite as multinational as the old 'prisons of nations' they replaced. Czechoslovakia, Poland, Romania and Yugoslavia are cases in point. German, Slovene and Croat minorities in Italy took the place of Italian minorities in the Habsburg empire. The main change was that states were now on average rather smaller and the 'oppressed peoples' within them were now called 'oppressed minorities'. The logical implication of trying to create a continent neatly divided into coherent territorial states each inhabited by a separate ethnically and linguistically homogeneous population, was the mass expulsion or extermination of minorities. Such was and is the murderous *reductio ad absurdum* of nationalism in its territorial version, although this was not fully demonstrated until the 1940s. However, mass expulsion and even genocide began to make their appearance on the southern margins of Europe during and after World War I, as the Turks set about the mass extirpation of the Armenians in 1915 and, after the Greco-Turkish war of 1922, expelled between 1.3 and 1.5 millions of Greeks from Asia Minor, where they had lived since the days of Homer.[1] Subsequently Adolf Hitler, who was in this respect a logical Wilsonian nationalist, arranged to transfer Germans not living on the territory of the fatherland, such as those of Italian South Tyrol, to Germany itself, as he also arranged for the permanent elimination of the Jews. After World War II, the Jews having virtually disappeared from the large belt of Europe between

[1] See C. A. Macartney, 'Refugees' in *Encyclopedia of the Social Sciences* (New York 1934), vol. 13, pp. 200–5; Charles B. Eddy, *Greece and the Greek Refugees* (London 1931). In fairness it should be added that Greece expelled 400,000 Turks.

France and the Soviet interior, it was the turn of the Germans to be expelled *en masse*, notably from Poland and Czechoslovakia. The homogeneous territorial nation could now be seen as a programme that could be realized only by barbarians, or at least by barbarian means.

One paradoxical result of the discovery that nationalities and states could not be made to coincide was that the frontiers of the Versailles settlement, absurd though they were by Wilsonian standards, proved to be permanent, except where great-power interests required them to be changed, i.e. in the interests of Germany before 1945, in the interests of the USSR after 1940. In spite of various shortlived attempts to redraw the frontiers of the succession states of the Austrian and Turkish empires, they are still more or less where they ended up after World War I, at least south and west of the Soviet borders, except for the transfer of those areas on the Adriatic taken over by Italy after 1918 to Yugoslavia.

However, the Wilsonian system also produced some other significant and not entirely expected results. First, it demonstrated to no great surprise that the nationalism of small nations was just as impatient of minorities as what Lenin called 'great-nation chauvinism'. That, of course, was not a new discovery to watchers of Habsburg Hungary. More novel, and more significant, was the discovery that the 'national idea' as formulated by its official champions, did not necessarily coincide with the actual self-identification of the people concerned. The plebiscites organized after 1918 in various regions of mixed national composition to decide on their inhabitants' membership of rival nation-states, revealed significant bodies of those who spoke one language but opted to join the state of those who spoke another. This could sometimes be explained away by political pressure or electoral fraud, or dismissed as political ignorance and immaturity. Neither hypothesis was entirely implausible. Nevertheless the existence of Poles who preferred living in Germany to living in reborn Poland, of Slovenes who chose Austria over the new Yugoslavia could not be denied, though it was *a priori* inexplicable to believers in the necessary identification of the members of a nationality with the territorial state that claimed to embody it. This, it is true, was a theory which was now gaining ground rapidly. Twenty years later it was to lead the British government to intern most Germans resident in the United Kingdom *en bloc*, including Jews and anti-fascist emigrants, on the ground that anyone born in Germany must be presumed to owe an overriding loyalty to that country.

A more serious divergence between definition and reality emerged in Ireland. In spite of Emmet and Wolfe Tone, the majority community in the six counties of Ulster refused to see themselves as 'Irish' in the manner of the bulk of the inhabitants of the twenty-six counties – even of the small Protestant minority south of the border. The assumption that a single Irish nation existed within a single Ireland, or rather that all the inhabitants of the island shared the aspiration of a single, united and independent Fenian Ireland, proved mistaken, and while, for fifty years after the establishment of the Irish Free State (and later Republic), Fenians and their sympathizers could dismiss the division of the country as a British imperial plot and the Ulster Unionists as misguided dupes led by British agents, the past twenty years have made it clear that the roots of a divided Ireland are not to be found in London.

Again, the establishment of a South Slav kingdom revealed that its inhabitants did not possess the single Yugoslav consciousness posited by the (Croatian) pioneers of the Illyrian idea in the early nineteenth century, and could be more easily mobilized under slogans strong enough to produce massacre, as Croats, Serbs or Slovenes. Indeed mass Croatian national consciousness appears to have developed only after the establishment of Yugoslavia, and against the new kingdom, or more precisely the alleged Serb predominance within it.[2] Within the new Czechoslovakia the Slovaks persistently evaded the brotherly embrace of the Czechs. Similar developments were to become even more obvious in many of the states produced by national and colonial liberation, and for similar reasons. The peoples did not identify with their 'nation' in the way prescribed for them by their leaders and spokesmen. The Indian National Congress, committed to a single united sub-continent, had to accept the partition of India in 1947, as Pakistan,

---

[2] Mirjana Gross, 'On the integration of the Croatian nation: a case study in nation building' (*East European Quarterly*, 15, 2 June 1981, p. 224).

committed to a single state for the Muslims of that subcontinent, had to accept the partition of Pakistan in 1971. Once Indian politics was no longer monopolized by a small and highly anglicized or westernized elite, it had to confront the demand for linguistic states, which the early national movement had given no thought to, although some Indian communists began to draw attention to it just before World War I.[3] Linguistic rivalries were to maintain English as the official language of India to the present day, though it is spoken by an insignificant fraction of the country's 700 millions, because other Indians are unwilling to accept the domination of Hindi, spoken by 40% of the population.

The Versailles settlement revealed another new phenomenon: the geographical spread of nationalist movements, and the divergence of the new ones from the European pattern. Given the official commitment of the victorious powers to Wilsonian nationalism, it was natural that anyone claiming to speak in the name of some oppressed or unrecognized people – and they lobbied the supreme peacemakers in large numbers – should do so in terms of the national principle, and especially of the right to self-determination. Yet this was more than an effective debating argument. The leaders and ideologues of colonial and semi-colonial liberation movements sincerely spoke the language of European nationalism, which they had so often learned in or from the west, even when it did not suit their situation. And as the radicalism of the Russian Revolution took over from that of the French Revolution as the main ideology of global emancipation, the right to self-determination, now embodied in Stalin's texts, henceforth reached those who had been beyond the range of Mazzini. Liberation in what was not yet known as the Third World was now seen everywhere as 'national liberation' or, among the Marxists, 'national and social liberation'.

However, once again, practice did not conform to theory. The real and growing force of liberation consisted in the resentment against conquerors, rulers and exploiters, who happened to be

---

[3] See G. Adhikari, *Pakistan and Indian National Unity* (London 1942) *passim*, but esp. pp. 16–20. This abandoned the earlier Communist Party line which was, like that of Congress, in favour of Hindustani as the single national language (R. Palme Dutt, *India To-day*, London 1940, pp. 265–6).

recognizable as foreigners by colour, costume and habits, or against those who were seen as acting for them. It was anti-imperial. Insofar as there were proto-national identifications, ethnic, religious or otherwise, among the common people, they were, as yet, obstacles rather than contributions to national consciousness, and readily mobilized against nationalists by imperial masters; hence the constant attacks on the imperialist policies of 'Divide and rule', against the imperial encouragement of tribalism, communalism, or whatever else divided peoples who should be, but were not, united as a single nation.

Moreover, apart from a few relatively permanent political enti-ties such as China, Korea, Vietnam, and perhaps Iran and Egypt which, had they been in Europe, would have been recognized as 'historic nations', the territorial units for which so-called national movements sought to win independence, were overwhelmingly the actual creations of imperial conquest, often no older than a few decades, or else they represented religio-cultural zones rather than anything that might have been called 'nations' in Europe. Those who strove for liberation were 'nationalists' only because they adopted a western ideology excellently suited to the overthrow of foreign governments, and even so, they usually consisted of an exiguous minority of indigenous évolués. Cultural or geo-political movements like pan-arabism, pan-Latinamericanism or pan-Africanism, were not nationalist even in this limited sense, but supra-nationalist, though no doubt ideologies of imperialist expan-sion born in the heartlands of national Europe, such as pan-Germanism, suggested an affinity with nationalism. These were entirely the constructs of intellectuals who had nothing closer to a real state or nation on which to focus. The early Arab nationalists were to be found in Ottoman Syria, which had only the faintest reality as a country, rather than in Egypt, where movements were much more Egypt-oriented. In any case such movements expressed little more than the undoubted fact that men educated in a particularly widespread language of culture are linguistically quali-fied to take intellectual posts anywhere within that culture-area, which is still fortunate for Latin American intellectuals, most of whom may expect a spell of political exile at some time in their lives, and for Palestinian graduates who can readily be employed anywhere between the Gulf and Morocco.

On the other hand territory-oriented movements for liberation could not avoid building on the foundation of what common elements had been given to their territory by its colonial power or powers, since often this was the only unity and national character the future country had. The unity imposed by conquest and administration might sometimes, in the long run, produce a people that saw itself as a 'nation', just as the existence of independent states has sometimes created a sense of citizen patriotism. Algeria has nothing in common as a country except the French experience since 1830 and, more to the point, the struggle against it, yet one would guess that its character as a nation is at least as well-established today as that of the 'historic' political units of the Maghreb, Tunisia and Morocco. It is even more patent that the common experience of Zionist settlement and conquest is what has created a Palestinian nationalism associated with a territory which, until 1918, did not even have any significant regional identity within southern Syria, to which it belonged. However, this is not sufficient to call the states which have emerged from decolonization, mainly after 1945, 'nations', or the movements that led to their decolonization – assuming this was a response to actual or anticipated pressure for it – 'nationalist' movements. More recent developments in the dependent world will be considered below.

Meanwhile, let us turn back to the original home of nationalism, Europe.

Here the reconstruction of the map on national lines deprived nationalism of its liberating and unifying content, since for most of the hitherto struggling nations these aims had been substantially achieved. In a way the European situation now anticipated the situation of the politically decolonized 'Third World' since World War II, and resembled that laboratory of premature neo-colonialism, Latin America. Political independence for territorial states had been largely achieved. Consequently it ceased to be as easy as before to simplify, or conceal, the problems of the future by postponing their consideration until after the achievement of independence or self-determination, which, as now became evident, did not automatically solve all of them.

What remained of the old liberating and unifying nationalism? On the one hand, and for most nationalities, there remained unredeemed minorities outside the frontiers of the national state, such as the Hungarians in Romania and the Slovenes in Austria; on the other there remained national expansion by such national states at the expense of foreigners or domestic minorities. Naturally there were still some nationalities without states in both eastern and western Europe, for instance the Macedonians and Catalans. However, whereas before 1914 the characteristic national movement had been directed against states or political agglomerations seen as multinational or supranational, such as the Habsburg and Ottoman empires, after 1919 it was on the whole, in Europe, directed against national states. It was therefore, almost by definition, separatist rather than unifying, though separatist aspirations might be mitigated by political realism or, as in the case of the Ulster Unionists, concealed behind attachment to some other country. But this had long been so. What was new, was the emergence of such aspirations in nominally national but actually plurinational states of western Europe in a political rather than a primarily cultural form, though one or two of such new nationalist bodies, as for instance the Welsh and Scottish national parties which emerged between the wars, as yet lacked mass support, having only just entered, let alone passed through, 'phase B' of their evolution.

Indeed, leaving the Irish aside, lesser nationalisms in western Europe had kept rather a low profile before 1914. The Basque National Party which acquired some mass support after 1905 and virtually swept the local elections in 1917-19 (except for the working-class voters of Bilbao) was somewhat exceptional. Its young militants took their inspiration directly from the revolutionary nationalism of the Irish in the 1916-22 period, and its popular base was reinforced by and under the centralizing dictatorship of Primo de Rivera, and eventually by the more ruthless and centralizing repression of General Franco. Catalanism still belonged primarily to the local middle classes, to small-town provincial notables and to intellectuals, for the militant and predominantly anarchist working class, both Catalan and immigrant, remained suspicious of nationalism on class grounds. The literature of the anarchist movement was consciously and deliberately published in Spanish. Once again, the regional left and right only came together under Primo de Rivera, via a sort of popular front against the Madrid monarchy on the basis of autonomy for Catalonia. The Republic and the Franco dictatorship were to reinforce mass Catalanism, which, in the last years of the dictatorship and since Franco's death may actually have led to a mass linguistic shift towards what is now not only a spoken idiom but the established and institutionalized language of culture, even if in 1980 the solid Catalan circulations were to be found in intellectual and middle-class journals, a remarkably flourshing genre. In that year only 6.5% of the daily papers circulating in Barcelona were in Catalan.[4] However, while 80% of all inhabitants of Catalonia speak the language and 91% of the inhabitants of Galicia (which has a much less active regional movement) speak the local Gallego, only 30% of the inhabitants of the Basque country spoke the language in 1977 – the latest figures appear not to have changed[5] – a fact wich may not be unconnected with the Basque nationalists' greater zeal for total independence as against autonomy. The divergence between Basque and Catalan nationalism, of which this is one indication, have probably grown wider over time, largely because Catalanism became, and could become, a mass force only by moving to the left in order to integrate a powerful and independent labour movement, while Basque nationalism succeeded in isolating and eventually practically eliminating the traditional working-class socialist movements, a fact not concealable by the revolutionary Marxist phraseology of the separatist ETA. It is perhaps not surprising that Catalanism has been spectacularly more successful in assimilating the (mainly working-class) immigrants to its country than the Basque movement, held together largely by xenophobia. While in 1977 54% of the inhabitants of Catalonia

---

[4] *Le Monde*, 11 January 1981.
[5] H.-J. Puhle, 'Baskischer Nationalismus im spanischen Kontext' in H. A. Winkler (ed.), *Nationalismus in der Welt von Heute*' (Göttingen 1982), pp. 53–4.

born outside that country spoke Catalan, only 8% of those living in the Basque country but born outside, spoke Basque, though allowance ought to be made for the considerably greater difficulty of that language.[6]

As for the other west European nationalism which was becoming a serious political force, the Flemish movement entered a new and more dangerous phase in 1914 when a part of it collaborated with the Germans who had conquered and occupied most of Belgium. It collaborated even more dramatically in World War II. However, it was not until some time after 1945 that Flemish nationalism appeared to put Belgian unity seriously at risk. The other small west European nationalisms remained negligible. Scottish and Welsh nationalist parties just emerged above the surface during the years of the inter-war depression, but they remained on the outer margins of their countries' politics, as witness the fact that the founder of Plaid Cymru was by affinity a continental reactionary of the stamp of Charles Maurras, and a Roman Catholic to boot.[7] Neither party got any electoral support until the second post-war era. Most other movements of the kind hardly got beyond folkloric traditionalism and provincial resentment.

However, a further observation must be made about post-1918 nationalism, which takes us – and it – outside the traditional areas of frontier disputes, elections/plebiscites and linguistic demands. National identification in this era acquired new means of expressing itself in modern, urbanized, high-technology societies. Two crucial ones must be mentioned. The first, which requires little comment, was the rise of the modern mass media: press, cinema and radio. By these means popular ideologies could be both standardized, homogenized and transformed, as well as, obviously, exploited for the purposes of deliberate propaganda by private interests and states. (The first Ministry specifically described as

6 For a full contrast between Catalan and Basque opinion and linguistic practices, based on sample surveys, see M. García Ferrando, *Regionalismo y autonomías en España* (Madrid 1982) and E. López Aranguren, *La conciencia regional en el proceso autonómico español* (Madrid 1983).
7 See E. Sherrington, 'Welsh nationalism, the French Revolution and the influence of the French right' in D. Smith (ed.), *A People and a Proletariat: Essays in the History of Wales 1780–1980* (London 1980), pp. 127–47.

concerned with Propaganda and 'Public Enlightenment' was set up in Germany in 1933 by the new government of Adolf Hitler.) However, deliberate propaganda was almost certainly less significant than the ability of the mass media to make what were in effect national symbols part of the life of every individual, and thus to break down the divisions between the private and local spheres in which most citizens normally lived, and the public and national one. The evolution of the British royal family into a domestic as well as a public icon of national identification, would have been impossible but for the modern mass media, and its most deliberate ritual expression was actually devised specifically for radio – later adapted to television: the royal Christmas broadcast, instituted in 1932.

The gap between private and public worlds was also bridged by *sport*. Between the wars sport as a mass spectacle was transformed into the unending succession of gladiatorial contests between persons and teams symbolizing state-nations, which is today part of global life. Until then such occasions as the Olympic Games and international football matches had interested chiefly a middle-class public (though the Olympic Games began to acquire an air of national competition even before 1914), and international matches had actually been established with the object of integrating the national components of multinational states. They symbolized the unity of such states, as friendly rivalry among their nations reinforced the sense that all belonged together by the institutionalization of regular contests that provided a safety-valve for group tensions, which were to be harmlessly dissipated in symbolic pseudo-struggles. It is difficult not to recognize this element of ritual defusion in the first regular international football matches organized on the European continent, namely those between Austria and Hungary.[8] One is naturally tempted to see the extension of the Rugby internationals from England and Scotland to Wales and Ireland in the 1880s as a reaction to the intensification of national sentiment in Britain at this period.

[8] E. J. Hobsbawm, 'Mass-Producing traditions' in E. J. Hobsbawm and T. Ranger (eds.), *The Invention of Tradition* (Cambridge 1983), pp. 300–1.

Between the wars, however, international sport became, as George Orwell soon recognized, an expression of national struggle, and sportsmen representing their nation or state, primary expressions of their imagined communities. This was the period when the Tour de France came to be dominated by national teams, when the Mitropa Cup set leading teams of the states of Central Europe against each other, when the World Cup was introduced into world football, and, as 1936 demonstrated, when the Olympic Games unmistakably became occasions for competitive national self-assertion. What has made sport so uniquely effective a medium for inculcating national feelings, at all events for males, is the ease with which even the least political or public individuals can identify with the nation as symbolized by young persons excelling at what practically every man wants, or at one time in life has wanted, to be good at. The imagined community of millions seems more real as a team of eleven named people. The individual, even the one who only cheers, becomes a symbol of his nation himself. The present writer remembers nervously listening to the radio transmission of the first Anglo-Austrian football international played in Vienna in 1929 in the house of friends, who promised to take revenge on him if England beat Austria, which, on the record, seemed very probable. As the only English boy present I was England, as they were Austria. (Fortunately the match was a draw.) In this manner did twelve-year-old children extend the concept of team-loyalty to the nation.

What dominated inter-war nationalism in Europe, therefore, was the nationalism of established nation-states and their *irredentas*. Among the ex-belligerents nationalism had, of course, been reinforced by the war, especially after the tide of revolutionary hope had ebbed away in the early 1920s. Fascist and other right-wing movements were quick to exploit it. They did so in the first instance to mobilize the middle strata and others fearful of social revolution, against the red menace which could be – especially in its Bolshevik form – readily identified with militant internationalism and, what seemed to be much the same, an anti-militarism reinforced by the experiences of warfare in 1914–18. The appeal of such nationalist propaganda was all the more effective, even among workers, insofar as it put the blame for failure and weakness on enemies outside and traitors within. And there was plenty of failure and weakness to be explained away.

It is too much to claim that such militant nationalism was no more than a reflex of despair, even though it was patently failure, frustration and resentment that swept many people into the Nazi party, and into other movements of right-wing ultras elsewhere in Europe, during the Great Slump. Nevertheless, the difference between the German reactions to defeat after 1918 and those of West Germans after 1945 is significant. Under the Weimar Republic virtually all Germans, including the communists, were profoundly convinced of the intolerable injustice of the Versailles treaty and the fight against that treaty was one of the major forces of mass mobilization in all parties, right or left. Yet the terms imposed on Germany after 1945 were immeasurably harsher and more arbitrary than in 1919. Moreover, Federal Germany contained millions of resentful and nationalist Germans, brutally expelled from central and eastern Europe, unconvinced that this was a just punishment for the far greater horrors perpetrated on other peoples by Nazi Germany. Nevertheless, militant political revisionism was never to play more than a modest and rapidly diminishing part in the politics of Federal Germany, and is certainly not a major factor there today. The reason for the difference between Weimar and Bonn is not hard to find. In the Federal Republic things have gone strikingly well for most citizens since the late 1940s, whereas Weimar was plunged into an appalling depression when it had hardly done more than emerge, for a half decade, from defeat, revolution, slump and galloping inflation.

All the same, even if we do not see the resurgence of militant nationalism as a mere reflex of despair, it was plainly something that filled the void left by failure, impotence, and the apparent inability of other ideologies, political projects and programmes to realize men's hopes. It was the utopia of those who had lost the old utopias of the age of Enlightenment, the programme of those who had lost faith in other programmes, the prop of those who had lost the support of older political and social certainties. We shall return to this point below.

Yet, as the last chapter has tried to argue, nationalism cannot, and could not in this period, be identified with those for whom it was an exclusive, all-consuming, overarching political imperative. This was, as we have seen, not the only form taken by a sense of national identification or, to put it in terms of citizen rights and duties, of patriotism. It is important to distinguish between the exclusive nationalism of states or right-wing political movements which substitutes itself for all other forms of political and social identification, and the conglomerate national/citizen, social consciousness which, in modern states, forms the soil in which all other political sentiments grow. In this sense 'nation' and 'class' were not readily separable. If we accept that class consciousness in practice had a civic-national dimension, and civic-national or ethnic consciousness had social dimensions, then it is likely that the radicalization of the working classes in the first post-war Europe may have reinforced their potential national consciousness.

How else are we to explain the extraordinary success of the left in non-fascist countries, in recapturing national and patriotic senti-ment during the antifascist period? For it can hardly be denied that resistance to Nazi Germany, particularly during World War II, tended both to appeal to national feelings and to hopes of social renewal and liberation. Certainly in the mid-1930s the communist movement deliberately broke with the traditions of both the Second and the Third Internationals, which had abandoned the symbols of patriotism – even those as intimately associated with the revolutionary, and indeed the socialist, past as the 'Marseillaise'[9] – to bourgeois states and petty-bourgeois politicians. The subsequent attempts to recapture these symbols and, as it were, to refuse the devil's armies the monopoly of the best marching tunes, had its bizarre aspects, at least when seen from outside and in retrospect, as when the Communist Party of the USA declared – unsuccess-fully, to few observers' surprise – that communism was twentieth-century Americanism. Nevertheless, the role of the communists in

[9] For the substitution of the 'Internationale' for the 'Marseillaise' in Germany as well as France, see M. Dommanget, *Eugène Pottier* (Paris 1971), ch. III. For the patriotic appeal, see e.g. Maurice Thorez, *France To-day and the People's Front* (London 1936), XIX, pp. 174–85, esp. 180–1.

the antifascist resistance lent considerable plausibility to their reclamation of patriotism, particularly after 1941; certainly quite enough to worry General De Gaulle.[10] Moreover, both within and outside the movement, the combination of the red and national flags was genuinely popular.

Whether there was a genuine upsurge of national sentiment on the left, or whether it was simply that traditional revolutionary patriotism of the Jacobin kind was allowed once again to appear centre-stage, having been banished into the wings for so long by the official anti-nationalism and anti-militarism of the left, is hard to decide. There has been little research on such questions, though they are not beyond serious enquiry and the contemporary political documentation is as poor a guide in these matters as the memory of contemporaries. What is evident is that the remarriage of social revolution and patriotic sentiment was an extremely complex phenomenon. While we await further study, it is at least possible to sketch some of these complexities.

First, antifascist *nationalism* emerged in the context of an *international* ideological civil war, in which a part of numerous national ruling classes appeared to opt for an international political alignment of the right, and for the states identified with it. Such domestic parties of the right thus jettisoned the appeal to xenophobic patriotism, which had once served it so well. As the French phrase had it: 'Better Hitler than Léon Blum'. The phrase may well have been intended to mean: rather a German than a Jew, but it could only too easily be read as: rather a foreign country than our own. This made it easier for the left to take back the national flag from the now slackened grip of the right. Similarly in Britain opposition to the policy of appeasing Hitler was a great deal easier for the left than for Conservatives who could not fail to see him, quite correctly, as a powerful bulwark against Bolshevism rather than as a threat to the British empire. In a sense the rise of antifascist patriotism was thus part of what could legitimately be seen as the triumph of a kind of internationalism.

---

[10] Charles De Gaulle, *Mémoires de Guerre*, II (Paris 1956), pp. 291–2. For the USA, Earl Browder, *The People's Front in the United States* (London 1937), esp. pp. 187–96, 249–69.

Second, both workers and intellectuals also made an *international* choice, but one which happened to reinforce national sentiment. Recent research on both British and Italian communism in the 1930s has underlined the role of antifascist mobilization in attracting both young workers and intellectuals to it, and above all the role of the Spanish Civil War.[11] But support for Spain was not a simple act of international solidarity, like the anti-imperialist campaigns for India or Morocco, which had a much more restricted appeal. In Britain the fight against fascism and war concerned the British, in France the French – but after July 1936 the main front on which it was waged happened to be near Madrid. Issues which were essentially domestic in each country were, by the accidents of history, being fought out on battlefields in a country so remote and unknown to most workers that it had virtually no association for the average Briton other than those of the struggle which concerned them. Moreover, inasmuch as fascism and war were identified with particular foreign states, Germany and Italy, what was at stake in this struggle was not only the domestic future of Britain or France, or war and peace in general, but the defence of the British or French nations against the Germans.

Third, antifascist nationalism was patently engaged in a social as well as a national conflict, as became clear towards the end of World War II. Both among the British and among the resistance movements on the European continent victory and social transformation were inseparable. That the war ended in Britain with the electoral defeat of Winston Churchill, the loved and admired war-leader and symbol of British patriotism, and the massive victory of the Labour Party, demonstrates the point beyond argument; for, whatever the euphoria of liberation elsewhere, as a considered expression of public opinion the British general election of 1945 was beyond challenge. Both Conservatives and Labour had been equally committed to victory, but only one party had been formally committed to victory and social transformation.

Moreover, for many British workers the war itself had a social dimension. It is no accident that the German attack on the USSR in

---

[11] Hywel Francis, *Miners Against Fascism: Wales and the Spanish Civil War* (London 1984); Paolo Spriano, *Storia del Partito Cominista Italiano*, vol. III (Turin 1970), ch. IV.

1941 released a massive wave of philo-sovietism among British workers in and out of uniform; a wave quite unaffected by the behaviour of both the USSR and native communists between September 1939 and June 1941. It was not simply that, at long last, Britain was no longer fighting alone. To those of us who experienced this turn of events as rank-and-file soldiers in working-class units of the British Army, it is perfectly clear that the bulk of politically conscious, i.e. Labour and trade unionist, soldiers in such units still somehow thought of the Soviet Union as in some way 'a workers' state'. Even so firmly and formidably anti-communist a union leader as Ernest Bevin did not abandon this presumption until some time during World War II.[12] To this extent the war itself seemed to have elements of a war between both classes and states.

Nationalism thus acquired a strong association with the left during the antifascist period, an association which was subsequently reinforced by the experience of anti-imperial struggle in colonial countries. For colonial struggles were tied to the international left in various ways. Their political allies in metropolitan countries were to be found, almost invariably, in these quarters. Theories of imperialism (i.e. of anti-imperialism) had long formed an organic part of the corpus of socialist thinking. That Soviet Russia was itself largely an Asian country, and saw the world largely in a non-European – between the wars primarily an Asian – perspective, could not but strike activists from what was not yet called the 'Third World'. Conversely, since Lenin's discovery that the liberation of oppressed colonial peoples was an important potential asset for world revolution, communist revolutionaries did what they could for colonial liberation struggles, which in any case appealed to them on the grounds that anything that metropolitan imperialists abhorred, must be welcome to the workers.

The relations between the left and the nationalism of dependent countries were, of course, more complex than a simple formula might suggest. Quite apart from their own ideological preferences, anti-imperial revolutionaries, however internationalist in theory, were concerned with winning independence for their own country

---

[12] Cf. the 1941 speech in A. Bullock, *The Life and Times of Ernest Bevin*, vol. 2 (1967), p. 77. H. Pelling, *The Labour Governments 1945–51* (London 1984), p. 120.

and with nothing else. They were unreceptive to suggestions that they should postpone or modify their objective in the interests of some wider global purpose – such as winning the war against Nazi Germany and Japan, their empire's enemies which (following a traditional Fenian principle) many of them regarded as their nation's allies, especially during the years when they looked almost certain to win. From the point of view of the antifascist left someone like Frank Ryan was difficult to understand: an Irish Republican fighter so much on the left that he fought for the Spanish Republic in the International Brigades, but who, after being captured by General Franco's forces, turned up in Berlin where he did his best to bargain IRA support for Germany against the unification of Northern and Southern Ireland after a German victory.[13] From the point of view of traditional Irish Republicanism Ryan could be seen as someone pursuing a consistent policy, though perhaps not a well-judged one. There was a case to be made against Subhas C. Bose ('Netaji'), the hero of the Bengali masses and formerly an important radical figure in the Indian National Congress, who joined the Japanese and organized an anti-British Indian National Army from among the Indian servicemen taken prisoner in the early months of the war. However, it cannot be on the grounds that in 1942 the Allies looked an obviously better bet to win the war in Asia: a successful Japanese invasion of India was far from improbable. More leaders of anti-imperialist movements than we like to recall saw Germany and Japan as the way to get rid of the British and French, especially until 1943.

Nevertheless, the general movement towards independence and decolonization, especially after 1945, was unquestionably identified with socialist/communist anti-imperialism, which is perhaps why so many decolonized and newly independent states, and by no means only those in which socialists and communists had played an important part in the struggles for liberation, declared themselves to be in some sense 'socialist'. National liberation had become a

---

[13] See Sean Cronin, *Frank Ryan, The Search for the Republic* (Dublin 1980); but also, Frank Ryan (ed.), *The Book of the XV Brigade* (Newscastle on Tyne 1975, first published Madrid 1938).

slogan of the left. Paradoxically, the new ethnic and separatist movements in western Europe thus came to adopt the social-revolutionary and Marxist-Leninist phraseology which fits in so badly with their ideological origins in the pre-1914 ultra-right, and the pro-fascist and even, during the war, collaborationist record of some of their older militants.[14] That young intellectuals of the instant left rushed into such movements when 1968 failed to produce the expected millennium, gave an additional impetus to this transformation of nationalist rhetoric, by which the old-fashioned peoples prevented from exercising their natural right to self-determination were reclassified as 'colonies' also liberating themselves from imperialist exploitation.

It may be argued that from the 1930s to the 1970s the dominant discourse of national emancipation echoed the theories of the left, and in particular developments in Comintern Marxism. That the alternative idiom of national aspiration had been so discredited by its association with fascism as to be virtually excluded from public use for a generation, merely made this hegemony of left-wing discourse more obvious. Hitler and decolonization appeared to have restored the alliance of nationalism with the left which had seemed so natural before 1848. Only in the 1970s did alternative legitimations for nationalism re-emerge. In the west the major nationalist agitations of the period, being primarily directed against communist regimes, returned to simpler and more visceral forms of national assertion, even when they did not actually reject any ideology emanating from ruling communist parties. In the 'Third World' the rise of religious integralism, notably in various İslamic forms but also in other religious variants (e.g. Buddhism among the Sinhalese ultras in Sri Lanka), provided a foundation for both revolutionary nationalism and national repression. In retrospect the ideological hegemony of the left since the 1930s may appear as an interim, or even an illusion.

An important question remains to be asked: how have the fortunes of nationalism been affected by the spread of nationalist

[14] For the former collaborationism of many of the 'ethnic' activists in France, see William R. Beer, 'The social class of ethnic activists in contemporary France' in Milton J. Esman (ed.), *Ethnic Conflict in the Western World* (Ithaca 1977), p. 157.

sentiments and movements beyond the geographic regions where they first appeared? Although European observers in the 1920s began to take nationalism in the dependent world – i.e. in practice, in Asia and the Islamic countries – seriously, perhaps more so than we do in retrospect,[15] they did not regard it as requiring a modification of the European analysis. The greatest collection of independent states outside Europe, the Latin American republics, attracted very little attention except in the USA, and nationalism in this area was either regarded as a Ruritanian joke, or assimilated to *indigenismo*, the cultural rediscovery of suitable Indian civilizations and traditions, until certain groups in the 1930s and 1940s appeared to show sympathy for European fascism, thus allowing them to be easily pigeon-holed. Japan, though patently *sui generis*, could be considered an honorary western imperial power, and thus a national and nationalist state somewhat like its western models. Except for Afghanistan and perhaps Siam (Thailand), the rest of the Afro-Asiatic regions which were not actually owned and administered from a metropole, contained only one state which had genuine room for independent manoeuvre, namely post-imperial Turkey.

Virtually all the anti-imperial movements of any significance could be, and in the metropoles generally were, classified under one of three headings: local educated elites imitating European 'national self-determination' (as in India), popular anti-western xenophobia (an all-purpose heading widely applied, notably in China), and the natural high spirits of martial tribes (as in Morocco or the Arabian deserts). In the last case imperial administrators and intellectuals, not unmindful of the possibility of recruiting such sturdy, and usually unpolitical, fellows into imperial armies, tended to be indulgent, reserving their real hostility for urban agitators, especially those with some education. None of these cases seemed to require much theoretical reconsideration, though the example of popular movements in Islamic countries, and even

[15] Hans Kohn's *History of Nationalism* in the East (New York 1933) and *Nationalism and Imperialism in the Hither East* (New York 1932), originally published in German in 1928 and 1930 respectively, are probably the first major treatments of the subject. The author was perhaps moved to focus on this region by his Zionist interests.

Gandhi's appeal to the Indian masses, suggested a greater mobilizing role of religion than was usual in modern Europe. Perhaps the nearest thing to thought about nationalism inspired by the Third World – outside the revolutionary left – was a general scepticism about the universal applicability of the 'national' concept. It seemed, to imperial observers, that in the dependent world it was often an intellectual import, taken up by minorities of *évolués* out of touch with the mass of their countrymen, whose ideas of community and political loyalty were quite different. Such reflections were often just, even though they tended to cause imperial rulers or European settlers to overlook the rise of mass national identification when it did occur, as Zionists and Israeli Jews notably did in the case of the Palestinian Arabs.

Much the most interesting inter-war thinking about the 'national question' in the dependent world took place in the international communist movement, though it did not go outside the rigid frame of Leninist Marxism, as codified between the war. However, the problem that chiefly preoccupied Marxists was the relation of classes (including those which should have been engaged in class struggle against one another like the bourgeoisie and proletariat of a colonial country) within the broad anti-imperialist movement for national and social liberation; that is, insofar as indigenous colonial societies possessed a class structure which lent itself to analysis in western-derived terms, a situation which raised further complexities for Marxist analysis. The actual definition of the 'nations' fighting for their freedom, on the other hand, was generally taken over from such nationalist movements as existed without much enquiry. Thus the Indian nation was the population of the Indian subcontinent, as claimed by the Indian National Congress, the Irish nation was what the Fenians regarded as such.[16]

---

[16] *Die nationale Frage und Österreichs Kampf um seine Unabhängigkeit: Ein Sammelband*, Foreword by Johann Koplenig (Paris 1939), documents the chief exception: Austria. Its German-speaking inhabitants had hitherto been seen by Marxists as members of the German nation, the main reason for the Austrian Social Democratic Party's attachment to union with Germany, which raised problems once Germany was in the hands of Hitler. While the Social Democrats maintained their position, to the point where Karl Renner (subsequently first President of the second Austrian Republic) actually hailed the *Anschluss* in 1938, the Austrian communists evolved a theory of separate Austrian nation-hood which avoided these embarrassments.

For the present purposes we need not go further into this interesting area.

Since few Third World anti-imperial 'national' movements coincided with a political or ethnic entity existing before the coming of the imperialists, the development of nationalism in the nineteenth-century European sense of the term has occurred largely since decolonization, i.e. mainly since 1945. Most of it, therefore, has been directed not against a foreign imperialist oppressor, but against newly emancipated states claiming a national homogeneity which they did not possess. In other words they protested against the 'national', i.e. ethnic, or cultural, unreality of the territories into which the imperial era had partitioned the dependent world, though sometimes also against the unreality of the western-derived ideologies taken over by the modernizing elites which inherited the former rulers' power.

But did they – do they – protest in the name of something that corresponds to the old 'principle of nationality' and the demand for self-determination? In some instances they evidently speak the same language, probably derived no longer directly from Mazzini but indirectly via inter-war Marxism, the major ideological influence on intellectuals in large zones of the dependent world. This is plainly the case in Sri Lanka, both among Sinhala and Tamil extremists, though Sinhala communalism also relied on nineteenth-century western linguistic/racial ideas to demonstrate Aryan superiority.[17] Yet it does not follow that communal conflicts and rivalries and ethnic group-assertion in the Third World are best seen in this light, namely as movements of potential state creation whose logical end is the establishment of territorial states. The inability of 'tribalism' which has evidently very strong support in many parts of Africa 'to stand up against the sanctioning apparatus even of relatively rudimentary states'[18] should give us pause. So, to turn the coin, should the inability of areas disintegrating into their

[17] Kumari Jayawardene, *Ethnic and Class Conflicts in Sri Lanka* (Dehiwala 1985); by the same author, 'The national question and the left movement in Sri Lanka' (*South Asia Bulletin*, VII, 1 and 2, 1987, pp. 11–22); Jayadeva Uyangoda, 'Reinterpreting Tamil and Sinhala nationalism' (*ibid*. pp. 39–46); R. N. Kearney, 'Ethnic conflict and the Tamil separatism movement in Sri Lanka' (*Asian Survey*, 25, 9 September 1985, pp. 898–917).
[18] Fredrik Barth (ed.); *Ethnic Groups and Boundaries* (Boston 1989), p. 34.

communal components, like Lebanon, to maintain anything that could be even faintly described as a nation-state or any other state.

Of course new states have been created since 1945 which obviously divide into a small number – say two to four – regions which differ markedly in socio-political structure, culture, ethnicity, or other politically relevant characteristics, and might, but for the international situation, fall apart along such fracture lines, as has occasionally happened (e.g. East and West Pakistan, Turkish and Greek Cyprus). The Sudan and Chad (Muslim/Arab North, Christian/Animist Negro South) and Nigeria (Muslim and Hausa North, Yoruba Southwest, Ibo Southeast) are cases in point. However, it is significant that the Nigerian situation has been apparently defused since the failed secession of (Ibo) Biafra in 1967, by breaking up the three dominant communities and replacing the original tripartite division with nineteen smaller states, incidentally underlining the fact that Hausa, Yoruba and Ibo between them represented less than 60% of the total Nigerian population. It is also clear that the internal situation of states is unstable in which power rests with a single hegemonic community, especially if it is still in the process of establishing dominance over the entire territory of the state. This seems to be the case in Ethiopia, where the nineteenth-century rise of an empire based on a minority Christian community – Amhara-speakers represent 25% of a population divided into 40% Christians, 40% Muslims and 20% others – was interrupted by a brief period as an Italian colony, the restoration of an extended empire, and the revolution of 1974. Even so, it is unlikely that the territorial unity of this unhappy, famine- and war-wracked country, would be at serious risk but for the attempt to incorporate Eritrea, which was in a position to develop its own separate political movements, and territorial identity, as an Italian colony and under British administration, before being added, for the sake of international convenience, to Ethiopia, to which it had never previously belonged.

There are evidently plenty of ethnic, tribal or communal tensions within a number of the newly independent states, both in Africa and Asia, but – quite apart from countries which appear to have established what seems to be a workable multi-ethnic *modus vivendi* – it is far from clear that state separatism is what each of the peoples composing them or even their leaders and spokesmen have in mind.

The real problem of ethnic and communal groups, especially those facing dramatic socio-economic changes for which their history has not prepared them, is quite different. It is much less like that of the formation of new nations than it is like that of mass migration into old (or new) industrial countries: how to adapt to the new world in an ethnically plural society. Of course such immigrants are, as we have seen, naturally drawn into groups with others from 'the old country' or 'down home', out of insecurity and nostalgia, for mutual aid, by reaction against outside hostility to people like themselves and, not least, through the powerful organizing medium of electoral politics, where this is available. As any ward-politician in North America knows, they respond strongly to ethnic appeals and to support for whatever is seen as the national cause in their countries of origin, especially when migration is partly political or ideological: to support for the IRA among the Irish, hostility to Yasser Arafat among the Jews, the restoration of the Baltic states among Latvians. Yet as every politician also knows, making the right noises about Sinn Fein, the PLO and Stalinism is only a minor part of the political task of the representatives of such constituencies, the major task being to look after their interests as *Americans* or *Canadians*. In a pluri-ethnic or communal society this means essentially bargaining for the group's share of the resources available in the state against other groups, defending the group against discrimination and, in general, maximizing its members' chances and minimizing its disadvantages. Nationalism in the sense of the demand for a separate territorial state or even linguistic autonomy is irrelevant to this, though it may make a diaspora feel good.

The case of the Negroes in the USA makes the point with particular clarity, because race so clearly dominates their situation as a group, and because, in spite of their marked degree of social segregation or ghettoization, territorial separatism is so evidently beside the point for them, quite apart from its impracticability – either in the form of a mass exodus to some other (African) country or in the form of setting aside some part of the USA for them. The former has sometimes won a good deal of emotional support among blacks in the western hemisphere, but has never been considered a serious programme except by the crazy ultra-right which envisages the mass expulsion ('repatriation') of coloured immigrants.

The latter was at one time briefly proposed, in line with the orthodox doctrine of 'national self-determination' by the Communist International, but without raising any interest among blacks. By mapping the distribution of counties in the southern states where the Census showed black majorities, a more or less continuous belt could be shown to exist on paper (with a number of enclaves and exclaves) which could thus claim to be a 'national territory' for American Negroes that could become a black republic.[19] The absurdity of this cartographic fantasy lay in the assumption that the problem of living in the (predominantly white) USA could somehow be eliminated from the life of American blacks by separatism. Moreover, it was already evident that even if a black republic could be established somewhere in the country blues zone, it could have very little bearing on the city ghettoes of the north and west into which blacks were already pouring. Concentration in cities, where 97% of non-southern blacks lived in 1970 – a third of southern blacks were still rural – has given US blacks considerable electoral leverage, from which they have derived some advantage, but by concentrating on winning a larger share of the resources and facilities of the entire society for their ethnic group. The territorial segregation of ghettoes in plural societies may be a formidable force for ethnic cohesion as witness both Belfast and Beirut, but it actually *eliminates* the classic perspective of self-determination by the formation of territorial states, in all but very exceptional cases.

---

[19] 'The Party strengthened the struggle for the equal rights of the Negroes and the right to self-determination up to and including secession for the "black belt".' (*Die Kommunistische Internationale vor dem VII Weltkongress: Materialien.* Moscow–Leningrad 1935, p. 445), reporting on 'decisions in the autumn of the year 1930'. On the 'sharp divergences' about the slogan favouring a black republic for the Negro population in the USA, at the discussion of the relevant sub-commission of the VI Congress of the International in 1928, see the contributions of Ford and Jones at the Congress (*Compte-Rendu Sténographique du VIe Congrès de l'Internationale Communiste 17 juillet–1*

What is more, urbanization and industrialization, resting as they do on massive and multifarious movements, migrations and transfers of people, undermine the other basic nationalist assumption of a territory inhabited essentially by an ethnically, culturally and linguistically homogeneous population. The sharp xenophobic or racist reaction of the native population in receiving countries or regions to the mass influx of 'strangers' has been, unfortunately, familiar in the USA since the 1890s and in western Europe since the 1950s. Yet xenophobia and racism are symptoms, not cures. Ethnic communities and groups in modern societies are fated to coexist, whatever the rhetoric which dreams of a return to an unmixed nation. Mass murder and mass expulsion ('repatriation') did indeed drastically simplify the ethnic map of Europe, and might be tried in some other regions. Yet the movement of peoples has since restored the ethnic complexity which barbarism sought to eliminate. Only today the typical 'national minority' in most countries receiving migration, is an archipelago of small islands rather than a coherent land-mass. Otto Bauer may have some relevance to their problem, but not Mazzini.

Fundamentally, this is the situation of ethnic groups in poly-ethnic and poly-communal states of the Third World, i.e. in most ex-colonial states larger than small Caribbean islands – and even in some mini-states. Ethnic or communal groups within them are often strongly organized as such – mainly, in new states, through political parties and pressure-groups which are *de facto* spokesmen for ethnic interests. Access to positions in the state and public service which, in many such states, are the chief road to wealth and capital accumulation for those not versed in modern entrepreneurial skills – traditionally practised by some minority communities and whites[20] – is the chief objective. Insofar as such access is acquired through schooling (except in the rare case of military coups not made by commissioned officers), 'contending ethnic groups', as Fredrik Barth observes with his usual acuteness,

---

septembre 1928. In *La Correspondance Internationale*, no. 125, 19 October 1928, pp. 1292–3; no. 130, 30 October 1928, p. 1418).
[20] Such minorities, of course, also operate by privileged access to those in state power.

'... become differentiated with respect to educational level and attempt to control or monopolize educational facilities'.[21]

To the extent that this group competition is for access to, or control of, positions in the machinery of the (territorial) state, such ethnic contests have something in common with the rise of 'petty-bourgeois' nationalism discussed in chapter 4. In extreme cases it may indeed lead to separatism, as among Tamils in Sri Lanka, a (geographically in part separable) minority which was over-represented in public service under the British and probably in higher education, and has since been under pressure from the heavily dominant Sinhalese majority, not least through the adoption of Sinhalese as the *only* official national language in 1956. If Hindi had been the language of 72% instead of 40% of the population of India, the temptation to eliminate English for official purposes would have been greater, as would the danger of Tamil and other separatisms on the Indian mainland.[22] However, territorial nationalism is a special and limiting case. Even in Sri Lanka separatist aspirations did not replace federalist ones until twenty-five years or so after independence. The general case is competitive coexistence buttressed where necessary by various brands of decentralization and autonomy. And the more a society is urbanized and industrialized, the more artificial the attempt to confine ethnic communities operating in the wider economy to territorial homelands. The South African attempt to do so is correctly seen not as an exercise in classical nation-building for Africans, but as a project to perpetuate racial oppression.

Yet, as Barth once again points out,[23] group relations in such complex poly-ethnic/communal societies are both different from and less stable than such relations tended to be in traditional societies. In the first place groups entering modern or more advanced societies have three possible (perhaps not entirely distinct) strategies. Their members may seek to assimilate or 'pass' as

[21] See Barth (ed.) *Ethnic Groups*, pp. 34–7.
[22] See Sunil Bastian, 'University admission and the national question' and Charles Abeysekera, 'Ethnic representation in the higher state services' in *Ethnicity and Social Change in Sri Lanka* (Papers presented at a seminar organized by the Social Scientists' Association, December 1979), Dehiwala 1985; pp. 220–32, 233–49.
[23] Barth (ed.), *Ethnic Groups*, pp. 33–7.

members of the advanced society, with the result that some may succeed, but the community as a whole will be 'denuded of its source of internal diversification and will probably remain as a culturally conservative ... group with low rank in the larger social system'. Alternatively, it may accept minority status and seek to reduce minority disabilities, but insist on maintaining its specific character 'in sectors of non-articulation'. There will hence be no clear emergence of a poly-ethnically organized society, and in industrial societies, probably, eventual assimilation. Lastly, the group may choose to emphasize its ethnic identity, 'using it to develop new positions and patterns ... not formerly found in their societies or not adequately there for the new purposes'. This is the strategy that, in Barth's view, comes nearest to generating post-colonial ethnic nationalism or possible state-building, though, as I have argued, this is not the normal objective nor the necessary implication of this strategy. In any case it is not helpful to analysis to put all these modes of ethnic group survival under the same heading of 'nation' and 'nationalism': Québécois, Greek and Baltic immigrants, Algonquin Indians, Inuit, Ukrainians and Anglo-Scots – to take merely one multi-ethnic case.

In the second place, traditional inter-ethnic relations were often, perhaps in most cases, stabilized by developing into a segmented social division of labour, so that the 'stranger' has a recognized function and, whatever 'our' frictions with his community, complements, rather than competes with, 'us'. Left to itself, such ethnically segmented labour markets and service-patterns develop naturally, even in the history of western industrialization and urbanization, partly because specific niches in such markets are there to be filled, mainly because the informal mutual aid network of migrants from particular regions fills them with friends, kin and clients from back home. Thus even today in New York one expects to see Korean faces in a greengrocer's shop, and Mohawk Indians to be over-represented among skyscraper steel-erectors, and (as in London) newsagents to be of Indian origin and the staff in Indian restaurants to be immigrants from the Sylhet area of Bangladesh.

Given that 'traditional poly-ethnic systems are so often markedly economic' (Barth), it is striking that the movements in plural states which emphasize ethnic identity are so rarely concerned with this kind of social division, but rather with the competitive position of their group in an inter-communal free-for-all within the state. Much of what passes for post-colonial nationalism reflects the consequent instability of group relations which are based not on a real ethno-economic division of labour or function but on a balance (or preponderance) of political power.

Ethnic and communal frictions and conflicts are therefore visible enough in the world outside the original zone of nationalism, and may look as though they fitted the 'national' model.

And yet, it must be said again, all this is not the same as 'the national question' about which the Marxists argued, and in terms of which maps were redrawn. Or, if we prefer, the extension of 'nationalism' beyond its region of origin moves it beyond the range of the original analysis of the phenomenon – as witness the spontaneous emergence of new terms to grasp it, such as the word *ethnie* (for 'ethnic group' or what would have been called a 'nationality'), which appears to be quite recent.[24] This has long been understood, though earlier observers of non-western nationalism, while quite aware 'that we are confronted with a phenomenon quite different from European nationalism', regarded it as 'futile' to eschew the term 'in view of its adoption on all sides'.[25] Nevertheless, whether the term is used or not, the phenomenon raises novel questions in several respects. One of these may be briefly mentioned at the conclusion of the chapter: language.

It is by no means clear that the classic pattern of linguistic nationalism, that of developing an ethnic idiom into a new all-purpose standard 'national' literary language, which will then become official, will, or can, continue. (Even within old-established standard languages of this kind there has been a recent tendency to disintegrate them by turning spoken sub-variants or dialects into

24 The *Trésor de la Langue Française* (vol. VIII, Paris 1980), while recording the word *ethnie* for 1896 also shows no use for it before 1956. Anthony D. Smith, *The Ethnic Origins of Nations* (Oxford 1986) uses the term extensively, but clearly regards it as a French neologism not yet fully anglicized. I doubt whether it can be found, except freakishly, in the discussion of nationality before the late 1960s.

25 John H. Kautsky, 'An essay in the politics of development' in John H. Kautsky (ed.), *Political Change in Underdeveloped Countries: Nationalism and Communism* (New York–London 1962), p. 33.

possible media of school instruction, e.g. 'black English' or the strongly anglicized French *joual* of the Montreal lower-class neighbourhoods.) For practical purposes multilinguality is unavoidable in most states today, either because migration fills virtually all western cities with 'ethnic' colonies, or because most new states today contain so large a number of mutually non-intelligible spoken languages that media of national (and today preferably of international) intercommunication are indispensable, without counting more modest lingua-francas. (Papua New Guinea with more than 700 languages for a population of some 2½ milion may be the extreme case.) In the latter case it is already clear that the politically most acceptable languages are communication constructs without local ethnic identification, like pidgin or Bahasa Indonesia, or foreign (preferably world culture) languages, notably English, which do not put any ethnic group at a special advantage or disadvantage. This situation, which may explain 'what seems to be a remarkable linguistic flexibility among the Indonesian elite and lack of intense emotional commitment to a "mother tongue"'[26] is evidently not the same as that familiar in European nationalist movements. Nor is the politics of modern multi-ethnic census-taking in Canada, if we compare it with that of the old Habsburg empire (see above pp. 98–9). For, knowing that members of immigrant ethnic groups, if asked to choose between ethnicity and Canadianness, see themselves as Canadians, and knowing the attraction of English to them, ethnic pressure groups oppose census questions about language or ethnic self-identification, and, until recently, the census insisted on a declaration of patrilineal ethnic *origin* and rejected 'Canadian' or 'American' as an answer except from Amerindians. This 'census artifact' ethnicity, originally pressed by French Canadians to swell their numbers outside the core area of Quebec, also served the purposes of ethnic and immigrant leaders, since it muffles the fact that of the 315,000 who claimed Polish origin in the Census of 1971, only 135,000 claimed Polish as their mother tongue and only

[26] N. Tanner, 'Speech and society among the Indonesian elite' in J. B. Pride and J. Homes (eds.), *Sociolinguistics* (Harmondsworth 1972), p. 127.

70,000 actually spoke it at home. The figures for the Ukrainians are comparable.[27]

In short, ethnic and linguistic nationalism may be on divergent routes, and both may now be losing their dependence on national state power. What may be called non-competing multi-lingualism or bilingualism analogous to the relation in the nineteenth century between official culture/state languages and subaltern dialects and patois, already seems common. The tendency to give vernaculars official status by the side of national/international culture-languages – Spanish in Latin America, French in parts of Africa, more generally English (which is the medium of secondary education in the Philippines and is, or until the revolution was, in Ethiopia) – should not mislead.[28] The model may no longer be a struggle for supremacy, as in Quebec, but a division of function, as in Paraguay, where both Spanish and Guaraní are taught and spoken by the urban elite, but Spanish is the medium of communication for all written purposes other than, perhaps, *belles lettres*. It is unlikely that Quechua, given equal official status in Peru since 1975, will seek to replace Spanish as the language of, say, daily press and university, or that, whatever official standing of some vernacular in African or Pacific British ex-colonies, the way to education, wealth and power will not continue to pass through English.[29]

This speculation brings us to some concluding reflections on the future of nations and nationalism.

[27] Robert F. Harney, '"So great a heritage as ours." Immigration and the survival of the Canadian polity' (*Daedalus*, vol. 117/4, Fall 1988), pp. 68–9, 83–4.

[28] On the significance of English, see François Grosjean, *Life with Two Languages* (Cambridge MA 1982), where it is stated that in only 38 states had English no official standing whatever in 1974. In 20 (non-English-speaking) countries was it the only official language, in another 36 it was used in courts and as principal medium of instruction in schools (p. 114). For the problems of competing with English, see also L. Harries, 'The nationalization of Swahili in Kenya' (*Language and Society*, 5, 1976, pp. 153–64).

[29] In some ways the modern (oral and visual) mass media 'which do not require the arduous steps of literacy' (David Riesman, Introduction to Daniel Lerner, *The Passing of Traditional Society* (New York 1958), p. 4, have diminished the utilitarian case for vernacular literature for the monoglot, who is now no longer cut off from information about the wider world. The transistor radio has been the chief agent of this cultural revolution. See e.g. Howard Handelman, *Struggle in the Andes: Peasant Political Mobilization in Peru* (Austin, 1974), p. 58. My attention was first drawn to this revolution in the early 1960s by the late José María Arguedas, who pointed to the multiplication of local radio broadcasts in Quechua for the immigrants to Lima, usually operating at the time when only the labouring Indians were awake.

CHAPTER 6

Nationalism in the late twentieth century

I

Since this book was first published in early 1990, more new nation-states have been formed, or are in the process of formation, than at any time in this century. The break-up of the USSR and Yugoslavia have so far added sixteen to the number of internationally recognized sovereign entities, and there is no immediately foreseeable limit to the further advance of national separatism. All states are today officially 'nations', all political agitations are apt to be against foreigners, whom practically all states harry and seek to keep out. It may therefore seem wilful blindness to conclude this book with some reflections on the *decline* of nationalism as a vector of historical change, compared to its role in the century from the 1830s to the end of World War II.

It would indeed be absurd to deny that the collapse of the Soviet Union and the regional and international system of which, as one super-power, it was a pillar for some forty years marks a profound, and probably permanent, historical change, whose implications are, at the time of writing, entirely obscure. However, they introduce *new* elements into the history of nationalism only insofar as the break-up of the USSR in 1991 went far beyond the (temporary) break-up of Tsarist Russia in 1918–20, which was largely confined to its European and transcaucasian regions.[1] For, basically, the 'national questions' of 1989–92 are not new. They belong overwhelmingly to the traditional home of national causes, Europe. There is so far no sign of serious political

---

[1] Even so, the 'pan-Turanian' ambitions of Turkey in central Asia, fortunately pursued not by Kemal Atatürk but by his defeated political rivals like Enver Pasha, and the Japanese interest in Russia's Pacific Far East, anticipate themes of which a lot more will be heard in the 1990s.

separatism in the Americas, at least south of the US–Canadian border. There is little sign that the Islamic world, or at least the rising fundamentalist movements within it, are concerned with multiplying state frontiers. They want to return to the true faith of the founders. In fact, it is hard to see how separatism could interest them as such. Separatist agitations (largely terrorist) are clearly shaking corners of the South Asian sub-continent, but so far (except for the secession of Bangladesh) the successor states have held together. In fact, the post-colonial national regimes not only in this region still overwhelmingly accept the nineteenth-century traditions of nationalism, both liberal and revolutionary-democratic. Gandhi and the Nehrus, Mandela and Mugabe, the late Zulfikhar Bhutto and Bandaranaike, and, I would wager, the imprisoned leader of Burma (Myanmar), Ms Aung-San Su Xi, were or are not nationalists in the sense of Landsbergis and Tudjman. They are or were on exactly the same wavelength as Massimo d'Azeglio: nation-builders not nation-splitters (see p. 44 above).

Many more post-colonial African states may collapse into chaos and disorder, as has recently happened to some; including – though one hopes not – South Africa. Yet it is to stretch the sense of words to see the collapse of Somalia or Ethiopia as being brought about by the inalienable right of peoples to form independent sovereign nation-states. Friction between ethnic groups and conflicts, often bloody ones, between them, are older than the political programme of nationalism, and will survive it.

In Europe the outburst of separatist nationalism has even more specific historical roots in the twentieth century. The eggs of Versailles and Brest Litowsk are still hatching. Essentially the permanent collapse of the Habsburg and Turkish empires and the short-lived collapse of the Tsarist Russian empire produced the same set of national successor-states with the same sort of problems, insoluble in the long run, except by mass murder or forced mass migration. The explosive issues of 1988–92 were those created in 1918–21. Czechs were then yoked to Slovaks for the first time, and Slovenes (formerly Austrian) with Croats (once the military frontier against the Turks) and – across a millennium of divergent history, with the Serbs who belonged to Orthodoxy and the Ottoman empire. The doubling of Romania's size produced friction between its component nationalities. The victorious Germans set up three small Baltic nation-states for which there was no historical precedent at all, and – at least in Estonia and Latvia – no noticeable national demand.[2] They were maintained in being by the Allies as part of the 'quarantine belt' against Bolshevist Russia. At the moment of Russia's greatest weakness, German influence encouraged the setting up of an independent Georgian and Armenian state, and the British the autonomy of oil-rich Azerbaijan. Transcaucasian nationalism (if such a term is not too strong for the grassroots anti-Armenian resentment of the Azeri Turks) had not been a serious political issue before 1917: the Armenians were, for obvious reasons, worried about Turkey rather than Moscow, the Georgians supported a nominally Marxist all-Russian party (the Mensheviks) as their national party. However, unlike the Habsburgs and the Ottoman empire, the multi-national Russian empire survived for another three generations, thanks to the October Revolution and Hitler. Victory in the Civil War eliminated the possibility of Ukrainian separatism, and the recovery of Transcaucasia eliminated local nationalisms, though – since it was achieved partly through negotiations with Kemalist Turkey – it left a few sensitive issues for future nationalist resentment, notably the problem of the Armenian enclave of Mountain Karabakh in Azerbaijan.[3] In 1939–40 the USSR in practice recovered all that Tsarist Russia had lost, except for Finland (which had been allowed to secede peacefully by Lenin) and former Russian Poland.

The simplest way to describe the apparent explosion of separatism in 1988–92 is thus as 'unfinished business of 1918–21'. Conversely, ancient and deep-seated national questions

[2] This emerges from the voting figures for the Russian Constituent Assembly in November 1917, analysed by O. Radkey, *Russia Goes to the Polls* (Ithaca 1989).

[3] The Armenians illustrate the difficulties of tying nationality to territory. The present Republic of Armenia (with Yerevan as its capital) had not been of particular significance to that unhappy people before 1914. 'Armenia' was primarily in Turkey. The Russian Armenians were both a rural transcaucasian people, and a substantial urban population – probably the majority of the population in Tbilisi and Baku – as well as a large national and international diaspora. 'Armenia', one might say, was what was left when Armenians had been exterminated or expelled from everywhere else.

which actually seemed dangerous to European chanceries *before* 1914, have not proved explosive. It was not 'the Macedonian Question', well known to scholars as leading to battles between rival experts in a half-dozen fields at international congresses, which provoked the collapse of Yugoslavia. On the contrary, the Macedonian Peoples Republic did its best to stay out of the Serb-Croat imbroglio, until Yugoslavia was actually collapsing, and all its components, in sheer self-defence, had to look after themselves. (Characteristically enough, its official recognition has been hitherto sabotaged by Greece, which had annexed large parts of Macedonian territory in 1913). Similarly, the only part of Tsarist Russia which contained a genuine national movement before 1917, though not a separatist one, was Ukraine. Yet Ukraine remained relatively quiet while Baltic and Caucasian republics demanded secession, remained under the control of the local Communist Party leadership, and did not resign itself to separation until after the failed coup of August 1991 destroyed the USSR.

Moreover, the definition of 'the nation' and its aspirations which, paradoxically, Lenin shared with Woodrow Wilson, automatically created the fracture lines along which multi-national units constructed by communist states were to break, just as the colonial frontiers of 1880–1950 were to form the state frontiers of post-colonial states, there being no others available. (Most of their inhabitants did not know what frontiers were, or took no notice of them.) In the Soviet Union we can go further: it was the communist regime which deliberately set out to *create* ethno-linguistic territorial 'national administrative units', i.e. 'nations' in the modern sense, where none had previously existed or been thought of, as among the Asian Moslem peoples – or, for that matter, the Bielorussians. The idea of Soviet Republics based on Kazakh, Kirghiz, Uzbek, Tadjik and Turkmen 'nations' was a theoretical construct of Soviet intellectuals rather than a primordial aspiration of any of those central-Asian peoples.[4]

The idea that these peoples, whether because of 'national oppression' or Islamic consciousness, were putting the Soviet

[4] Cf. Graham Smith (ed.), *The Nationalities Question in the Soviet Union*, part IV: 'Muslim Central Asia' (London and New York 1990), e.g. pp. 215, 230, 262.

system under the intolerable strain which led to its collapse seems to be merely another expression for some western observers' justified horror of the Soviet system and their belief that it could not last long. In fact, central Asia remained politically inert until the collapse of the Union, except for some pogroms of the national minorities whom Stalin had tended to banish into those remote regions. Such nationalism as is developing in those republics is a post-Soviet phenomenon.

The changes in and after 1989 were thus essentially not due to national tensions, which remained under effective control even where they genuinely existed, as in Poland and among the Yugoslav peoples, so long as central party operated, but primarily to the decision of the Soviet regime to reform itself, and in doing so (a) to withdraw military support from its satellite regimes, (b) to undermine the central command and authority structure which allowed it to operate, and consequently also (c) to undermine the foundations of even the independent communist regimes in Balkan Europe. Nationalism was the beneficiary of these developments but not, in any serious sense, an important factor in bringing them about. Hence, indeed, the universal amazement at the sudden collapse of the eastern regimes, which had been entirely unexpected, even in Poland, where a deeply unpopular regime had shown that it could keep a massively organized opposition movement under control for almost a decade.

One has only to compare the German unifications of 1871 and 1990 to note the differences. The first was seen as the long-awaited achievement of an objective which, in one way or another, was the central concern of everyone interested in politics in the German lands, even those who wanted to resist it. Even Marx and Engels felt that Bismarck '(tut) jetzt, wie im 1866, ein Stück von unserer Arbeit in *seiner* Weise'[5]. But until the autumn of 1989 none of the major parties in the Federal Republic had paid more than lip-service to the creation of a single German state for many years. This was not only because it was obviously not practicable until Gorbachev made it so, but because nationalist

[5] Engels to Marx, 15 August 1870 (Marx–Engels, *Werke* vol. 33 (Berlin 1966), p. 40.

organizations and agitations were politically marginal. Nor did the desire for German unity motivate the political opposition in the DDR, or the ordinary East Germans, whose mass exodus precipitated the collapse of the regime. No doubt, among all their doubts and uncertainties about the future, most Germans welcome the unification of the two Germanies, but its very suddenness, and the patent lack of serious preparation for it, demonstrate that, whatever the public rhetoric, it was the by-product of unexpected events outside Germany.

As for the USSR, it collapsed not, as some Sovietologists had predicted, under its internal national tensions[6], undeniable as these were, but under its economic difficulties. *Glasnost*, which the reform-communist leadership of the country regarded as a necessary condition of *perestroika*, reintroduced freedom of debate and agitation and also weakened the centralized command system on which both regime and society rested. The failure of *perestroika*, i.e. the growing deterioration of living conditions for ordinary citizens, undermined faith in the all-Union government, made responsible for it, and indeed encouraged or even imposed regional and local solutions to problems. It is safe to say that before Gorbachev no Soviet republic envisaged secession from the USSR except the Baltic states, and even there independence was then obviously a dream. Nor can it be argued that only fear and coercion kept the USSR together, though it undoubtedly helped to stop ethnic and communal tensions in mixed regions from degenerating into mutual violence, as they have subsequently done. Indeed, in the long Brezhnev era local and regional autonomy was by no means illusory. Moreover, as the Russians never ceased to complain, most of the other republics were rather better off than the inhabitants of the RSFSR. The national disintegration of the USSR, and incidentally of its constituent republics, almost all effectively multinational, is plainly more the consequence of events in Moscow than their cause.

Paradoxically, the case for nationalist movements with the power to undermine existing regimes is rather stronger in the west, where such agitations disrupt some of the most ancient

---

[6] Helène Carrère d'Encausse, *L'empire éclaté* (Paris 1978); *idem, La gloire des nations, ou La Fin de l'empire sovietique* (Paris 1990).

nation-states: the United Kingdom, Spain, France, even in a more modest way Switzerland, not to mention Canada. Whether complete secession of Quebec, Scotland or some other region will actually take place is at present (1992) a matter for speculation. Outside the former Euro-Soviet red belt, successful secessions since World War II are extremely rare, and peaceful separations virtually unknown. Nevertheless, the possible secession of Scotland or Quebec can today be discussed as a realistic possibility, which it was not twenty-five years ago.

II

Yet nationalism, however inescapable, is simply no longer the historical force it was in the era between the French Revolution and the end of imperialist colonialism after World War II.

In the 'developed' world of the nineteenth century, the building of a number of 'nations' which combined nation-state and national economy was plainly a central fact of historical transformation and seen to be such. In the 'dependent' world of the first half of the twentieth century, and for obvious reasons especially in the colonized part of it, movements for national liberation and independence were the main agents for the political emancipation of most of the globe, that is to say for an elimination of imperial administration and, more significantly, direct military domination by the imperial powers, a situation that would have appeared almost inconceivable even half a century ago.[7] While, as we have seen, these national liberation movements in the Third World were in theory modelled on the nationalism of the west, in practice the states they attempted to construct were, as we have also seen, generally the opposite of the ethnically and linguistically homogeneous entities which came to be seen as the standard form of 'nation-state' in the west. Nevertheless, even in this respect they were *de facto* more like than unlike the western nationalism of the liberal era. Both were typically unificatory as

---

[7] Wars waged on a considerable scale by super-powers using all except their nuclear (and chemical/biological) weaponry, have been spectacularly less successful than pre-World War II history would have led one to suppose – e.g. in Korea and Vietnam.

well as emancipatory, though in the latter case the reach exceeded the grasp more frequently than in the earlier.

The current phase of essentially separatist and divisive 'ethnic' group assertion has no such positive programme or prospect. This is demonstrated by the mere fact that, for want of any genuine historical project, it attempts to recreate the original Mazzinian model of the ethnically and linguistically homogeneous territorial nation-state ('every nation a state – only one state for each nation'). This is unrealistic as a matter of observation – and, as we have seen (pp. 160–2) it is also completely out of line with late twentieth-century linguistic and cultural developments.

It is, as we shall see, entirely irrelevant to the problem of the late twentieth century, for which it provides no general solution, or, except by a rare and happy accident, no local solutions. It merely complicates the task of addressing these problems.

Nevertheless, the force of the sentiments which leads groups of 'us' to give themselves an 'ethnic'/linguistic identity against the foreign and threatening 'them' cannot be denied. Least of all in the late twentieth century, when a crazy war has been fought, to widespread patriotic enthusiasm, by an imaginary British 'we' against a symbolic Argentinian 'they' over some South Atlantic bog and rough pasture, and when xenophobia has become the most widespread mass ideology in the world. However, xenophobia, readily shading into racism, a more general phenomenon in Europe and North America in the 1990s even than it was in the days of fascism, provides even less of an historic programme than Mazzinian nationalism. Indeed, it rarely even pretends to be more than a cry of anguish or fury. Moreover, even the romantic sympathisers with the sovereign independence of selected small peoples are rarely found insisting on the Janus-like characteristics of M. Le Pen's National Front. It has one face, and most of us would prefer it to have none.

What is the nature of this cry of distress or fury? Time and again such movements of ethnic identity seem to be reactions of weakness and fear, attempts to erect barricades to keep at bay the forces of the modern world, similar in this respect to the resentment of Prague Germans pressed into a corner by Czech immigration rather than to that of the advancing Czechs. This is not only the case of small linguistic communities vulnerable to quite modest demographic changes, such as the thinly populated hills and coasts of Welsh-speaking Wales, or Estonia, whose one million or so Estonian speakers would in any case place it at the very lower limit of populations capable of maintaining a modern linguistic culture at all levels. It is not surprising that the most explosive issue in both areas is the uncontrolled immigration of monoglot speakers of the English or Russian language respectively. However, similar reactions are to be found among much larger populations whose linguistic/cultural existence is not, or does not seem, in any way threatened. The most absurd example of this is the movement, which acquired political clout in some states of the USA in the late 1980s, to declare English as the only *official* language of the US. For while hispanophone immigration is indeed sufficiently massive in some parts of the USA to make it desirable, and sometimes necessary, to address this public in its own language, the idea that the supremacy of English in the USA is, or is likely to be, in jeopardy, is political paranoia.

What fuels such defensive reactions, whether against real or imaginary threats, is a combination of international population movements with the ultra-rapid, fundamental and unprecedented socio-economic transformations so characteristic of the third quarter of our century. French Canada may illustrate this combination of an intensified petty-bourgeois linguistic nationalism with mass future shock. On paper the French language, spoken as a native tongue by a quarter of Canada's population, a community about half the size of Canada's native anglophones, and buttressed by the official bilingualism of the federation, the international backing of French culture and upwards of 130,000 students in francophone universities (1988), seems safe enough. And yet the stance of Quebec nationalism is that of a people in headlong retreat before historical forces which threaten to overwhelm it; a movement whose very advances are viewed in terms of potential weakness rather than as success.[8] Indeed, Quebec

---

[8] Léon Dion, 'The mystery of Quebec' (*Daedalus*, vol. 117/4, Fall 1988, pp. 283–318) is a good example: e.g. 'This new generation does not show the same desire to stand up for the French language as its elders did, partly because it feels protected by . . . the French Language Charter . . . and partly because Canada's Anglophones and speakers of other languages are becoming more tolerant of French' (p. 310).

nationalism has *de facto* abandoned the large francophone minorities in New Brunswick and Ontario in order to barricade itself within an autonomous or even separatist province of Quebec. The sense of the *Canadiens'* insecurity is indicated by the belief that Canada's now official 'multiculturalism' is simply a plot aimed at 'crushing *Francophonie's* special needs under the political weight of multiculture',[9] and it is, of course, reinforced by the patent preference of the 3.5 million post-1945 immigrants to have their children educated in English, which opens far wider career perspectives in North America than the French language does. Yet on paper the threat of immigration is less in francophone than in anglophone Canada, since between 1946 and 1971 only about 15% of newcomers settled in Quebec.

What lies behind the fear and insecurity of French Canadians is patently a social cataclysm which is indicated by the dramatically sudden collapse of the Catholic Church in what had for so long been a conservative, Catholic, clerical, child-producing society not only among the farmers but among townspeople. It seems that in the course of the 1960s church attendance in the province dropped from well over 80% to 25%, while the Quebec birth-rate has become one of the lowest in Canada.[10] Whatever lies behind such a startling transformation in Québécois mores could hardly fail to create a disoriented generation hungry for new certitudes to replace the collapsing old ones. It has even been argued that the rise of militant separatism was a surrogate for the lost traditional Catholicism. The guess – it would hardly lend itself to convincing verification or falsification – is not implausible, at all events for someone like this author who has observed an entirely non-traditional, indeed, in its liking for pubs and alcohol, an entirely counter-traditional, Welsh nationalist militancy emerging among a younger generation in one part of North Wales; as the chapels have emptied, the preacher and amateur scholar is no longer the community's voice, and the decline of a public commitment to temperance has removed the most obvious

---

9 R.F. Harney, '"So great a heritage as ours." Immigration and the survival of the Canadian polity' (*Daedalus*, vol. 117/4, Fall 1988), p. 75.

10 Gérard Pelletier, 'Quebec: different but in step with North America' (*Daedalus*, vol. 117/4, Fall 1988, p. 271); Harney, '"So great a heritage as ours"', p. 62.

way in which individuals demonstrated their membership of a puritan culture and community.

Massive population mobility naturally intensifies this disorientation, as do economic shifts, some not unconnected with the rise of local nationalism.[11] Wherever we live in an urbanized society, we encounter strangers: uprooted men and women who remind us of the fragility or the drying up of our own families' roots.

In the case of the western ex-communist societies, this social disorientation is intensified by the collapse of life as most of the inhabitants have known it and learned to live it. Nationalism or ethnicity – to quote Miroslav Hroch, writing about contemporary central Europe – is 'a substitute for factors of integration in a disintegrating society. When society fails, the nation appears as the ultimate guarantee.'[12]

In the socialist and ex-socialist economies, governed essentially, in Janos Kornai's phrase, by the 'economics of shortage'[13] ethnicity, like kinship, and other networks of potential reciprocity or patronage, already had a more concrete function. It gave 'members of the same group an edge over claimants from "other" groups'[14] for scarce resources; and, conversely, defined the 'others' whose claims came second to 'ours'. Where the former

[11] Quebec nationalism in the 1970s produced a large business exodus from Montreal, hitherto both the largest Canadian city and the centre of Canadian business, to the advantage of Toronto. 'The city is coming to grips with a more modest destiny as a regional center for Quebec and eastern Canada.' Even so, the notably smaller impact of minority languages on Montreal than on other cities does not seem to have lessened linguistic militancy. In Toronto and Vancouver white Anglo Protestants no longer form the majority of the population, whereas in Montreal French Canadians form 66% of the population. Cf. Alan F. J. Artibise, 'Canada as an urban nation' (*Daedalus*, vol. 117/4, Fall 1988, pp. 237–64).

[12] M. Hroch, 'Nationale Bewegungen früher und heute. Ein europäischer Vergleich' (unpublished paper 1991) p. 14. Hroch, I need hardly add, insists that the apparent revival of old national agitation in east-central Europe is not (usually) the continuation of an old nationalist tradition, but a sort of re-invented tradition, an 'Illusion der Reprise'. 'As e.g. the nineteenth-century Czech patriots dressed up as Hussite fighters, so today the patriots of contemporary east-European national movements dress up as nineteenth-century patriots' (p. 11).

[13] J. Kornai, *The Economics of Shortage* (Amsterdam 1980).

[14] Katherine Verdery, unpublished draft on 'Nationalism and the "Road to Democracy"', p. 36.

nation-wide society and government disintegrates entirely, as in the ex-USSR, the 'outsider' is helpless. 'Towns, [administrative districts], republics, are fencing themselves off in defence against migratory demand'; local food cards divide the market into separate mini-economies 'and protect resources... from "aliens"'.[15]

However, in post-communist societies ethnic or national identity is above all a device for defining the community of the innocent and identifying the guilty who are responsible for 'our' predicament; especially once communist regimes are no longer there to function as scapegoats. As someone has said about Czechoslovakia: 'The country is swarming with otherness. Everyone's first finger is sore from pointing at Others and calling them names.'[16] But this is a universal rather than merely a post-communist situation. 'They' can be, must be, blamed for all the grievances, uncertainties and disorientations which so many of us feel after forty years of the most rapid and profound upheavals of human life in recorded history. And who are 'they'? Obviously, and virtually by definition, those who are 'not us' – the strangers who, by their very alienness, are enemies: present aliens, past aliens, even purely notional aliens as in Poland where anti-Semitism continues to explain Polish ills in the total absence of Jews. If the foreigners with their knavish tricks did not exist, it would be necessary to invent them. But at the end of our millennium they rarely have to be invented: they are universally present and recognizable within our cities, as public dangers and agents of pollution, universally present, beyond our borders and control, but hating and conspiring against us. In the unhappier countries they are, and have always been, our neighbours, but our very co-existence with 'them' now undermines the exclusive certainties of belonging to *our* people and *our* country.

What, if anything have such ethnic/nationalist reactions in common with the recent rise of 'fundamentalism' in many parts of the globe, which has been described as appealing to 'people who cannot tolerate random and haphazard existence and

<hr />

[15] Caroline Humphrey, '"Icebergs", barter and the mafia in provincial Russia' (*Anthropology Today*, 7(2) 1991, pp. 8–13.
[16] Andrew Lass, quoted by Verdery, 'Nationalism and the "Road to Democracy"', p. 52.

unexplained conditions (and thus) often converge on those who offer most complete, inclusive and extravagant world views'.[17] It is seen as 'always reactive, reactionary'. 'Some force, tendency, or enemy must be perceived as potentially or actually eroding, corroding, or endangering one's movement and what it holds dear.' The 'fundamentals' that fundamentalism stresses 'always come from some earlier, presumably primal and pure . . . stage in one's own sacred history'. They 'are used for setting boundaries, for attracting one's kind and alienating other kinds, for demarcating'. And they conform to George Simmel's old observation that

> Groups, and especially minorities, which live in conflict . . . often reject approaches or tolerance from the other side. The closed nature of their opposition, without which they cannot fight on, would be blurred . . . Within certain groups, it may even be a piece of political wisdom to see to it that there be some enemies in order for the unity of the members to be effective and for the group to remain conscious of this unity as its vital interest.[18]

The similarities with a number of recent ethnic/nationalist phenomena are evident, especially where these are themselves linked with, or seek to re-establish links with, a group-specific religious faith – as among (Christian) Armenians opposing (Muslim) Azeri Turks, or in the recent and markedly Old Testament phase of Likud Zionism in Israel, so different from the aggressively secularist, and even anti-religious, ideology of the movement's founders.[19] It seems probable that the visiting extraterrestrial would see ethnic exclusiveness and conflict, xenophobia and fundamentalism as aspects of the same general phenomenon. Nevertheless, there is one important distinction. Fundamentalism, whatever its religious version, provides a

---

[17] Martin E. Marty, 'Fundamentalism as a social phenomenon' (*Bulletin, The American Academy of Arts and Sciences*, 42/2 November 1988, pp. 15–29).
[18] *Ibid.* pp. 20–1.
[19] It is not clear how far genuinely traditional Jewish religious orthodoxy, which is, of course, opposed to the establishment of a state for all the Jews in Israel before the return of the Messiah, has attenuated or dropped its opposition to Zionism. At all events Jewish settlers in the occupied territories, advertising the paraphernalia of religious practice, must not be automatically identified with the other (and probably growing) wing of Jewish fundamentalism which seeks to reimpose the full rigours of ritual on a secularized society.

detailed and concrete programme for both individuals and society, even if it is one selected from texts or traditions whose suitability for the late twentieth century is not obvious. What the alternative to the present, degenerate and evil, society is, presents no immediate problem: women are once again hidden from sight, or married ones have their hair shorn; thieves are once again punished by having hands or legs cut off; alcohol, or whatever else is ritually prohibited, is banned; and Koran, or Bible, or whatever constitutes the authoritative compendium of eternal wisdom, provides complete practical and moral guidance on all subjects, as interpreted by those whose business it is to do so. The call of ethnicity or language provides no guidance to the future at all, even when new states are formed on the basis of these criteria. It is merely a protest against the status quo or, more precisely, against 'the others' who threaten the ethnically defined group. For, unlike fundamentalism which, however narrow and sectarian in its actual appeal, draws its strength from the claim to *universal* truth, theoretically applicable to all, nationalism by definition excludes from its purview all who do not belong to its own 'nation', i.e. the vast majority of the human race. Moreover, while fundamentalism can, at least to some extent, appeal to what remains of genuine custom and tradition or past practice as embodied in religious practice, as we have seen nationalism in itself is either hostile to the real ways of the past, or arises on its ruins.

On the other hand nationalism has one advantage over fundamentalism. Its very vagueness and lack of programmatic content gives it a potentially universal support within its own community. Except in genuinely traditional societies reacting against the initial impact of modernity, fundamentalism appears to be, universally, a minority phenomenon. This may be concealed either by the power of regimes which impose it on their peoples, whether they like it or not (as in Iran), or by the capacity of fundamentalist minorities to mobilize strategically placed votes effectively in democratic systems, as in Israel and the USA. But it may be taken for granted that nowadays the 'moral majority' is not a real (electoral) majority, just as a 'moral victory' (the traditional euphemism for defeat) is not a real victory. Yet ethnicity *can* mobilize the vast majority of its community

– provided its appeal remains sufficiently vague or irrelevant. There is little doubt that most non-Israeli Jews in the world are 'for Israel'; that most Armenians support the transfer of Nagorno-Karabakh from Azerbaijan to Armenia; and that most Flemings do their best not to speak French. Of course this unity crumbles as soon as the national cause is identified not with generalities, but with much more divisive specifics: not with 'Israel' in general, but with the policies of Begin, Shamir or Sharon; not with Wales in general but with the supremacy of the Welsh language; not with Flemishness as against Frenchness, but with a specific Flemish nationalist party.[20] To this extent movements or parties specifically committed to a 'nationalist' programme, mostly separatist, are likely to be the expression of sectional or minority interests, or to be politically fluctuating and unstable. The rapid changes in the membership and electoral fortunes of Scots, Welsh, Québécois and no doubt other nationalist parties of the past twenty years illustrate this instability. Such parties, as always, like to equate themselves with the sense of collective separateness, hostility to 'them' and the 'imagined community' which may be almost universally felt in their 'nation', but they are very unlikely to be the only expressions of such a national consensus.

III

The anguish and disorientation which finds expression in this hunger to belong, and hence in the 'politics of identity' – not necessarily national identity – is no more a moving force of history than the hunger for 'law and order' which is an equally understandable response to another aspect of social disorganization. Both are symptoms of sickness rather than diagnoses, let alone therapy. Nevertheless, they create the illusion of nations and nationalism as an irresistibly rising force ready for the third millennium. This force is further exaggerated by the semantic illusion which today turns all states officially into 'nations' (and members of the United Nations), even when they are patently not. Consequently, all movements seeking territorial autonomy tend to

[20] From 1958 to 1974 the three main Belgian parties (in their Flemish versions) never totalled less than 81.2% of the vote in Flanders. See A. Zolberg in M. Esman (ed.), *Ethnic Conflict in the Western World* (Ithaca 1977), p. 118.

think of themselves as establishing 'nations' even when this is plainly not the case; and all movements for regional, local or even sectional interests against central power and state bureaucracy will, if they possibly can, put on the national costume, preferably in its ethnic-linguistic styles. Nations and nationalism therefore appear more influential and omnipresent than they are. Aruba plans to break away from the rest of the Netherlands West Indies, because it does not like to be yoked to Curaçao. Does that make it a nation? Or Curaçao, or Surinam, which is already a member of the United Nations? The Cornish are fortunate to be able to paint their regional discontents in the attractive colours of Celtic tradition, which makes them so much more viable, even though it leads some of them to reinvent a language not spoken for 200 years, and even though the only popular public tradition with genuine roots in the county is Wesleyan Methodism. They are luckier than, say, Merseyside, which can mobilize in defence of the equally or more hard-hit local interests only the memory of the Beatles, of generations of Scouse comedians, and the proud tradition of its rival football teams, while taking care to keep away from anything that reminds its inhabitants too obviously of the divisive colours Orange and Green. Merseyside cannot blow a national trumpet. Cornwall can. But are the situations which produce discontent in one area substantially different from those which do so in the other?

In fact, the rise of separatist and ethnic agitations is partly due to the fact that, contrary to common belief, the principle of state-creation since World War II, unlike that after World War I, had nothing to do with Wilsonian national self-determination. It reflected three forces: decolonization, revolution and, of course, the intervention of outside powers.

Decolonization meant that, by and large, independent states were created out of existing areas of colonial administration, within their colonial frontiers. These had, obviously, been drawn without any reference to, or sometimes even without the knowledge of, their inhabitants and therefore had no national or even protonational significance for their populations; except for colonial-educated and westernized native minorities of varying, but generally exigous, size. Alternatively, where such territories were too small and scattered, as in many colonized archipelagos, they were combined or broken up according to convenience or local politics. Hence the constant, and eventually often vain, calls of the leaders of such new states to surmount 'tribalism', 'communalism', or whatever forces were made responsible for the failure of the new inhabitants of the Republic of X to feel themselves to be primarily patriotic citizens of X rather than members of some other collectivity.

In short, the appeal of most such 'nations' and 'national movements' was the opposite of the nationalism which seeks to bond together those deemed to have common ethnicity, language, culture, historical past, and the rest. In effect it was *internationalist*. The internationalism of the leaders and cadres of national liberation movements in the Third World is more obvious where such movements played a leading part in the liberation of their countries than where countries were decolonized from above, for the post-independence breakdown of what previously operated, or seemed to operate, as a united movement of 'the people' is more dramatic. Sometimes, as in India, the unity of the movement has already cracked before independence.

More commonly, soon after independence tensions develop between the component parts of the independence movement (e.g. in Algeria, Arabs and Berbers), between peoples actively involved in it and those not, or between the emancipated non-sectional secularism of the leaders and the feelings of the masses. However, while the cases where multi-ethnic and multi-communal states have fractured, or are close to breaking, naturally attract most attention – the partition of the Indian subcontinent in 1947, the splitting of Pakistan, the demands for Tamil separatism in Sri Lanka – it should never be forgotten that these are special cases in a world where multi-ethnic and multi-communal states are the norm. What was written almost thirty years ago remains substantially true: 'Countries including many language and culture groups, like most African and Asian ones, have not split up, and those taking in only part of a single language group, like the Arab ones and North Africa, have . . . not united.'[21]

[21] John H. Kautsky, 'An essay in the policies of development' in John H. Kautsky (ed.), *Political Change in Underdeveloped Countries: Nationalism and Communism* (New York–London 1962), p. 35.

The intervention of outside powers, finally, has obviously been non-nationalist in both motivation and effect, except by pure accident. This is so evident that it does not require illustration. However, so also has been the impact of social revolution, though rather less effectively. Social revolutionaries have been keenly aware of the force of nationalism, as well as ideologically committed to national autonomy, even when it is not actually wanted, as among the Lusatian Slavs, whose language is slowly retreating, in spite of the admirable efforts of the German Democratic Republic during its period of independent existence to foster it. The *only* form of constitutional arrangements which socialist states have taken seriously since 1917 are formulas for national federation and autonomy. While other constitutional texts, where they existed at all, have for long periods been purely notional, national autonomy has never ceased to have a certain operational reality. However, inasmuch as such regimes do not, at least in theory, identify with any of their constituent national-ities[22] and regard the interests of each of them as secondary to a higher common purpose, they are non-national.

Hence, as we can now see in melancholy retrospect, it was the great achievement of the communist regimes in multinational countries to limit the disastrous effects of nationalism within them. The Yugoslav revolution succeeded in preventing the nationalities within its state frontiers from massacring each other almost certainly for longer than ever before in their history, though this achievement has now unfortunately crumbled. The USSR's potential for national disruption, so long kept in check (except during World War II), is now patent. In fact, the 'discrimination' or even 'oppression' against which champions of various Soviet nationalities abroad used to protest, was far less[23] than the consequences of the withdrawal of Soviet power. Official Soviet anti-Semitism, which has undoubtedly been

[22] The deliberate policy of Romanization in Ceausescu's Romania is among the rare exceptions. It breaks with the elaborate arrangements for national autonomy which were instituted when the communists took power after World War II.
[23] This statement is not to be understood as condoning the mass transfer of entire populations on the grounds of their nationality that took place during the war. This cannot be condoned under any circumstances, except to save such populations from extermination.

observable since the foundation of the state of Israel in 1948, must be measured against the rise of popular anti-semitism since political mobilization (including that of reactionaries) became permitted again, not to mention the massacre of Jews on a considerable scale *by local elements* in the Baltic states and Ukraine as the Germans marched in but *before the systematic German killing of Jews began.*[24] Indeed, it may be argued that the current wave of ethnic or mini-ethnic agitations is a response to the overwhelmingly non-ethnic and non-nationalist principles of state formation in the greater part of the twentieth-century world. However, this does not mean that such ethnic reactions provide in any sense an alternative principle for the political restructuring of the world in the twenty-first century.

A third observation confirms this. 'The nation' today is visibly in the process of losing an important part of its old functions, namely that of constituting a territorially bounded 'national economy' which formed a building block in the larger 'world economy', at least in the developed regions of the globe. Since World War II, but especially since the 1960s, the role of 'national economies' has been undermined or even brought into question by the major transformations in the international division of labour, whose basic units are transnational or multinational enterprises of all sizes, and by the corresponding development of international centres and networks of economic transactions which are, for practical purposes, outside the control of state governments. The number of *intergovernmental* international organizations grew from 123 in 1951 through 280 in 1972 to 365 in 1984; the number of international *non-governmental* organizations from 832 through 2,173 in 1972, more than doubling to 4,615 in the next twelve years.[25] Probably the only functioning 'national economy' of the late twentieth century is the Japanese.

Nor have the old (developed) 'national economies' been replaced as the major building-blocks of the world system only by larger associations or federations of 'nation-states' such as the European Economic Community, and collectively controlled

[24] Arno Mayer, *Why Did the Heavens not Darken? The 'Final Solution' in History* (New York 1989), pp. 257–62.
[25] David Held, 'Farewell nation state' (*Marxism Today*, December 1988), p. 15.

international entities like the International Monetary Fund, even though the emergence of these is also a symptom of the retreat of the world of 'national economies'. Important parts of the system of international transactions, such as the Eurodollar market, are outside any control whatever.

All this has, of course, been made possible both by technological revolutions in transport and communication, and by the lengthy period of free movements of the factors of production over a vast area of the globe which has developed since World War II. This has also led to the massive wave of international and intercontinental migration, the largest since the decades before 1914, which has, incidentally, both aggravated inter-communal frictions, notably in the form of racism, and made a world of national territories 'belonging' exclusively to the natives who keep strangers in their place, even less of a realistic option for the twenty-first century than it was for the twentieth. At present we are living through a curious combination of the technology of the late twentieth century, the free trade of the nineteenth, and the rebirth of the sort of interstitial centres characteristic of world trade in the Middle Ages. City states like Hong Kong and Singapore revive, extraterritorial 'industrial zones' multiply inside technically sovereign nation-states like Hanseatic Steelyards, and so do offshore tax-havens in otherwise valueless islands whose only function is, precisely, to remove economic transactions from the control of nation-states. The ideology of nations and nationalism is irrelevant to any of these developments.

This does not mean that the economic functions of states have been diminished or are likely to fade away. On the contrary, in both capitalist and non-capitalist states they have grown, in spite of a tendency in both camps to encourage private or other non-state enterprise in the 1980s. Quite apart from the continued importance of state direction, planning and management even in countries dedicated in theory to neo-liberalism, the sheer weight of what public revenue and expenditure represent in the economies of states, but above all their growing role as agents of substantial redistributions of the social income by means of fiscal and welfare mechanisms, have probably made the national state a more central factor in the lives of the world's inhabitants than before. National economies, however, undermined by the trans-national economy, coexist and intertwine with it. However, except for the most self-sealed at one end – and how many of these are left after even Burma appears to consider re-entering the world? – and perhaps Japan at the other extreme, the old 'national economy' is not what it was. Even the USA, which in the 1980s still seemed sufficiently vast and dominant to deal with its economic problems without taking any notice of anyone else, at the end of that decade became aware that it 'had ceded considerable control over its economy to foreign investors . . . [who] now hold the power to help keep the US economy growing, or to help plunge it into recession' (*The Wall Street Journal*, 5 December 1988, p. 1). As for all small and practically all medium-sized states their economies had plainly ceased to be autonomous, insofar as they had once been so.

Another observation also suggests itself. The basic political conflicts which are likely to decide the fate of the world today have little to do with nation-states, because for half a century there has not existed an international state system of the nineteenth-century European type.

Politically the post-1945 world was bi-polar, organized round two super-powers which may just be describable as jumbo-sized nations, but certainly not as parts of an international state system of the nineteenth century or pre-1939 type. At most, third-party states, whether aligned with a super-power or non-aligned, could act as a brake on superpower action, though there is no strong evidence that they did so to much effect. Moreover, as far as the USA was concerned – but vestigially this was probably also true of the USSR before the Gorbachev era – the basic conflict was ideological, the triumph of the 'right' ideology being equated with the supremacy of the appropriate super-power. Post-1945 world politics were basically the politics of revolution and counter-revolution, with national issues intervening only to underline or disturb the main theme. Admittedly this pattern broke down in 1989 when the USSR ceased to be a super-power; and indeed the model of a world divided by the October Revolution had ceased to have much relation to the realities of the late twentieth century for some time before then. The immediate result was to leave the world without any international system or principle of order, even though the remaining super-power attempted to impose itself singlehanded as the global policeman, a role probably beyond its, or any other single state's, economic and military power.

There is thus at present no system at all. That ethnic-linguistic separation provides no sort of basis for a stable, in the short run even for a roughly predictable, ordering of the globe is evident in 1992 from the merest glance at the large region situated between Vienna and Trieste in the west, and Vladivostock in the east. All maps for one fifth of the world's surface are uncertain and provisional. And the only thing clear even about its cartographic future is that it will depend on a handful of major players outside the region, except for Russia (which is likely to remain a political entity of some substance). They are major players precisely because they have not so far been disrupted by separatist agitations: Germany, Turkey, Iran, China, Japan and – at one remove – the USA.[26]

For a new 'Europe of nations', and still more a 'world of nations', would not even create an ensemble of independent and sovereign states. In military terms the independence of small states depends on an international order, whatever its nature, which protects them against rapacious stronger neighbours, as the Middle East immediately demonstrated after the ending of the super-power balance. Until a new international system emerges at least a third of the existing states – those with populations of two and a half million or less – have no effective guarantees of independence. The establishment of several additional small states would merely increase the number of insecure political entities. And when such a new international system emerges, the small and the weak will have as little real role in it as Oldenburg or Mecklenburg-Schwerin had over the politics of the German Federation in the nineteenth century. Economically, as we have seen, even much more powerful states depend on a global economy over which they have no control and which determines their internal affairs. A Latvian or Basque 'national' economy

[26] At the time of writing the European Community as such has not demonstrated an ability for collective action in international diplomacy, and the United Nations is an adjunct to US policy. This may, of course, not be a lasting situation.

separate from some larger entity of which it forms a part is as meaningless a concept as a Parisian economy considered in separation from France.

The most that could be claimed is that small states are today economically no less viable than larger states, given the decline of the 'national economy' before the transnational one. It may also be argued that 'regions' constitute more rational sub-units of large economic entities like the European Community than the historic states which are its official members. Both observations are correct, in my view, but they are logically unconnected. West European separatist nationalisms like the Scottish, Welsh, Basque or Catalan are today in favour of bypassing their national governments by appealing directly to Brussels as 'regions'. However, there is no reason to suppose that a smaller state *ipso facto* forms more of an economic region than a larger one (say Scotland than England) and conversely there is no reason why an economic region should *ipso facto* coincide with a potential political unit constituted according to ethnic-linguistic or historic criteria.[27] Moreover, when separatist small-nation movements see their best hope in establishing themselves as sub-units of a larger politico-economic entity (in this case the European Community) they are in practice abandoning the classical aim of such movements, which is to establish independent and sovereign nation-states.

However, the case against *Kleinstaaterei* today, at least in its ethnic-linguistic form, is not only that it provides no solution for the actual problems of our day, but that, insofar as it has the power to carry out its policies, it makes these problems more difficult. Cultural freedom and pluralism at present are almost certainly better safeguarded in large states which know themselves to be plurinational and pluricultural than in small ones pursuing the ideal of ethnic-linguistic and cultural homogeneity. It is far from surprising that the most immediate demand of Slovak nationalism in 1990 was to 'make Slovak the only official language and force the population of 600,000 ethnic Hungarians

---

[27] This should be clear from Sydney Pollard, *Peaceful Conquest: The Industrialization of Europe 1760–1970* (Oxford 1981), which treats its subject as 'essentially one of regions in a European context' (p. vii).

to use only Slovak in dealing with the authorities'.[28] The Algerian nationalist law of late 1990 'making Arabic the national language and exacting heavy fines for using anything else in official transactions' will be seen in that country not as a liberation from the French influence, but as an attack on the third of Algerians speaking Berber.[29] It has been rightly observed that

> A modern version of the pre-nineteenth century world of uprejudiced local attachments sounds good, but that does not seem to be the direction in which today's nation-state unbuilders are pointing . . . They are all aiming towards states based not on tolerant and fairly open little countries, but on the blinkered view that what should hold people together is ethnic, religious or linguistic sameness.[30]

Monolithic aspirations of this kind are already leading to autonomist and separatist aspirations of threatened minorities within such nationalist entities, and to something better described as Lebanization than Balkanization. Turks and Russians attempt to secede from Moldavia, Serbs declare their independence from a nationalist Croatia, other Caucasian peoples reject the domination of the Georgians, while conversely ultra-ethnic noises are to be heard in Vilnius doubting whether a leader whose name indicates a German ancestry can properly understand the deepest ancestral aspirations of Lithuanians. In a world in which probably not much more than a dozen states out of some 180 can plausibly claim that their citizens coincide in any real sense with a single ethnic or linguistic group, nationalism based on the establishment of such homogeneity is not only undesirable, but also largely self-destructive.

In short, in the classic Wilsonian-Leninist form, the slogan of self-determination up to and including secession as a *general* programme can offer no solution for the twenty-first century. It can be best understood as a symptom of the crisis of the nineteenth-century concept of the 'nation-state', caught between

[28] Henry Kamm, 'Language bill weighed as Slovak separatists rally', *New York Times*, 25 October 1990.

[29] 'Algerians hit at language ban', *Financial Times*, 28 December 1990

[30] 'The state of the nation state', *Economist*, 22 December 1990 – 14 January 1991, p. 78.

what *The Economist* has called 'supranationalism' and 'infra-nationalism'.[31] But the crisis of the large nation-state is also the crisis of small ones, old or new.

So what is in doubt is not the strength of men's and women's longing for group identity, of which nationality is one expression, but (as the Islamic world shows) not the only one. Nor is it the strength of the reaction against the centralization and bureau-cratization of state, economic or cultural power, i.e. against its remoteness and uncontrollability. Nor need we doubt the fact that almost any local or even sectional discontent capable of wrapping itself in coloured banners, finds it attractive to claim national justification.[32] What sceptics doubt is the alleged irresis-tibility of the desire to form homogeneous nation-states and the usefulness of both the concept and the programme in the twenty-first century. Even in regions where the classic aspiration for separate nation-states might be expected to be strong, effec-tive devolution or regionalization has pre-empted it, or even reversed it. State separatism in the Americas, at any rate south of Canada, has declined since the American Civil War. And it is significant that the states defeated in World War II, on which a high degree of devolution was imposed – presumably in reaction against fascist centralization – lack most of the separatist move-ments of the rest of western Europe, though on paper Bavaria and Sicily are at least as obvious breeding-grounds for such move-ments as Scotland and the francophone parts of the Bernese Jura. In fact, the separatist movement which developed in Sicily after 1943 proved short-lived, though its disappearance is still mourned by a few as 'the end of the Sicilian nation'.[33] It was killed by the regional autonomy legislation of 1946.

Thus nationalism today reflects an only half-acknowledged crisis of the old Wilsonian-Leninist ideology and programme. As

[31] *Ibid.*, pp. 73–8.
[32] 'The class make-up of the activist leaders ... [of the Occitanian movement] indicates that the causes of this discontent lie less in regionally uneven economic development than in grievances felt by professions and white-collar classes ... throughout France. William R. Beer, 'The social class of ethnic activists in contemporary France' in Milton J. Esman (ed.), *Ethnic Conflict in the Western World* (Ithaca 1977), p. 158.
[33] Marcello Cimino, *Fine di una nazione* (Palermo 1977); G. C. Marino, *Storia del separatismo siciliano 1943–1947* (Rome 1979).

we have seen, even many old, strong and determined nationalist movements have their doubts about actual state independence, even when they maintain the aim of total separation from the states of which they form part at present (as the Basques and Scots nationalists do). The old and still not adequately answered 'Irish Question' illustrates this uncertainty. On the one hand the independent Irish Republic, while insisting on its total political autonomy from Britain – underlined by remaining neutral in World War II – in practice accepts considerable mutual involvement with the United Kingdom. Nor has Irish nationalism found it difficult to adjust to the curious situation in which Irish citizens, when in Britain, enjoy full citizen rights in the United Kingdom as though they had not separated from it, i.e. *de facto* dual nationality. On the other hand, faith in the classic programme of a single united independent Ireland has rapidly waned. Thus probably both the governments in Dublin and London would agree about the (relative) desirability of a single united Ireland. However, few, even in the Irish Republic, would see such a union as anything except the least bad of a selection of bad solutions. Conversely, if Ulster were in such a case to declare its independence from both Britain and Ireland, most Ulster Protestants would also see this ultimate refusal of the Pope as a lesser evil. In short, only a handful of fanatics would, it is safe to say, regard this achievement of national/communal self-determination as more than marginally better than an acutely unsatisfactory status quo.

We may also detect a crisis of national consciousness in the old nations, and for similar reasons. That consciousness, as it emerged in nineteenth-century Europe, was situated somewhere in the quadrilateral described by the points People–State–Nation–Government. In theory these four elements coincided. In Hitler's phrase (where the word *Volk* stands for both 'people' and 'nation') Germany consisted of 'Ein Volk, ein Reich, ein Fuehrer', i.e. one people/nation, one state, one government. In practice the ideas of state and government tended to be determined by political criteria typical of the period since the era of great eighteenth-century revolutions, but the idea of 'people' and 'nation' largely by pre-political criteria which were helpful in the creation of the imagined and imaginary community. Politics constantly tended to take over and remould such pre-political elements for its own purposes. The organic connection between the four elements was taken for granted. But that is no longer possible in the historical or old-established large nation-states.

This may be illustrated from a public opinion survey in the Federal Republic of Germany in 1972.[34] This is admittedly an extreme case since Germany had passed from the, in theory, most complete pan-German political unity under Hitler to a situation where at least two states coexisted which could claim to be all or part of the German nation. However, it is just this situation which allows us to detect the uncertainties and ambiguities in the minds of most citizens, as they think about 'the nation'.

The first thing to emerge from this enquiry is considerable uncertainty. 83% of West Germans thought they knew what capitalism was, 78% were in no doubt about socialism, but only 71% ventured an opinion on 'the state' and 34% had not the least idea of how to define or describe 'the nation'. Among the less educated uncertainty was even greater. 90% of Germans who had completed secondary education felt they were informed about all four terms, but only 54% of (non-apprenticed, i.e. unskilled) Germans with only primary education felt they knew what 'the state' was, and only 47% felt they knew about 'the nation'. This uncertainty sprang precisely from the breakdown of the old congruence between 'people', 'nation' and 'state'.

When asked 'Are nation and state the same, or are we talking about different things?' 43% of West Germans – 81% among the most educated – gave the obvious answer that they were not the same, since two German states coexisted. However, 35% believed that nation and state were inseparable, and so, logically enough, 31% of workers – 39% among those under 40 years – concluded that the German Democratic Republic now formed a different nation, because it was a different state. Let us note also, that the group with the strongest conviction of the identity of state and nation – 42% – consisted of the skilled workers; the group with the strongest conviction that Germany consisted of one nation divided into two states were Social Democratic voters.

[34] Bundesministerium für innerdeutsche Beziehungen, *Materialien zum Bericht zur Lage der Nation*, 3 vols. (Bonn 1971, 1972, 1974), III, pp. 107–13, esp. p. 112.

52% of them held this view as against 36% of Christian Democratic voters. One might say that, a century after the unification of Germany, the traditional nineteenth-century concept of 'the nation' survived most strongly in the working class.

What this suggests is that the idea of 'the nation', once extracted, like the mollusc, from the apparently hard shell of the 'nation-state', emerges in distinctly wobbly shape. Not, of course, that Germans east and west of the Elbe had ceased to think of themselves as 'Germans' even before the two states were united, although probably most Austrians after 1945 no longer thought of themselves as part of a greater Germany, as a majority of them had done between 1918 and 1945; and certainly the German-speaking Swiss actively distanced themselves from any suggestion of German identity. What East and West Germans were uncertain about, with good reason, was the political or other implications of 'Germanness'. And it is far from clear that the establishment of a single Federal Republic of Germany in 1990 has removed these uncertainties entirely.

One suspects that similar enquiries in other historic 'nation-states' would produce similarly confused responses. What, for instance, is the relation between 'Frenchness' and *francophonie* (a term which did not even exist until recently – it is first recorded in 1959)? Whether he meant to be or not, General De Gaulle was completely at odds with what we have seen to be the traditional and non-linguistic definition of Frenchness, when he addressed the inhabitants of Quebec as Frenchmen abroad. Quebec nationalist thinking, in turn, has 'more or less abandoned the term *homeland* (*la patrie*) and has embroiled itself instead in interminable debate about the merit and demerit of such terms as *nation, people, society* and *state*'.[35] Until the 1960s 'Britishness', in terms of law and administration, was a simple matter of being born to British parents or on British soil, marrying a British citizen, or being naturalized. It is a far from simple matter today.

None of this means that nationalism is not very prominent in

[35] Dion, 'The mystery of Quebec', p. 302. The Gaullist version of Quebec as French, as given in a French cabinet statement on 31 July 1967, was that France could not 'disinterest herself in the present and future fate of a population descended from her own people and admirably faithful to their country of origin or consider Canada as a foreign country in the same sense as others' (*Canadian News Facts* vol. 1, no. 15, 14 August 1967), p. 114.

world politics today, or that there is less of it than there was once. What I am arguing is rather that, in spite of its evident prominence, nationalism is historically less important. It is no longer, as it were, a global political programme, as it may be said to have been in the nineteenth and earlier twentieth centuries. It is at most a complicating factor, or a catalyst for other developments. It is not implausible to present the history of the Eurocentric nineteenth-century world as that of 'nation-building', as Walter Bagehot did. We still present the history of the major European states of Europe after 1870 in this manner, as in the title of Eugene Weber's *Peasants into Frenchmen.*[36] Is anyone likely to write the world history of the late twentieth and early twenty-first centuries in such terms? It is most unlikely.

On the contrary, it will inevitably have to be written as the history of a world which can no longer be contained within the limits of 'nations' and 'nation-states' as these used to be defined, either politically, or economically, or culturally, or even linguistically. It will be largely supranational and infranational, but even infranationality, whether or not it dresses itself up in the costume of some mini-nationalism, will reflect the decline of the old nation-state as an operational entity. It will see 'nation-states' and 'nations' or ethnic/linguistic groups primarily as retreating before, resisting, adapting to, being absorbed or dislocated by the new supranational restructuring of the globe. Nations and nationalism will be present in this history, but in subordinate, and often rather minor roles. This does not mean that national history and culture will not bulk large – perhaps larger than before – in the educational systems and the cultural life of particular countries, especially the smaller ones, or that they may not flourish locally within a much broader supranational framework, as, say, Catalan culture today flourishes, but on the tacit assumption that it is Catalans who will communicate with the rest of the world through Spanish and English, since few non-residents in Catalonia will be able to communicate in the local language.[37]

[36] Eugen Weber, *Peasants into Frenchmen: The Modernization of Rural France, 1870–1914* (Stanford 1976).
[37] When abroad, two-thirds of Catalans considered themselves 'Spanish' in the 1970s. M. García Ferrando, *Regionalismo y autonomías en España* (Madrid 1982), Table II.

As I have suggested, 'nation' and 'nationalism' are no longer adequate terms to describe, let alone to analyse, the political entities described as such, or even the sentiments once described by these words. It is not impossible that nationalism will decline with the decline of the nation-state, without which being English or Irish or Jewish, or a combination of all these, is only one way in which people describe their identity among the many others which they use for this purpose, as occasion demands.[38] It would be absurd to claim that this day is already near. However, I hope it can at least be envisaged. After all, the very fact that historians are at least beginning to make some progress in the study and analysis of nations and nationalism suggests that, as so often, the phenomenon is past its peak. The owl of Minerva which brings wisdom, said Hegel, flies out at dusk. It is a good sign that it is now circling round nations and nationalism.

[38] Among the rare theorists who seem to share my doubts about the strength and dominance of nationalism is John Breuilly in *Nationalism and the State*. He criticizes both Gellner and Anderson for assuming 'that the self-evident success of nationalism means that nationalism is very strongly rooted in the thought or behaviour of people' ('Reflections on nationalism'(*Philosophy and Social Science*, 15/1, March 1985, p. 73)).

MAPS

Maps

ICELAND

independent, 1918 in personal union with Denmark

0 ——— 500 km
0 ——— 300 miles

Atlantic

Ocean

NORWAY

S W E D E N

Åland Is.
neutralised 1921

Londonderry
ULSTER
Belfast

North Sea

DENMARK

B a l t i c   S e a

③ MEMEL TERRITORY

SCHLESWIG HOLSTEIN ①

Danzig Free City 1920

IRISH FREE STATE
•Dublin

Cork•
Queenstown•

UNITED KINGDOM

NETHERLANDS

Hamburg

Marienwerder▲②
Allenstein

Berlin

Polish corridor

Posen
to Dec

RUHR ⑤

G E R M A N Y

⑦ UPPER SILESIA

BELGIUM

Spa 1920■

Eupen
Malmedy
to Belgium 1919

Rhein

BOHEMIA

CZECHOSLOVAK

LUXEMBOURG
▲
SAAR ⑥

RHINELAND ④

Paris•
1919

ALSACE-LORRAINE
to France 1919

Munich•

MORAVIA

Vienna•

Sopron
to Hungary 19

N

F R A N C E

SWITZERLAND

Lausanne 1922-23■

Montreux
1936■

Locarno 1925■

Stresa 1935■

TYROL

AUSTRIA
HUNG

Trieste•
Fiume
1919

SLOVENIA

CROATIA

Y U G O

ASTURIAS

Genoa 1922■
■Rapallo
1922

BOSNIA

HERZE-GOVINA

MON

BASQUE REP.
autonomous
1936-37

PORTUGAL

CATALONIA
autonomous
1932-38

S P A I N

I T A L Y

M e d i t e r r a n e a n

S e

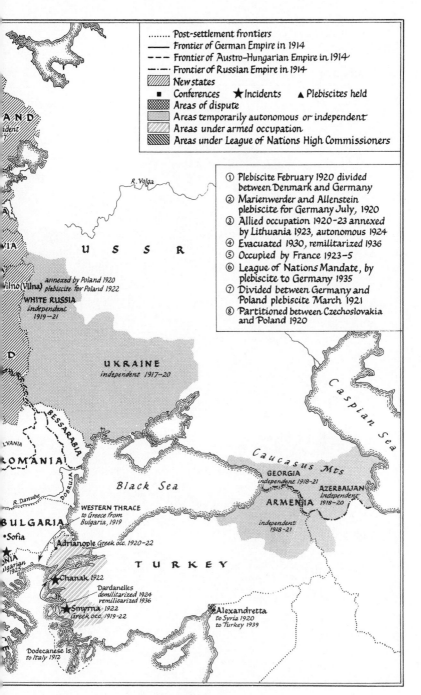

.... Post-settlement frontiers
——— Frontier of German Empire in 1914
– – – Frontier of Austro-Hungarian Empire in 1914
–·–·– Frontier of Russian Empire in 1914
▨ New states
■ Conferences ★ Incidents ▲ Plebiscites held
▨ Areas of dispute
▨ Areas temporarily autonomous or independent
▨ Areas under armed occupation
▨ Areas under League of Nations High Commissioners

① Plebiscite February 1920 divided
   between Denmark and Germany
② Marienwerder and Allenstein
   plebiscite for Germany July, 1920
③ Allied occupation 1920–23 annexed
   by Lithuania 1923, autonomous 1924
④ Evacuated 1930, remilitarized 1936
⑤ Occupied by France 1923–5
⑥ League of Nations Mandate, by
   plebiscite to Germany 1935
⑦ Divided between Germany and
   Poland plebiscite March 1921
⑧ Partitioned between Czechoslovakia
   and Poland 1920

R. Volga

U S S R

annexed by Poland 1920
Vilno (Vilna) *plebiscite for Poland 1922*
WHITE RUSSIA
independent 1919–21

UKRAINE
independent 1917–20

BESSARABIA

LVANIA
ROMANIA

R. Danube

DOBRUJA

Black Sea

Caspian Sea

Caucasus Mts

GEORGIA
independent 1918–21

AZERBAIJAN
independent 1918–20

ARMENIA
independent 1918–21

WESTERN THRACE
to Greece from Bulgaria, 1919

BULGARIA
•Sofia

NIA
Bulgarian 1925

Adrianople *Greek occ. 1920–22*

★Chanak 1922

Dardanelles
demilitarized 1924 remilitarized 1936

★Smyrna 1922
Greek occ. 1919–22

T U R K E Y

▲Alexandretta
*to Syria 1920
to Turkey 1939*

Dodecanese Is
to Italy 1912

1 National conflicts and frontier
disputes, 1919–1934.

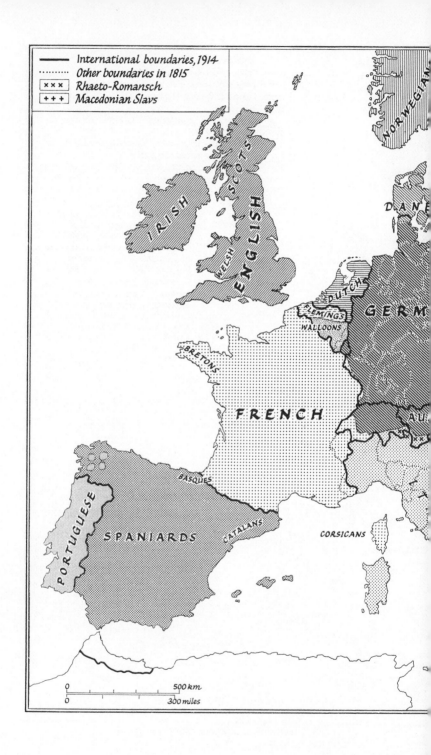

	International boundaries, 1914
	Other boundaries in 1815
×××	Rhaeto-Romansch
+++	Macedonian Slavs

NORWEGIAN

IRISH

SCOTS

WELSH

ENGLISH

DANE

DUTCH

GERM

FLEMINGS
WALLOONS

BRETONS

FRENCH

AU

BASQUES

PORTUGUESE

SPANIARDS

CATALANS

CORSICANS

0   500 km
0   300 miles

2 Peoples, languages and political divisions in the
nineteenth century: the East European linguistic jigsaw.

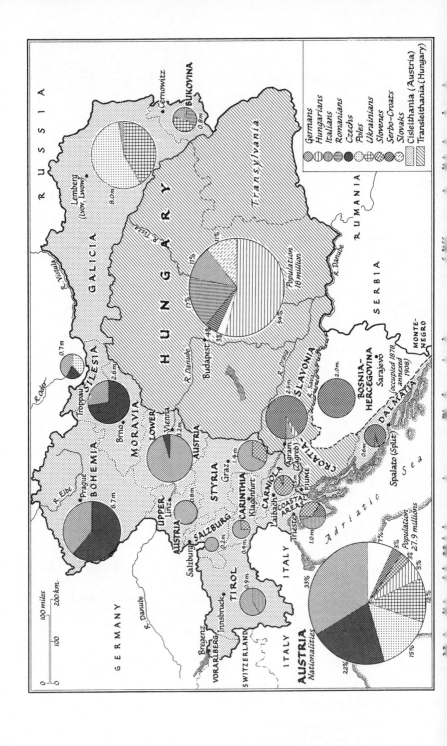

Legend:
- Germans
- Hungarians
- Italians
- Romanians
- Czechs
- Poles
- Ukrainians
- Slovenes
- Serbo-Croats
- Slovaks
- Cisleithania (Austria)
- Transleithania (Hungary)

RUSSIA

GALICIA
Cernowitz
Lemberg (Lvov, Lwow)
BUKOVINA 0.8m
8.0m

R. Vistula
R. Oder

GERMANY

SILESIA
Troppau 0.7m
Brno
MORAVIA
0.2m
Prague
R. Elbe
BOHEMIA
6.7m

R. Danube

UPPER AUSTRIA
Linz 0.8m
LOWER AUSTRIA
Vienna 3.2m

SALZBURG
Salzburg 0.2m

TIROL
Bregenz
VORARLBERG
Innsbruck 0.9m

SWITZERLAND

ITALY

STYRIA
Graz

CARINTHIA
Klagenfurt 0.4m

CARNIOLA
Laibach

COASTAL AREAS
Trieste
Gorizia
FIUME 1.0m

HUNGARY
Population 18 million
Budapest
R. Danube
R. Tisza
11%
4%
17%
3%
54%

TRANSYLVANIA

RUMANIA

R. Danube
R. Drava
R. Save
SLAVONIA
CROATIA
Agram (Zagreb) 2.6m

SERBIA

BOSNIA-HERCEGOVINA
Sarajevo (occupied 1878 annexed 1908)
2.0m

MONTE-NEGRO

DALMATIA
Spalato (Split) 0.6m

Adriatic Sea

AUSTRIA
Nationalities
Population 27.9 millions
33%
22%
15%
2%
5%
2%
3%
3%
7%

100 miles
200 km.
0   100
0   200

Index

Also of interest in Canto

The Invention of Tradition

Edited by ERIC HOBSBAWM and TERENCE RANGER

Many of the traditions which we think of as ancient in their origins were, in fact, invented comparatively recently. This book explores examples of this process of invention, including the creation of Welsh and Scottish 'national culture'; the elaboration of British royal rituals in the nineteenth and twentieth centuries; the origins of imperial rituals in British India and Africa; and the attempts by radical movements to develop counter-traditions of their own. This wide-ranging book addresses the complex interaction of past and present in a fascinating study of ritual and symbolism.

Contributors: DAVID CANNADINE, BERNARD S. COHN, HUGH TREVOR-ROPER, ERIC HOBSBAWM, PRYS MORGAN, TERENCE RANGER.

'... arouses admiration, annoyance, disagreement, delight, which testifies to its sustained interest and stimulus'.
The Times Literary Supplement

'... learned, funny and surprising essays'.
The New Yorker

1992   216 × 138 mm   328 pp   5 tables
Paperback 0 521 43773 3